12ML

D0079147

WITHDRAWN

The Death of Desire

WITHDRAWN

PSYCHOANALYTIC CROSSCURRENTS
General Editor: Leo Goldberger

616.89
T375d

THE DEATH
OF
DESIRE

A Study in Psychopathology

M. Guy Thompson

New York University Press
New York and London
1985

Copyright © 1985 by New York University
All rights reserved
Manufactured in the United States of America

Library of Congress Cataloging in Publication Data
Thompson, M. Guy, 1947–
The death of desire.

(Psychoanalytic crosscurrents)
Bibliography: p.
Includes index.
1. Psychology, Pathological. 2. Desire.
3. Psychoanalysis. 4. Freud, Sigmund, 1856–1939.
5. Phenomenological psychology. I. Title. II. Series.
RC454.4.T47 1985   616.89   85–13785
ISBN 0–8147–8173–X (alk. paper)

Clothbound editions of New York University Press books are Smyth-sewn
and printed on permanent and durable acid-free paper.

For Guy and Dashiell

CAT May 25 '87

5-6-87 MWS 33.46

86-7664
ALLEGHENY COLLEGE LIBRARY

Those who restrain desire do so because theirs is weak enough to be restrained, and being restrained it by degrees becomes passive, till it is only the shadow of desire.

—William Blake, *The Marriage of Heaven and Hell*

Contents

Foreword

The *Psychoanalytic Crosscurrents* series presents selected books and monographs that reveal the growing intellectual ferment within and across the boundaries of psychoanalysis.

Freud's theories and grand-scale speculative leaps have been found wanting, if not disturbing, from the very beginning and have led to a succession of derisive attacks, shifts in emphasis, revisions, modifications, and extensions. Despite the chronic and, at times, fierce debate that has characterized psychoanalysis, not only as a movement but also as a science, Freud's genius and transformational impact on the twentieth century have never been seriously questioned. Recently psychoanalytic thought has been subjected to dramatic reassessments under the sway of contemporary currents in the history of ideas, philosophy of science, epistemology, structuralism, critical theory, semantics, and semiology as well as in sociobiology, ethology, and neurocognitive science. Not only is Freud's place in intellectual history being meticulously scrutinized, his texts, too, are being carefully read, explicated, and debated within a variety of conceptual frameworks and sociopolitical contexts.

The legacy of Freud is perhaps most notably evident within the narrow confines of psychoanalysis itself, the "impossible profession" that has served as the central platform for the promulgation of official orthodoxy. But Freud's contributions—his original radical thrust—reach far beyond the parochial concerns of the clinical psychoanalyst as clinician. His writings touch on a wealth of issues, crossing traditional boundaries—be they situated in the biological, social, or humanistic spheres—that have profoundly altered our conception of the individual and society.

A rich and flowering literature, falling under the rubric of "applied psychoanalysis," came into being, reached its zenith many decades ago, and then almost vanished. Early contributors to this literature, in addition to Freud himself, came from a wide range of backgrounds both within and outside the medical/psychiatric field; many later became psychoanalysts themselves. These early efforts were characteristically reductionistic in their attempt to extrapolate from psychoanalytic theory (often the purely clinical theory) to explanations of phenomena lying at some distance from the clinical. Over the years, academic psychologists, educators, anthropologists, sociologists, political scientists, philosophers, jurists, literary critics, art historians, artists, and writers, among others (with or without formal psychoanalytic training) have joined in the proliferation of this literature.

The intent of the *Psychoanalytic Crosscurrents* series is to apply psychoanalytic ideas to topics that may lie beyond the narrowly clinical, but its essential conception and scope are quite different. The present series eschews the reductionistic tendency to be found in much traditional "applied psychoanalysis." It acknowledges not only the complexity of psychological phenomena but also the way in which they are embedded in social and scientific contexts that are constantly changing. It calls for a dialectical relationship to earlier theoretical views and conceptions rather than a mechanical repetition of Freud's dated thoughts. The series affirms the fact that contributions to and about psychoanalysis have come from many directions. It is designed as a forum for the multidisciplinary studies that intersect with psychoanalytic thought but without the requirement that psychoanalysis necessarily be the starting point or, indeed, the center focus. The criteria for inclusion in the series are that the work be significantly informed by psychoanalytic thought or that it be aimed at furthering our understanding of psychoanalysis in its broadest meaning as theory, practice, and sociocultural phenomenon; that it be of current topical interest and that it provide the critical reader with contemporary insights; and, above all, that it be high-quality scholarship, free of obsolete dogma, banalization, and empty jargon. The author's professional identity and particular theoretical orientation matters only to the extent that such facts may serve to frame the work for the reader, alerting him or her to inevitable biases of the author.

The Psychoanalytic Crosscurrents Series presents an array of works from the multidisciplinary domain in an attempt to capture the ferment of scholarly activities at the core as well as at the boundaries of psychoanalysis. The books and monographs are from a variety of sources:

authors will be psychoanalysts—traditional, neo- and post-Freudian, existential, object-relational, Kohutian, Lacanian, etc.—social scientists with quantitative or qualitative orientations to psychoanalytic data, and scholars from the vast diversity of approaches and interests that make up the humanities. The series entertains works on critical comparisons of psychoanalytic theories and concepts as well as philosophical examinations of fundamental assumptions and epistemic claims that furnish the base for psychoanalytic hypotheses. It includes studies of psychoanalysis as literature (discourse and narrative theory) as well as the application of psychoanalytic concepts to literary criticism. It will serve as an outlet for psychoanalytic studies of creativity and the arts. Works in the cognitive and the neurosciences will be included to the extent that they address some fundamental psychoanalytic tenet, such as the role of dreaming and other forms of unconscious mental processes.

It should be obvious that an exhaustive enumeration of the types of works that might fit into the *Psychoanalytic Crosscurrents* series is pointless. The studies comprise a lively and growing literature as a unique domain; books of this sort are frequently difficult to classify or catalog. Suffice it to say that the overriding aim of the editor of this series is to serve as a conduit for the identification of the outstanding yield of that emergent literature and to foster its further unhampered growth.

Leo Goldberger
Professor of Psychology
New York University

Preface

This book is a study of desire in psychopathology and its cure in psychoanalysis. Its purpose is to make psychoanalysis comprehensible, so the reader will have to judge for himself the success or failure of this aim. I would prefer, however, to be judged on what this book is intended to achieve and not on what it is not intended to. This book is not intended to provide an inventory of so-called "mental disorders," but rather to get to the root of what is manifest when pathos is ascribed to a specifically *human condition,* which is to say, the condition of man himself.

This work is theoretical and, as such, is intended to provide a way to understand human suffering as well as the unique task of the psychotherapist when he encounters, in his charge, the weight of this suffering. In the main, I have tried to demonstrate the efficacy of my theory from cases readily available in the literature, cases which have been discussed by numerous authors already. In choosing this course I hope this work provides an opportunity to compare my approach to psychoanalysis with those of others, an opportunity which would not be so feasible were I to rely on cases from my own practice.

A further purpose is to provide, in terms relatively free of jargon, an account of some forms of psychopathology, specifically neurosis, psychosis, and perversions. A brief statement about my intentions will, I hope, avoid misunderstanding.

In reviewing the major concepts of Freudian theory, I have attempted to bridge a gap between phenomenology and psychoanalysis, which is to say, between the phenomenologists who, in my opinion, have failed to account for the Freudian unconscious, and those psychoanalysts who have been unable to render the theory of the unconscious comprehensible. In trying to situate the significance of desire in psychoanalysis from a phenomenological perspective, I believe this work to be the first of its kind. In order to do this, I have abandoned Freud's conception of desire rooted, as it were, in the fulcrum of the body, and replaced it with Hegel's which conceives it in terms of the subject's existential appeal for recognition, in terms of the lack at the heart of man's being. Viewed from this perspective, psychoanalysis is in turn conceived as an undertaking which aims at the realization of desire and not merely its satisfaction, which is to say, its adaptation. I have thus defined man as the ensemble of his desires and, alternately, psycho-pathology as the subversion, that is, the deadening, of those desires.

The reader will recognize numerous authors cited from the phe-nomenological tradition in this work, yet it is not a direct application of any of them. While I have relied extensively on the theories of Hegel, Sartre, Heidegger, Scheler, Merleau-Ponty, Laing, and Lacan, my views express important points of divergence with each of them. I do not pretend to be a phenomenologist in the strictest sense of that term, but it is to the phenomenological tradition that I owe my greatest intellectual indebtedness. Having said this, it is psychoanalysis—not phenomenology—that is my calling, and it is to Freud that I ultimately turn for my inspiration. In my reading of psychoanalysis I have tried to situate my thought squarely in the Freudian tradition, and to return to that tradition by elaborating a theory of the unconscious in a language that is clear and to the point, and yet, not that easy to grasp. Many of Freud's earliest insights into the human condition have been lost due to the vocabulary that housed them, and due to the ideas themselves and their more disturbing implications.

Of course, the view that Freud's most radical views about human nature have been repressed or distorted is nothing new. R. D. Laing, Jacques Lacan, and others have been making this claim for decades. That this message has, in the main, fallen on deaf ears is not altogether surprising. Laing's attacks on conventional psychiatric treatment and Lacan's insistence that every psychoanalyst since Freud has misun-derstood him could hardly be expected to endear them to the hearts and minds of their colleagues. This argument does not rest on whether to follow Freud or to reject him, but whether we have managed to under-stand him in the first place. Further, having understood him, if only in an approximate way, what are we to make of the impossible vocabulary he has left us?

Beneath the sometimes bemusing and sometimes confusing termi-nology of the various schools and fashions of psychoanalysis, there emerges a somewhat unsettling thought that the more disturbing elements of Freud's earlier work—his critique of unconscious subjectivity and the irrepressible perversity of desire—have been tamed or altogether rejected by many of his inheritors, including the object relations theorists in Britain and the ego psychologists in the United States. If there is any validity in the taming of these theories, then it is precisely to these theories that we must turn in order to see what is there, which is a return to Freud himself.

Laing and Lacan, each in his own bombastic style, have tried to rescue Freud from the grasp of increasingly behavioristic interpretations of his message, interpreters who on the other extreme have taken his biological metaphors too literally. While Lacan emphasized his debt to Hegelian dialectics and Saussurian linguistic theory, Laing pointed to the enormous corruptive power that inhabits the family constellation—all in the name of "love." On the one hand, Lacan is telling us that humans are vastly more complex and unknowable than we are ready to admit, while, on the other, Laing is reminding us of our inherent human cruelty, the truth of which each of us must bear. Not a popular message, but one that is clearly at the heart of the Freudian vision of man. If these truths seem so hard to face, what price must be paid if we continue to ignore them?

My aim in this book has been to point to desire as the foundation of the human subject and to locate this desire in the heart of the unconscious, an unconscious which, after having been situated in phenomenology, reveals the nature of intersubjective relations. If my task has been less than successful, I have no one to blame but myself. I would add that while my questioning of psychoanalysis falls within a tradition occasioned by Laing and Lacan, my theories are not derivatives of either of them. They belong to no one but me.

I would like to express my deepest gratitude to R. D. Laing, John Heaton, and the late Hugh Crawford, from whom I received my psychoanalytic training at the Philadelphia Association in London from 1973 to 1980. It is to them that I owe the greatest measure of my analytic education and theoretical knowledge. This book is the culmination of some 15 years of research and therapeutic practice, half of which was carried out in London. The views expressed in this study were discussed with more individuals than I can conveniently list, but I would like to thank particularly Professor Douglas Kirsner, Mr. Chris Oakley, Mrs. Haya Oakley, Professor Steven Gans, Dr. Robin Cooper,

Dr. Martin Grotjahn, Professor Richard Lichtman, Professor Alan Swope, Professor Benjamen Tong, Dr. David Cooper, Professor Bernd Jager, Dr. Sanford Rosenberg, Dr. Karl Kracklauer, and especially to Dr. Leo Goldberger and to my editor at the New York University Press, Ms. Kitty Moore, for their support and encouragement.

M. Guy Thompson

CHAPTER ONE
THE IDOLATRY OF THE EGO

American psychoanalysts—and, more importantly, American psycho-therapists generally—have tended to interpret the Freudian notion of the ego as an agent of synthesis, integration, power, autonomy, and adaptation. American individualism and optimism, two values essential to the constitutional prerogatives of the individual in a society of others, have been adapted to (and adopted by) philosophical and psychological deliberations which tend to view the individual as an "entrepreneur of the self," and which approach psychoanalysis as a utilitarian instrument of change at the service of those who, by virtue of effort and will, endeavor to adapt themselves to, and ultimately to master, that situation in their lives which has become problematical.

Yet, in Europe, particularly in Britain, Germany, and France, a far more worrisome conception of the ego has enjoyed a certain credence, one in which it is perceived as being constituted of an identification with one's self-image. Perpetually threatened by that act of identification and misapprehension which created it, and which, due to the denatured and denaturing structure through which it is used to alienate the subject from himself, this ego becomes essentially suicidal and homicidal.

The prevailing American image of the ego as "monarch of the self" was ordained by early twentieth-century thinkers of the American Enlightenment—James, Pierce, Dewey, and Mead—who celebrated the belief that people can "change" themselves by acts of will. Americans are taught from an early age that if they want to be successful, they must be willing to change. According to Sherry Turkle, this view is based on a belief in the "plasticity of the individual," a sort of Heraclitean hero who is subject to change at a moment's notice.[1]

While sociological explanations never in themselves provide a foundation for the acceptance or rejection of beliefs, it is interesting to note that the success of ego psychology in this country has a number of resonances with the social fabric of American history and its inherent "pioneer spirit," as noted by Turkle. According to her,

> In the American nation of immigrants, psychoanalytic absorption in the history of the individual helped to compensate for the absence of a collective past. Many Americans shared an insecurity about their *parvenu* status that encouraged continual self-examination and the strong desire for self-improvement.[2]

Drawing on the views of Nathan Hale, Philip Rieff, John Burnham, and Paul Roazen, Turkle goes on to elaborate a sociological setting that was particularly ripe for the plucking of psychoanalytic ideas at the turn of the twentieth century:

> When the individual feels himself to be a part of a network of stable social relationships with family, ancestry, and religion, he can use these relationships to make sense of experience, and when he feels himself in pain or distress, they become natural reference points for trying to understand what is happening and sources of support for finding a way out of trouble. But with a mobility of place, profession, and status, and a new instability of values, old ways of looking at the world could no longer apply.[3]

Indeed, with no one to turn to but himself, an individual without tradition to rely upon would become especially susceptible to theories which promote a search for the meaning of his fears, doubts, dreams, and nightmares, precisely the sort of search that was being promoted by mystical orders and psychoanalytical societies. Further, with day-to-day living in greater flux, unseen forces appeared to play an increasingly dominant role. The idea of unconscious forces took on a greater reality, and the counterbalance of a conceivably powerful and potentially autonomous ego took on a greater urgency. In a word, the time for psychological therapy had come. American society was ready to look at a conception of the world which focused on a self or ego.

While Americans have tended to regard the ego (or self) as an agent of strength, a number of European philosophers and psychiatrists have viewed the ego as only an illusion of strength. Edmund Husserl in Germany, Jean-Paul Sartre, and Jacques Lacan in France, Ronald Laing in Great Britain, and Medard Boss in Switzerland all share a similar conception of the ego as an illusory support for false identifications. As a result, they emphasize the concept of a subject that is distinct from the ego, a subject that appears through the elusive intentional structure of unconscious motivations and, in that respect, bears a striking resemblance to George Groddek's conception of the unconscious, or the "It." Since this subject is never revealed and can only be apprehended indirectly, a psychotherapist, using this perspective, would, by necessity, have to tolerate working in the dark most of the time. Yet, there is no clearcut distinction in psychoanalysis—save for the work of Lacan—between the ego and the subject. Sometimes Freud speaks of the ego as a subject; sometimes he speaks of it as a false identification; sometimes he speaks of the unconscious as a second subject; and so on.

The recent tendency among psychoanalysts, especially in Britain and the United States, to prefer the use of the term "self" in place of or in contradistinction to the ego has resulted in more confusion than clarity since there is as yet no consistent definition of a concept of self in psychoanalytic literature. Our task at the present will be to examine some rough-and-ready uses in psychoanalysis of the terms "ego," "subject," and "self," and to set the way during the course of this book to examine the nature of subjectivity and desire, the deadening of desire, the relation between desire and dialectical knowledge, and the indications for therapeutic action.

The Ambiguity of the Ego

Freud's *Project for a Scientific Psychology* emphasizes from the very start of his career the view that the ego represents the repressive, defensive agency of the psychical apparatus.[4] In other words, the ego is not in the strict sense of the term a *subject*. It is not a subject in the classical sense of philosophy, nor is it the subject of wishing and desire. It is rather an *object* of unconscious influences that is said to be capable of action to the extent that it is the seat of multiple identifications which are "representative" of the individual's unacknowledged intentions. The ego participates in conflicts due to its inhibiting and defensive functions. Yet, a contradiction becomes immediately apparent if we want to believe—as did Freud—that the ego is capable of passing itself off as a subject, in a deceptive manner, in order to serve its own (rather than the subject's) defensive claims. This is rather like saying that a suit of armor has a mind of its own.

Later in his career, Freud spoke of the ego in an altogether different manner, one in which he attributes to its properties a certain synthetic function. Here he describes the ego "as an organization characterized by a very remarkable trend towards unification, towards synthesis."[5]

Even in its synthetic function Freud saw the defensive structure as paramount. His recognition of the defensive nature of the ego always played a dominant role in Freud's critique of his structural theory and continued to overshadow other aspects of the ego which arose from time to time. Rather than a separate "entity" entirely apart from the id, Freud sometimes characterized the ego as merely a facade of the id, as a sort of outer layer.[6] In *The Ego and the Id,* Freud specifies that "The ego is first and foremost a bodily-ego; it is not merely a surface entity, but it is itself the projection of a surface."[7] This rather enigmatic statement deserved a special note in the *Standard Edition:*

> The ego is ultimately derived from bodily sensations, chiefly from those springing from the surface of the body. It may thus be regarded as a mental projection of the surface of the body, besides, as we have seen above, representing the superficies of the mental apparatus.[8]

From the quotations, it is evident that Freud believed the root concept of the ego to be located in that bodily part of the organism, which is, above all, perceptible. The child spends a great deal of time and effort looking at and becoming perceptually familiar with the parts of its body. The continuity of these perceptions is often cited as the core of the individual's sense of selfhood. At the very least, it is regarded by all psychoanalysts as an extremely important aspect of the ego, if not its very foundation. What these statements suggest is nothing more or less than a conception of the ego as an imaginary structure of the subject, or id, which is constituted at some phase of the child's development, and whose seeming purpose is to defend the subject from the world of reality and other people.

This view, which is often attributed to Freud's early phase (although it can be found to exist to the very end), is in stark contrast to the majority of Freud's followers. Some analysts, such as Ronald Fairbairn of Great Britain, suggest that an ego is present from birth and that there is no such thing as an id. This extreme view has had its influence on the object-relations school in Britain and the ego psychology movement in America. There is no denying that the relations between id and ego, id and the unconscious, the ego and the unconscious, the ego and consciousness, the id and subjectivity, the ego and subjectivity, subjectivity and consciousness, and so on, are problematical to delineate, not least because each of these concepts has never been clarified. Since Freud's death, increasing attention has been paid to the ego and its mechanisms of defense. More recently, the ego has quite explicitly taken on the property of subjectivity, while the unconscious has taken on the property as a mere obstacle to autonomy. Thus, emphasis has shifted from the ego as an agency of defense to an ego as the organizing agency which organizes both the environment and inner psychic reality, becoming in the truest sense of the word a subject. The defensive functions of the ego were not lost sight of but became understood from the vantage point of psychical organization. This shift can be attributed to a growing influence of the concept of adaptation, a biological concept which was elaborated by Heinz Hartmann but which clearly existed in Freud's later formulations on the ego. According to Hans Loewald, in his essay on "Ego and Reality,"

> The trend of thought in the theory of the development of the ego appears to be as follows: The ego is pictured as a cortical layer of the psychic apparatus. This layer comes into being through increasing tension between the psychic apparatus of the organism and what later is experienced as the external world. This is an image borrowed from biology, in analogy to a biochemical system.[9]

Freud never used the term "adaptation" himself in his description of the ego's role. It was left to Heinz Hartmann and the ego-psychology movement in America to instigate and develop this concept in psychoanalytic theory. The root of this concept in its "psychological" aspect can be traced to the gradual development of object-relations theory in Britain, especially in the work of Ronald Fairbairn and Anna Freud. But England enthusiastically welcomed psychoanalysis due to the biographical and literary tradition in Britain and the historical imperative of Freud's case histories, miniature novels in themselves. The European disciples of Freud who were responsible for implanting his theories in the United States assumed that, in order for it to become Americanized, psychoanalysis would first of all have to be adapted to American society. While in Europe, psychiatrists had only to adapt themselves to Freud's views, in America it became necessary that analysis become adapted to American culture. And although the notion of adaptation had tentatively been introduced in Britain, the idea of adaptation differed in the United States from that of Darwin's homeland. Americans failed to emphasize the strictly scientific character of the term and substituted in its stead the notion of acculturation, a concept of primordial importance to the immigrant who was concerned with adapting himself to the reality of the American Dream.

Ernest Hilgard, the American psychologist, declared in 1949 that the "mechanisms of adjustment" were the aspects of Freudian theory which were the first to be domesticated into American psychology. This is an especially remarkable comment when one pauses to consider that Freud never regarded adjustment as a basic concept or a therapeutic goal. The term does not even appear in the index of the *Standard Edition*. To Hilgard, psychoanalysis itself became just another immigrant, like the practitioners who had themselves immigrated.

Freud never encouraged his patients to adapt or adjust to society. Rather he challenged them to solve their own problems or to learn to live with them. Their relation to society was one of these problems, and, given Freud's views on civilization, the last thing one would suspect is that he would influence anyone to "throw themselves to the masses."

This emphasis on assuming responsibility for oneself by becoming more independent and more reliable is a theme which must have struck a deep chord in the American psyche. But Americans are not as independent or autonomous as they would like to appear. Above all else, Americans want to be liked by others and generally get along with everyone. This is an attitude which is obviously rooted in the perpetual transformation from immigrant status to native American—a status which can never truly be achieved since their roots will always lie elsewhere. The lone figure of the cowboy or the hardboiled detective are deep-seated mythological symbols because everyone would like to be like that. In actual fact, America is essentially a conformist society which is willing to give up its desire for independence for the rewards of belonging to the establishment: the reward of the American Dream.

It was this fiercely independent aspect of Freud's vision that was at once welcomed and yet had to be accommodated to American society. Thus, the theory of adaptation was uprooted from a biological concept of evolutionary reform and transplanted onto a cultural milieu on the level of a faceless social morality: "Everyone should become like everyone else."

To stress adjustment is to treat the patient as a kind of immigrant undergoing *acculturation*—by stating it this way one can see the anachronistic
nature of that concept; it is explained as a trait of the individual or collective past and already constitutes a kind of survival in the present world.
[But] it must be recognized that an immigrant quite talented in criminal
activities adapts more quickly to the society he enters than the one who
reveals a docile honesty.[10]

It is perhaps revealing to note that European immigrants, such as
Hartmann, had the most profound effect on the development of psychoanalytic theory in America. They promoted the notion of adaptation as the crucial issue in psychotherapy. Before determining the
efficacy of such a concept in Freudian psychoanalysis, we will examine
the roots of Hartmann's theory to see precisely what he means by it.

The Adaptation of the Ego

In his *Ego Psychology and the Problem of Adaptation,* Hartmann says

The foundation on which Freud built his theory of neurosis was not
"specifically human" but "generally biological" so that for us the difference between animal and man is relative.[11]

One would think that, because animals cannot be psychoanalyzed and
that speech is a fundamental criterion of analysis, we are already talking
about a specifically rather than a relatively human discipline. Hartmann
does not make this assumption. For Hartmann, man is an adapting
organism rather than a subject of unconscious desire. He goes on to say

We call a man well-adapted if his productivity, his ability to enjoy life, and
his mental equilibrium are undisturbed and we ascribe failure to a lack of
adaptation. But degree of adaptiveness can only be determined with reference to environmental conditions. The conception of adaptation has no
precise definition. It was long cherished by biology . . . but recently has
been frequently criticized and rejected.[12]

It is interesting that Hartmann would take a concept that was already
losing favor in the biological sciences and adapt it to psychoanalysis in
his endeavor to promote a more general psychology than Freud's. Unfortunately, as had Freud, Hartmann failed to formulate a coherent

theory of the subject, placing in its stead Groddek's notion of an id who/which determines our behavior willynilly. As a result, subjectivity was at times attributed to the mechanisms of the id and at other times to the ego. If the id was considered to be the seat of unconscious (and presumably uncontrollable) desires, it is no wonder that the ego would have to be acknowledged as a regularity principle to prevent Groddek's It from living us at its whim. By compelling the id to bow to the ego's demand that the organism adapt to the environment, it was inevitable that it would become an "organ of adaptation."

Hartmann attempted to compensate for the failings of the id theory by distinguishing between "ego-functions involved in conflicts with the id and superego, and ego-functions concerned with coming to terms with the environment."[13]

Hartmann was concerned to demonstrate that, in addition to warding off the demands of the drives of the id, the ego was also capable of achieving autonomy by adapting to the outside world. This, of course, is something that Freud would have never presumed, so that Hartmann's theory may be regarded as a real advance in psychoanalytic theory or a serious error, depending on one's point of view. It is this area outside of the ego's conflict with the id that Hartmann calls a "conflict-free ego sphere." Nonetheless, Hartmann's theory is rooted, on the one hand, in a biological id, and, on the other hand, in the concept of adaptation, also a biological concept. While Freud stressed the ego's ultimate defensive posture against both the id and outer world, Hartmann proposed that the ego defends itself against the id but adapts to the other world.

While Hartmann adopts Freud's distinction between *autoplastic adaptation* (altering oneself to fit the environment) and *alloplastic adaptation* (altering the environment to fit oneself), he comments that neither is truly adaptive. A higher ego-function must ultimately decide what is appropriate.[14] But since ego functions have already been defined by Hartmann as essentially adaptive, how can a biological concept go *beyond* biology to determine what the terms "truly adaptive" and "appropriately adaptive" mean? If this higher ego function has the capacity to make moral choices and to determine the higher values of life that this particular individual subject is willing to choose and to stand upon—whatever the consequences—then we are talking about an entity which is far more sophisticated than a mere organ of adaptation. Such an organism would not restrict its concerns to physical survival or getting along with others but would be interested in the realization of unconscious motives and the defense of personal values. Nowhere does Hartmann's theory truly admit to such a possibility.

As close as Hartmann can stretch his theory to include a notion of subjectivity is his proposal for yet a third form of adaptation: "The *choice* of a new environment which is advantageous for the functioning of the organism."[15] Hartmann merely says that such an avenue of exploration appears to be fruitful, but, with little interest in the subtleties of the unconscious, he is ill equipped to pursue such a course.

The reason for biological adaptation is to fit into the environment for the sake of survival. Some species are so well adapted that they have not changed for millions of years. Once the concept of adaptation is stretched beyond its basic meaning, it begins to lose the biological basis which serves as its foundation. Hartmann is well aware of the fact that a human environment involves not just nature but other people. Society is not just a collection of organisms who are bound together for the purpose of sex, food, and survival. A home is not merely a sanctuary. A human may choose not to adapt to his environment for the sake of ideals he is prepared to die for. I do not believe that an organ of adaptation could conceive of such a possibility.

In contradistinction to Freud, Hartmann believed that the ego does not derive from the id but rather from a nondifferentiated point out of which ego and id both proceed. Further, the ego is said to bring with it a heredity which prepared it for adaptation to a probable reality. The biological inspiration is obvious. This primary adaptation—in relation to drives—makes way for a secondary autonomy which allows for adaptation to the environment. Although Hartmann does not specifically say it, this secondary autonomy allows for a position that could only be called one of objectivity. To his credit, Hartmann realized that this kind of objectivity was not nearly sufficient to account for the interplay of personal relationships. It would be necessary, first of all, to make a place for what we call subjectivity. The lack of such a concept produces certain contradictions which, given his hypothetical bases, are unavoidable.

Hartmann goes so far as to suggest that "the nature of the environment may be such that a pathological development of the psyche offers a more satisfactory solution than would a normal one."[16] Thus neurosis is a form of adaptation. But if we are to discern a pathological characteristic of this adaptation, by what standard are we to recognize it? By virtue of another environment? If we were to choose a different criterion (other than adaptation to an environment) against which to judge the pathological element which is inherent in it, then we would no longer have a hypothesis of an ego psychology from which to judge the intentional structure of the ego. If we were to say that the ego, in all its supposed plasticity, is able to adapt itself to an environment which is inherently pathological by refusing to adapt to it, then we are not speaking of adaptation in any conceivable aspect of the term. We would rather be referring to the subject's ability to disadapt himself, to refuse to be party to a situation which is even more pathological than the inevitable alienation he would suffer by opting out. Perhaps what Hartmann is missing in his search for a psychology of adaptation is the simple truth that man has always been adapted to his environment (in the strict Darwinian sense). He disadapts himself by manipulating the environment and by establishing the limits of his autonomy in relation to other people.

It should not be surprising that the ego would be conceived of as an organ of adaptation since—through its multiple identifications and attachments to objects in the environment—it is capable of nothing but adaptation. Survival is its only credo: There is no question of autonomy for this ego; there is only one of its dependence. What is lacking in the ego is what is lacking in Hartmann's theory of man: a subject of forbidden desires, invisible to the naked eye, unheeding to acts of will.

While Hartmann's theories may be regarded as passé by many contemporary psychoanalysts, his theories have served to provide the foundation for a particular trend in psychoanalysis which has more recently become joined to object-relations theory as conceived on the American continent. I am not suggesting that there is anything one could accurately refer to as an American school, per se. Certainly the work of Anton Kris, Stanley Leavy, Hans Loewald, Charles Brenner, and other Americans cannot be accused of being rooted in an ego-psychological interpretation of Freud. This trend, however, which has been perpetrated by David Rapaport and appropriated by Otto Kernberg in his conception of object-relations theory, remains perhaps the most distinctively "American" contribution to psychoanalytic theory and technique. Rapaport, who himself has exerted immeasurable influence on American clinical psychologists in their emphasis on the ego in applying psychoanalysis to the mainstream of psychological testing and diagnosis, never tired of expanding the significance of Hartmann's theory to what he called the mainstream of psychoanalysis itself, which for Rapaport includes Rudolph Lowenstein, Ernst Kris, Erik Erikson,

Edith Jacobson, Bruno Bettelheim, Margaret Mahler, and Merton Gill in particular. In a paper he wrote on "A Historical Survey of Psychoanalytic Ego Psychology," Rapaport delineates the evolution of psychoanalytic theory according to its faithfulness to—and deviation from—his conception of ego autonomy which he insists was implied (though certainly never stated) by Freud. Rapaport argued that Freud himself "repudiated the conception that the ego is totally subservient to the id."[17] Rapaport goes on to claim that Freud became increasingly concerned with reality relationships as opposed to his earlier emphasis on "the agent which creates fantasies and the processes by which this agent works."[18] This call to external reality, which has become the rallying cry of both ego psychologists and object-relations theorists, is for Rapaport limited to Hartmann's conception of adaptation: "The ego . . . is ultimately concerned with reality relationships (i.e., adaptation) and therefore curbs instinctual drives when action prompted by them would lend into reality danger."[19] Thus, Rapaport is not merely carrying the torch for all his presumed colleagues who believe that the environment is chiefly responsible for neurosis but more particularly for those who conceive of reality purely in terms of one's adaptability to it versus one's alienation from it, a conception—though not blatantly stated as it is by Rapaport—most certainly implied in those object relations theorists who, like Kernberg, attempt to incorporate the ego-psychological approach into their work.

The Ego and the Self

Before taking a closer look at the ego as an object of consciousness and in opposition to the subject, we might pause to reflect on a tendency of psychoanalysts during the past two decades, particularly in Britain and America, to pay concerted attention to the concept of a self in preference to an ego.

Freud deliberately used *Das Ich* to refer to both the self in the personal sense and as an abstract metapsychological component of the psychic apparatus. In English it has become common to retain the use of the word *ego* in the purely metapsychological aspect and to use the word *self* in the personal aspect. This tendency has led to major problems. One consequence has been the creation of two separate entities, each of which assume the abstract and personal roles, vying for ascendency in the international arena of psychoanalytical theory. The use of the term "self" has been extended (by Winnicott, Guntrip, Kohut, etc.) from the simply personal sphere to highly abstract levels, while the word *ego* has simultaneously—due to the influence of psychoanalysis in our everyday lives—become a part of our common vocabulary. As a result, it has become, for all intents and purposes, a current substitute for the word *self*. People are even beginning to talk about a possible relation between the two. Many analysts have suggested that Freud neglected to elaborate a theory of the self and that much work remains to be accomplished in this respect. As we shall see, the reason for this tendency is due to a neglect of a theory of the subject rather than the self, and Freud's critics have committed the same mistake in their zeal to address what they believed to be an oversight.

The fact is that Freud's entire work was concerned with developing an adequate theory of the self, though he chose to use the ambiguous *Ich,* which may be used in both personal and abstract ways. Since there is no comparable word in English, we have settled on the Latin *ego* instead—a practice which Freud studiously avoided in his development of a psychoanalytic vocabulary. The words *self, I,* and *me* have obvious similarities to *Ich,* but each lacks various shades of meaning which the German expression evokes. It is easy to see why the virginal "ego" offered a compromise term that could include all of the rich and diverse meanings of *Das Ich*. Freud continued to use the ego defined as self and ego defined as system throughout his work, relying on the context to determine its meaning. Some authors have suggested that he was not aware of the distinctions, but it seems more likely that what was lacking in Freud's deliberations was a decision as to whether the ego or the id was to be the final arbiter of subjectivity. His failure to make this decision has now been reincarnated as an argument between self or ego, with those in favor of the self theory promoting its use as a substitute for person—making it a subject—while the ego is demoted to an abstract entity. Winnicott even refers to a false self and a true self, an obvious substitute for the ego as a seat of the defenses and the ego as an organizing agency. It was again left to Hartmann to decide that Freud had failed to differentiate the concepts of ego, self, and person. What Hartmann and most of Freud's critics found objectionable about Freud's metapsychology was that it did not provide a term for the total person: a composite of the id, ego, and superego as a single entity and at the same time more personal than Freud's psychic apparatus.

It can easily be argued that Freud did not do this because he was convinced there was no such thing as a total person or total self. So why invent one? Again, it was Freud's inability to delineate the vicissitudes of subjectivity which left his followers bewildered and confused as to where such a concept belonged. Thus, in discussing the topic of narcissism, Hartmann suggested that the opposite of object cathexis is not ego cathexis but rather cathexis of one's own person, in other words, self-cathexis. He goes on to say that "it will be clarifying if we define narcissism as the libidinal cathexis not of the ego but of the self."[20] This formulation has been taken up by most analysts who like to use the self as a concept for subjectivity. Traces of this view can be found in the work of Jacobson, Kernberg, Kohut, Levin, Winnicott, Guntrip, and virtually all proponents of object relations theory and ego psychology.

But what does Hartmann, and others like him, mean by the term "self"? Alternately, he speaks of self as self representation, a collection of self representations, and of a person as a whole. But if the word *self* is used as a substitute for *person,* it becomes unnecessary. The same is true if he means by that term a psychic apparatus. The concept of a total person is itself problematical. This is the very concept that Freud chose to disavow since he wanted to emphasize that the person is not "master of his own house." Although a person may experience himself as an agent of his actions, it is questionable that he ever experiences himself as a whole. In Hartmann's haste to resolve what he perceived to be a theoretical ambiguity concerning the concept of the ego, he succeeded in nothing more than weakening the original concept. This has been pointed out by Laplanche and Pontalis:

> The attempt to identify and eliminate a supposed "terminological ambiguity" is merely a way of avoiding a fundamental problem. The danger . . . is that the real contributions of the Freudian usage may be lost. For Freud *exploits* traditional usages: He opposes organism to environment, subject to object, internal to external, and so on, while continuing to employ "Ich" at these different levels. He plays on the ambiguities thus created. . . . It is this complexity that is shunned by those who want a different word for every shade of meaning.[21]

Unless psychoanalysts come to terms with the proper role of subjectivity in contradistinction to an ego or self, it appears self-evident that confusion will continue to be substituted for what is intended to solve the inherent difficulties. We will now examine the perspective of Jacques Lacan in order to clarify this problem.

The Ego and the Subject

Lacan has chosen to define the ego as "that image the child encoun-ters in the mirror." In other words, a mistaken identity. Though the individual is not identical to his own image, he acts as though he were. Due to what he perceived as the inadequate theorizing of ego psychol-ogists, such as Hartmann, Lacan followed the phenomenological inves-tigations of Sartre and other philosophers of the existential persuasion by introducing the concept of a subject who is distinct from the ego. Essentially, the subject is the subject of unconscious desire, ultimately a speaking subject who speaks most truthfully in slips of the tongue and other errors which emerge when the censorship of the ego is suspended or decentered.

Lacan insists that the validity of his concept of the ego is confirmed in Freud's earlier emphasis on the unconscious and those wishes which are said to comprise it. Whereas the *Standard Edition* translates Freud's *Wunscherfüllung* as wish fulfillment, French analysts have chosen to emphasize the realization of desire, thus releasing the wish from its mentalist connotation by pointing to the intentional aspect of the un-conscious.

As far as Lacan is concerned the ego and the self are identical. The notion of a total person or total self is dismissed as a neurotic search for identity which can never be more than imaginary. Lacan believes that the child confuses others with his own mirror reflections, so that the self, or ego, is formed from a composite of introjections and false identifications which comprise a knot of "misrecognitions," or misun-derstandings. Thus, these sets of identifications can hardly comprise a unified person, even for so-called "normal persons." All of us, says Lacan, are profoundly divided. In order to come to terms with such a radical theory of the ego, we must first examine Lacan's theory of child development, which is centered around the emergence of the mirror phase of perceptual cognition.

Lacan accepts the view that the earliest stage of development is expe-rienced by the child as radically undifferentiated.[22] In other words, the child fails to distinguish between himself and the world of others, that is, his environment. This view is similar to that of Max Scheler who believes that a child's impulses and tendencies are essentially extroverted and initially directed outwards into his immediate surroundings.[23] In these early years, while the child interacts with his parents, siblings, and other members of his community, he is embued with a familial apprehension of the world, so that his being is virtually absorbed into and articulated by this world of the other.[24] The child's own self remains obscure. According to Scheler the child gradually begins to experience himself as himself, with feelings, ideas, and inclinations of his own, through a necessarily painful emancipation from his environmental attachments.[25] While this view is not unfamiliar to most developmental theorists, Lacan would propose just the opposite. That is, it is through the child's identifications and attachments to his environment that his self is formed—in bad faith. It is this move that sets Lacan apart from the mainstream of psychoanalytic theorists and paves the way for a radical theory of subjectivity.

We know that the infant can perceive human forms from the day of its birth, but Lacan, borrowing a concept from Hegel, traces the emergence of the phenomenon of recognition to the fateful day that the infant encounters its reflected image in a mirror, usually at six to eight months of age. It is this encounter which Lacan characterizes as the beginning of the mirror phase.[26] The peculiar aspect of this encounter is that the phenomenon of recognition is initiated through the apprehension of a mere image, yet the child takes this image to be himself. The paradox of this encounter is that the human infant should be initiated into his never-ending quest for the recognition of his desires through a device that is anything but the recognition by another human subject. It is this paradox that formalizes the ambiguities of human relationships generally. Why this paradox should be so important will soon become clear.

In the first few months of life the infant's visual perception is superior to his motor coordination. When presented with his image in a mirror, the child is capable of recognizing the image as his while simultaneously continuing to experience himself internally as a jumbled mess of fragmented impulses and chaotic sensations. Thus, he perceives himself outside himself as a unified gestalt in marked contrast to the internal fragmentation. At one stroke the child experiences for the first time both a formation of himself and the alienation of himself. The result is an ambivalent constitution of his self-identity as both exterior and interior, both perceptual and bodily. Thrilled by the loving apprehension of his narcissistic self-image, the infant also wants to destroy that self because it points to his inner chaos. For Lacan, this represents the birth of aggression. This specular capture of oneself in the mirror institutes

ALLEGHENY COLLEGE LIBRARY

object relations also, but this object, which Lacan characterizes as the ego, is not another human subject; rather it is imaginary.

This is not to say that one should take the mirror experience as a literal assumption of the child's self-identity. Winnicott, who was himself influenced by Lacan's theory of the mirror phase, points out that the baby's identity is more specifically created out of his experience of seeing himself in the mother's face, whose gaze upon her child serves to mirror to the baby his image of himself.[27] In a most informative analysis of Lacan's work, Muller and Richardson comment that, "the essential here apparently is that human form be the external image in which the infant discovers both himself and the 'reality' around him; but presumably that human form could also be—and in the concrete is more likely to be—the mothering figure."[28] But even more generally, it is the child's relation with external reality, i.e., its environment, to which the mirror phase refers, which situates that child into a particularly visual and spatial experience of his reality, since it is only at the birth of his separateness from the environment that he can begin to experience the world as a spacial and visual universe from which he is apart. According to Lacan, this must be tremendously bewildering to the child, since the world he resides in is outside of himself yet experienced as a part of himself and even as aspects of himself:

> Given the fact that the infant subject first discovers himself in an external image, it is easy to understand how he confuses his external image of himself with the images of other subjects among whom he finds himself. It is in such fashion that the "social dialectic" begins. This confusion leads to a misidentification of himself with the other and has far-reaching effects, not only on relationships with others but on knowledge of external things as well.[29]

In contrast to Hartmann's recognition of the ego as the center of perception and consciousness and as an autonomous agency, for Lacan the ego is merely a construct in the imaginary, a sort of mold into which is poured man's alienated self. Thus the mirror phase initiates the child's identification with the (reflected) image of his body—an identification which turns him inside out. It is this captivation by the image of his own form—the effects of which are said to continue for as long as 18 months—which continues to dominate his behavior, especially in the presence of children his own age. If the child strikes another, he may claim it is he who was struck; when another child is injured, the child who witnesses the injury cries out as if to say it had happened to himself. It is by means of this initial identification with others that the child begins to feel his way into the intersubjective world. And it is in the grip of this situation, through which the child fixes onto himself an image which is alienating, that the organization of the ego is established.

Lacan quite rightly observes that "We have only to understand the mirror-stage as an *identification,* in the full sense that analysis gives to the term, namely the transformation that takes place in the subject when he 'assumes' an image." However, the important point to remember is that "this form situates the agency of the ego, before its social determination, in a fictional direction, which will always remain irreducible for the individual alone."[30]

Furthermore, it is through the child's assumption of his own reflected image that we find symbolized the mental permanence of the ego as it constitutes an alienating destiny and the correspondences which unite the ego with that image in which the subject projects himself into a world where he seeks to establish his completion.

The transforming quality of the onset of the mirror phase lies in the observation that, when the child encounters the reflection of his body, there is formed for the first time an experience of wholeness and completeness which formalizes a sense of selfhood. Previously he felt fragmented with pieces of himself attached to the mother.[31] Now he experiences himself as an individual in his own right, who has the look about him that everyone else does.

It is instructive to note that, in terms of adaptation, Lacan says somewhere that some animals, particularly the chimpanzee, are perfectly capable of detecting their image in a reflected surface, testing its reality by various—and sometimes devious—methods, exhibiting an intelligence at least equal to that of a child of the same age. But after the chimp has been disappointed a few times in trying to grasp something that is not there, he loses interest! As far as his ability to adapt is concerned, it is perfectly obvious that the chimp is *better adapted* to his environment than the human creature will ever be, given that the latter will spend the rest of his life in search of something that does not even exist. It is clear that the human subject refuses to adapt by pursuing the limits of his knowledge.

Thus, this image of a body in the mirror, in formalizing a sense of selfhood, ushers into the world, through an imaginary structure, the ego of the human subject. While serving to integrate his world, this integration is grasped at the expense of a primal understanding: His ego is mistaken for the lure of a false unity. It is not at all surprising that the child's response to this encounter should be one of rapture, for we know that the result of this experience is the captivation of his marriage to an illusory narcissistic union, a disembodied love.

And it is through this dialectic of misapprehension that is born the emergence of a narcissistic love of self and enslavement to self which form the basis and support for the evolution of all forms of psychopathology, including normality. All the child is able to comprehend is that this image responds immediately and faithfully to his cues, creating the illusion of communion with himself, with the added bonus of serving as a barrier against his dread of fragmentation.

But it is here that lies the rub. Since the transforming quality of this narcissistic position situates the agency of the ego in a fictional direction, we now witness the dramatic emergence of an internal conflictual tension between the ego and the subject who created it, resulting in the child's experience of aggressiveness and competitiveness with himself. As he strives to become the ego he thinks he is and which also finds its support in the collusive confirmation of those significant others who attempt to solidify his personality, the child becomes the spectre of an ominous and perpetual failure to be real.

At the heart of this ambivalent aggression is the child's inability to discriminate between those others who are the support for his egoic creations and his own investment in multiple identifications which fix themselves onto anything that looks solid. It is precisely during this interaction that we discover a paranoiac structure of the ego which in turn seeks its analogue in a delusion through which the subject throws back onto the world that very disorder his ego is comprised of. When these two moments become confused, that is, when the child charges after himself and when he becomes fixed by others, we find the expressions of guilt and masochism which demonstrate the bondage of aggression to narcissism and the structure of systematic denial and objectification that characterizes the enslaving quality of the ego.[32]

Thus the ego represents the center of all the resistances to the treatment of symptoms and the subject's realization of his unconscious desires, a truth, says Lacan, which must prevent us from ever investing our faith in some kind of return to a preestablished harmony.[33] It is inconceivable that the subject's ego could be an instrument which

would aid in the removal of symptoms when it is precisely this ego
which supports the symptoms the subject is trying to unravel. Thus the
illusion of harmony is merely one more symptom of man's alienation
from himself.

If the Oedipus complex results in a sublimation and identification
with the image of the father, we must wonder why Freud ever relied
upon the Oedipus legend as the reference point around which this
identification becomes evident. It should be clear that the structural
effect of identification with the rival is not self-evident and that it can
only be conceived if the way is prepared for it by a primary identification that structures the subject as a rival with himself, that is, with his
ego.[34]

The position of the father is crucial in that the "murder of the father"
is prevented by the child's need to participate in his (the father's) world,
which in turn neutralizes the conflict of rivalry which had originated in
the subject himself. Thus, according to Lacan, "The Oedipal identification is that by which the subject transcends the aggressivity that is
constitutive of the primary subjective individuation."[35] The fact that
the "I" (as ego and not as subject) is alien to the subject himself is
evidenced in our culture's tendency to reduce subjectivity to that state
with which we identify, such as, for instance, when we say: "I am a
doctor"; or "I am an American"; or "I am a man." This is further proof
for Lacan that, "In the last resort, these various formulas are to be
understood only in reference to the truth of 'I am an other,' an observation that is less astonishing to the intuition of the poet than obvious to
the gaze of the psychoanalyst."[36]

Lacan's statement here is certainly enigmatic in that he uses the expressive *I* for ego rather than as the agent, or subject, of desire. In other
contexts, Lacan distinguishes between the I and me, which conveys the
distinction more obviously. Nonetheless, we should note the ambiguous manner in which, in using the first-person pronoun, we often speak
of ourselves and conceive of ourselves as egos in the objective—and
objectifying—sense, and it is this ambiguity which Lacan takes such
pains to point out.

Thus, the tension between a subject and the other he takes himself to
be constitutes that nucleus and ambivalent aggressivity which is best
characterized through the expression of specifically unpleasant emotions such as hatred, envy, spite, malice, and resentment, all of which
have the most deadening influence on desire.

The conception of the ego described above contains both the personal (imaginary) aspect of the Freudian ego as well as the abstract metapsychological entity which is represented as an abstraction. This concept also eliminates any notion of the ego as constituting the subject, since it is the subject that constitutes the ego. Whereas the ego is a reified product of successive imaginary identifications, the subject is not a thing at all. Rather, it is grasped as a set of mutations and dialectical upheavals which point toward objects of desire in a continuous intentional structure of transcendence and temporality.

It is easy to understand why Lacan would be ruthless in his condemnation of ego psychologists and others who recommend a strengthening of the ego in a quest for a consistent and reliable identity when it is this very identity which Lacan's theoretical position is determined to subvert. What is most unfortunate in the theories of analysts such as Hartmann and Erik Erikson is that they confuse identity with uniqueness. The feeling of uniqueness has its genesis in the family in which each person is, first, *irreplaceable* and, second, is recognized and loved simply because he is and not for who or what he is. The identifications which inevitably become intermingled with the unique structure of his desire do not really alter his desire but simply give him the power to repress it. When the socializing power of school takes its toll, the child discovers that he is merely one among others, absolutely and perpetually replaceable, and he is recognized simply for what he is able to achieve rather than for the unique structure of his being. Unless he achieves in the eyes of the others, he is condemned and made the object of ridicule. It becomes imperative that he become identified as a good student. Thus everyone is encouraged to be like everyone else for the sake of the perpetuation of a social machine whose purpose is to make everybody acceptable.

Inevitably, the adolescent is confronted with the double bind that he needs to conform to the expectations of his teachers, while having to assert his uniqueness for the recognition of his peers with exploits which are often antisocial. If it becomes necessary that he achieve an identity which stands out, it is only because his uniqueness has been repressed. And this holds equally true whether his identity takes the form of a troublemaker or that of the most popular student. Thus, Hartmann's concern for the individual's adjustment to society takes the form of a collusion the purpose of which is to repress the uniqueness of the individual. It is not surprising that the ego would become the

THE IDOLATRY OF THE EGO

vehicle of this adjustment, since its role as the seat of identifications has no other purpose but to become like everybody else.

This is clearly not the role for the ego that Freud stressed or even accepted. He emphasized that the ego is an object of narcissism and that it is an image in which we consistently alienate ourselves. Ironically, this ego is in no way conscious but, in the strictest and truest sense of the term, essentially unconscious. It is a role played but not the player himself. The ego does not play a part but is a part that is adopted and enacted by the subject—a subject who lies hidden behind the veil of his personality. Thus, it is the id—the subject—which is the conscious, constituting agency, and the ego—which is always an object, or an other, to the subject—which is one aspect of "unconsciousness" itself.

In short, when speaking of the ego in terms of its relation to a reality, we are not describing an agent who perceives or experiences reality so much as a structure and set of identifications through which reality is reflected and distorted by an imaginary assumption which the subject takes to be "himself."

So what or who is the subject, if not a self or identity? According to phenomenologists, such as Sartre in his early thought and Merleau-Ponty, the subject is consciousness itself, not consciousness in a supposed purity of itself—that would lead to Hartmann's conception of the autonomous ego—but consciousness of the objects in the world in which it discovers its subjectivity. Lacan himself has attacked this conception because, rooted as it is in the perceptual field, he takes this to be but one instance of the imaginary order which ushers one's mirror phase itself. Adding to the confusion, Hartmann has even described his theory of the ego as a phenomenological one, and the existentialists, who roundly condemn the Freudian notion of the unconscious, perpetuate the view that phenomenology is incapable of conceiving the unconscious as anything other than an article of bad faith, or at best what Freud characterized as the "preconscious." Structuralists such as Lacan accuse phenomenologists of failing to do justice to a subjectivity situated outside the province of an ego, though Sartre himself, in his essay, *The Transcendence of the Ego,* separated himself from this view by positing a subjectivity which is transcendent to the ego itself:

> For most philosophers the ego is an "inhabitant" of consciousness. Some affirm its formal presence at the heart of *Erlebnisse* (i.e., experience), as an empty principle of unification. Others—psychologists for the most part—

claim to discern its material presence, as the center of desires and acts, in
each moment of our psychic life. We should like to show here that the ego
is neither formally nor materially *in* consciousness: It is outside, in the
world. It is a being of the world, like the ego of another.[37]

This quotation could be inserted, word for word, into Lacan's description of the mirror phase as a perfect example of his definition for the
formation of the ego. But Lacan has rejected what he refers to as the
"transparency of consciousness" to which Sartre alludes, in that the
subject is neither in the ego nor in the objects of its gaze, but rather in
the subject's apprehension of the objects of its gaze. As we shall see
later, Lacan and phenomenologists diverge markedly in their conceptions of the unconscious, particularly when it comes to describing the
nature of language and its significance to the Freudian unconscious.
For the present it is sufficient to speak of the subject in terms of a
desiring subject, a concept which found its original expression in
Hegel's *The Phenomenology of Mind*. That Lacan and Sartre were both
profoundly influenced by Hegel as interpreted by Kojève should not be
lost on us. Also, the fact that Sartre's essay on the ego exerted a particular influence on Lacan has been noted by numerous authors.

Briefly, in Kojève's rendering of Hegel, the question of subjectivity is
central in man's misconceived search for a verifiable identity.[38] Being
himself "no-thing," man can hardly look within himself via introspec-
tion to discover his subjectivity. All he would find is an ego which, as
Lacan pointed out, is constructed in the gaze (e.g., objectification) of
the others. In the midst of man himself is an emptiness—a concept that
Sartre called "nothingness," or no-thing—a lack at the heart of being.
This lack constitutes man's desire to be something for the other and, of
course, ultimately for himself. Equating desire with self-consciousness
per se, man looks to others in order to see what they see in him, while
resisting their gaze for objectifying him into a thing which would
negate his specifically human reality. This leads to a paradox, since, if
man wants to be recognized by others as something other than a thing,
what then can he be recognized as?

If the subject is a desiring subject as conceived by Hegel, his relation
to the world is situated in his wanting something from others, as they,
in turn, want something from him. This process is, indeed, essential to
life, since we can equate this same principle in terms of man's appetite to
consume food. This process is also transformative in the sense that we
become what we eat. Thus, I become what I assimilate and in other

respects—such as in my egoic identification—take on the characteristics of what I assimilate. All this depends on what it is I direct my attention toward. If I cast my desire toward things, I will, in turn, become a thing. It is cravings and appetite that Kojève refers to as "animal desires," because, unlike humans, animals are incapable of asking who or what they are. So, if man wants to rise above self-objectification, he must turn, not to objects to discover himself (the credo which serves as the foundation of modern advertising), but rather to desire itself, which can only be another human desire. Finally, to desire another's desire is to desire to be the object of the other's desire, in order to be recognized by the other as desirable or, as a subject of desire. This leads to recognition of my desire which, according to Kojève, is the fundamental project of all human beings. The problem of becoming recognized as someone other than a something (or ego) is, of course, the dilemma of all human relationships—particularly if we already conceive of ourselves as things to be identified. This conception of the subject obviously makes for difficulties for the question is raised, How do we conceptualize something which must ultimately defy objectification? It is this question that the remainder of this study of the objectifying—e.g., "psychopathological"—tendencies in man will address.

THE PRIMORDIAL SUBJECT OF UNCONSCIOUS DESIRE: A RECONNAISSANCE OF THE UNCONSCIOUS

Of an Unconscious Psychology

Phenomenology brings to psychoanalysis categories and means of acquiring knowledge that it needs in order to be complete. Phenomenology permits psychoanalysis to formalize a world of psychic reality (the desire of the Other); an intersubjectivity of death (psychopathology); the fantastic operations which construct an imaginary world (the ego); and, in our encounter with others, a lived history which coincides with an archeology of suffering, which is called "experience." Together phenomenology and psychoanalysis constitute a science of ambiguity which attempts to transcend the material world by embracing the elusive frontiers of an uncertain epistemology of truth.

Thus transformed, Freud may be read as a classic or as a mythology, if the reader is willing to take his words and concepts, not literally, but as the enigmatic source of a tradition which demands to be recognized and interpreted according to the structures of contemporary knowledge.

We should remember that Freud was legion in his ability to listen to the enigmatic words of life. Freud sometimes described his categories of transformative logic in an unbelievable language; sometimes he enslaved himself to and sometimes merely alluded to the medical and mechanistic terms of his time. Misunderstandings arose over his use of words and, sometimes, between Freud himself and his own presuppositions. It is from the brink of these misunderstandings that I will attempt a clarification.

It has been suggested that Marx, Nietzsche, and Freud held in common positions as protagonists of suspicion, who tore away the masks of the obvious and posed instead the problem of consciousness as a lie.[1] Freud believed that Man is incapable of being unreservedly true to either himself or others. In his hypothesis of a second thinking subject, Freud proposed that Man's official existence is at the service of an imposter, and that the true author of our acts and inclinations lie buried. This concept of an anonymous author situates the significance of Freud's peculiar notion of the unconscious.

His clinical experience convinced Freud that his patients—mostly neurotic—were unaware of quite specific characteristics about themselves which were nonetheless evident to his keen eye. Moreover, Freud discovered, like Socrates before him, that people are generally resistant to discovering the truth about themselves, despite their protests to the contrary. These observations led Freud to conclude that only a portion of the psyche was capable of being aware of its thoughts. As a result, certain contents of mental life were unconscious yet capable of becoming conscious after the resistances to knowledge were overcome.

In other words, Freud believed that the mental life of the individual is possessed of active, but unconscious ideas and that neurotic symptoms proceeded from the unconscious repression of these ideas, or desires. Thus, Freud adopted the hypothesis of a topographical unconscious, occupying a physical locality which was not merely a second thinking consciousness in competition with the first but rather a structured epistemological retreat which was in possession of its own contents, mechanisms, and volitions.

Freud insisted that the topographical dimension of the unconscious was constituted by those repressed contents which it somehow contrived to take into itself, rather like the snake that swallows its tail and, ultimately, itself. Not surprisingly, Freud admitted to certain reservations as to how this was indeed possible.

In Freud's elaborate and, in some ways, occult account of the unconscious, a series of topographical, dynamic, and economic models are fused together. But after years of speculative considerations, while Freud was formulating the vicissitudes of the unconscious, he was still using a technical vocabulary in which biology, mechanics, and language each made a contribution. For instance, in describing these dynamics,

Freud suggested that the unconscious has at its core a set of instinctual impulses which coexist without mutual influence or contradition; that it knows no negation, no doubt, and no degrees of certainty; that it can only say yes; that it is guided by the primary processes in which physical energy is freely transmissible between ideas; and that it is timeless, yet impervious to external reality while having as its aim the achievement of pleasure and the avoidance of displeasure.

In the midst of the rather incredible intermixing of biological, mechanical, and psychical terminology we sometimes lose sight of the essential message—and with it, the essential confusion—which dominated Freud's position vis-à-vis his topographical paradigm. If the unconscious is merely a receptacle into which unpleasurable thoughts and emotions can be discarded, it still remains mysterious just how the unconscious can also assume the posture of a dynamic agent which is capable of performing this very task. In other words, Freud insisted that the unconscious is constituted of its contents, yet it is capable of taking these very contents into itself. Thus, it constitutes its own existence as well as its constituting activities.

As we shall see, Freud's conception of the unconscious is replete with logical errors, not the least of which is his description of the psyche in purely mechanistic and physicalist terms. What is far more promising in Freud's theory of the unconscious is his notion of the instinctual drives, or urges, which he elaborates in his dynamic theory of unconscious energy. Yet, this theory also is held captive by the limits of Freud's crude scientistic training and becomes a casualty of his reluctance to form a credible theory of consciousness and unconsciousness in interpersonal terms, terms which might strive to constitute a language of desire.

The crux of Freud's theoretical problems lies in meditations which suggest, on one hand, that the unconscious is a force which attracts thoughts into itself while combating their reemergence into consciousness via repression. On the other hand, the unconscious is an alternate force that tries to bring its derivatives back into consciousness while struggling against the mediating function of a censor. Thus, discussion of the Freudian unconscious is sometimes reduced to that which we decide not to assume. Since this decision supposes that we are still in contact with the repressed, the unconscious is conceived as nothing more than a particular instance of bad faith or a betrayal of desire.

Freud assumed that repression constituted a situation in which the subject repels certain thoughts, memories, and other representations of the real world from conscious experience to unconscious limbo. In his paper on repression Freud explains that "The essence of repression lies simply in turning something away, and keeping it at a distance, *from* the conscious."[2] Yet Freud never managed to explain just how it is possible to keep something at a distance while remaining unconscious of it, short of reducing the whole argument to a physicalist conception of human desire and intentionality.

Sometimes Freud speaks of the unconscious as if it had wishes and desires of its own and which it tries to get satisfied. We might ask what purpose the subject serves if it is the unconscious that does the desiring? And if we are to equate subjectivity with unconsciousness, then how can the unconscious subject keep things at a distance while remaining unconscious of it? It was precisely this dilemma that led Freud to propose the existence of a second thinking subject. But now we have an unconscious that is just as conscious as the conscious, while this second (unconscious) conscious is unknown by the first so that it is unconscious to it.

The problem with this explanation is that it places two minds inside one person: the consciousness which I am aware of and which represents my official existence; and an unconscious consciousness which I am not aware of, yet influences—and in some cases determines—the attitudes that my conscious consciousness takes up and assumes in its official acts. But if my conscious sensibilities are inhabited by an unconscious consciousness which is unknown to me, then how could I possibly ever come to recognize the contents of this unconsciousness as they reemerge into consciousness? As Freud realized, the notion of forgetfulness does not account for this problem, since what is implied in Freud's conception of the unconscious is an active force which seeks to prevent the coming to awareness which is being resisted.

In order to account for this paradox, Freud introduced yet a third thinking subject which serves as mediator between the former two. He calls this the censor, or the ego in its capacity to utilize mechanisms of defense which, in turn, are unconscious. According to Freud, quite specific contents of the unconscious ae kept unconscious by the censor, whose function is to keep out of consciousness any thoughts which are too painful for our conscious egos to bear. Yet, this censor is admittedly rather crude, since it is always being misled by the contents of the unconscious, which manage to make their way to the surface by means of disguises in the form of dreams and parapraxes. In this way, the unacceptable contents excape the ever-watchful surveillance of the censor and manifest themselves ambiguously by wearing a mask.

But this solution to Freud's previous difficulty creates still more difficulties. Just who, precisely, is the person in question? The unconscious, the conscious, or the censor? Although we are confronted with an obvious fragmentation of the individual into three aspects, Freud insists that it is the censor which prevents fragmentation because it serves as a bridge between the conscious and the unconscious. The censor, due to its stated role, must be intimately aware of the contents of the conscious and the unconscious in order to repress those painful objects of consciousness in the first place. Further, the censor must be forever on guard to insure that none of the contents buried in the unconscious escape into consciousness which, after all, had got rid of these contents to begin with. Consequently, the censor must be intimately aware of what is going on in the unconscious, for how else would it know what to keep there?

Similarly, the censor must know the values and concerns of the conscious in order to know what is and is not permissible for it to accept. Thus, it is this third thinking subject—the censor—which assumes the cognitive responsibilities of the individual—responsibilities we generally confer upon the conscious self—since it is the censor which knows more about me than either the unconscious or the conscious. Yet, if the censor is capable of knowing all that is going on in the conscious and unconscious dimensions of my life, while acting as the vehicle of repression, then it must render Freud's concept of the unconscious to absurdity since the censor is aware of everything that is happening to me. By virtue of its role as a bridge between the conscious and the unconscious dimensions of my life, it is the censor which commands the treacherous powers of betrayal Freud attributes to the unconscious. Can this mean that the censor is really me and that I am lived, not by unconscious desires but by a merciless censor?

Only by splitting the censor itself into conscious and unconscious domains can Freud's original conception of unconscious forces be maintained. Only now, it is the unconscious aspect of the censor, the mechanism of defense, which embodies a repressive force. And so on.

Thus, Freud's censor cannot succeed as a process "in the third person," since it is presumably the unconscious subject that chooses which aspect of our being is admitted to official existence, which avoids the thoughts and situations we are resisting, and which, therefore, is not unknowing but, rather, an unrecognized and unformulated knowing that we struggle to bring into and keep out of our world.

Freud's structural model constituted a considerable advance over the topographical conception because the question of agency—or subjectivity—eventually came to the forefront of his speculation. Rather than a polarity between a presumably unconscious and conscious subject—who in turn was divided into conscious and unconscious components—Freud posited first two, then three, specific agencies of subjectivity. The trilogy of the id, ego, superego emphasized the degree to which each was now unconscious—save for the reflective capacities of the ego—and, further, that *each*—and not all three combined—was to be regarded as subjectivity. Resisting the notion of a unified person or an integrated self, Freud insisted on the primacy of divided mastery in the house of being. In addition, this division could never be united but they could conceivably, to the extent that their operations be made conscious, work in relative harmony. Thus, psychopathology was defined as that situation in which any one of these three agencies was to become dominant in the life of the individual, though precisely what an individual could possibly be in Freud's structural theory remained a mystery.

Still, the question of unconsciousness versus consciousness remained. Were it not for Freud's insistence that the id remain the seat of desire and—in that respect—occupy the position of subjectivity of the most primordial kind, one could have dismissed the id and superego as merely instinctual and cultural incentives and prohibitions from which the courageous ego, in attempting to gain mastery of its own house, could be designated as the only subject in the house. This was the path chosen by ego psychologists and, as we have seen, is rooted in the most elementary misconceptions regarding the nature of desire itself—a concept which has been virtually eradicated from the development of the theory of ego psychology. To his credit, Freud never followed suit—no matter how much people such as Rapaport believed was implied—and remained steadfast in his insistence that desire lay at the heart of man's being, while psychopathology could be conceived in terms of its distortion. Since the concept of unconsciousness lies at the heart of Freud's topological and structural theories, what are we to make of this conception?

The Psychoanalysis of Desire

The unconscious, which is the specific domain of psychoanalysis, is in direct contrast to consciousness, the preconscious and the pre-psychoanalytic notion of the subconscious. Freud never wavered in his insistence on these distinctions.

Phenomenologists have traditionally contrasted consciousness with all those potential objects of consciousness which, therefore, are unconscious to the subject. Further, phenomenologists generally prefer to avoid altogether distinctions between consciousness and un-consciousness, emphasizing instead those phenomena which the subject is reflectively aware of. The thread of the argument tends to suggest that the subject is nonetheless conscious of potential objects of consciousness that have not yet been reflected upon. In other words, each of us is conscious of things which we are only potentially aware of, since we would otherwise be incapable of perceiving the world in the first place. Thus, to be conscious of something, in the Freudian sense, is to be aware that we are conscious of it in the phenomenological sense. In other words, we own up to it.

Freud, with his concept of censorship, makes rather more ambitious claims than do the supporters of the phenomenological unconscious because the censor's constituent—the unconscious—is supposed to be comprised of contents which are inaccessible to consciousness. However, the preconscious is available to consciousness and is somewhat identical to the potentially conscious, unconscious phenomena of the phenomenologist. Constituted by inactivated memories, general knowledge, or one's stock of opinions, the preconscious implies a sort of nascent consciousness or shadowy half-consciousness which precedes realization. The preconscious refers to that area of potential knowledge that was designated the subconscious or unconsciousness before Freud.

Freud's rather novel approach to the unconscious was intended to convey those objects which actually recoil from consciousness, a sort of counterconsciousness, which resists its own contents from emerging into full recognition, thus remaining unto itself. It is thus secretive, unadmitted, unconfessed, potentially dangerous, and destructive. The whole body of our repressions comprises the unconscious. Moreover, Freud's approach disregards any concern with a possible psychology of consciousness or phenomenology of consciousness, since, in his view, it is the unconscious which holds the key to the understanding of human behavior and pathology. Thus, the psychoanalytic unconscious is not defined by an intentional field in which the subject may hope to find himself eventually. Rather, it is defined by an opposition to the subject and designates that domain which is counter to the subject's chances of adapting to reality. Now we can begin to appreciate the significance of the tremendous gap which separates the Freudian unconscious from the phenomenological method: a science of so-called "appearances." For Freud, the unconscious is that which refuses to appear.

Unfortunately, phenomenologists have not been especially sympathetic with the psychoanalytic conception of the unconscious, probably due to Freud's intolerable mechanistic and positivistic theoretical orientation. Those philosophers who have attempted to give Freud his due, such as Ricouer, Merleau-Ponty, Scheler, and Habermas have had to dismiss Freud's theory and focus instead on his clinical studies which, in practice, tend to ignore the scientistic and energic explanations which Freud and his followers favored. Other phenomenologists have not been so kind.

Sartre's rather critical remarks on psychoanalysis appear to misconstrue Freud's formulation of the unconscious by reducing unconsciousness to those fringes of awareness (nascent consciousness) which Freud clearly designates as preconscious.[3] Thus, Sartre's concept of bad faith, as provocative and useful as it is, fails to account for Freud's argument while reducing the concept of repression to a mere hesitation of freedom. Yet, Sartre's intent is far more instructive than the fruit of his labors might suggest, since his aim was to expose Freud's philosophically impossible "receptacular" notion of the unconscious and to demonstrate further the consequent psychology of negativism on which psychoanalytic theory can be interpreted.

The heart of the divergences between phenomenology and psychoanalysis lies in the location of consciousness per se, that is, the lived space of unconsciousness. Psychoanalysts tend to place consciousness somewhere in the mind, which is located somewhere in the body. Moreover, the mind then presumably brings into itself contents which merely represent the external world. Thus, psychoanalysis is founded on a representational theory. Its proponents insist that a person first perceives an object in the world which is distinct and apart from himself, so that then a representational image of that object is reflected—as in a mirror—in the conscious component of the mind. The conscious mind is thus conceived every bit as much as being a receptacle as the unconscious is. This results in the conscious receptacle and the unconscious recpetacle, each of which trade between themselves representational images of the outside world. According to this view, should a perception of an event in the world (such as the scene of parents locked in the act of love) be so emotionally charged that the subject deems it intolerable, then the memory of that perception is repressed.

Any such notion as a receptacular consciousness is inconceivable to the adherents of phenomenology who hold that consciousness is, by its very nature, intentional. Thus, consciousness is rooted in the world, not in the mind. In other words, consciousness is nothing in itself, since it relies for its own composition on an object to constitute it. Thus, consciousness, by inhabiting the world, realizes its material expression in all those objects it takes stock of. A representational theory of consciousness is unnecessary because, if consciousness is indeed located in the world, we have no need to look inside a receptacle mind in order to locate refractions of objects which exist in the world to begin with.

We see things precisely where they are. But this is not to suggest that an intentionally based theory of consciousness is a realism which holds that we can enter into communication with the objects perceived. We would require a language in order to do that, and things cannot talk to us. Instead, consciousness runs after the things it takes stock of and in that sense discovers itself in those objects it perceives. According to Sartre,

> Intentionality is not the way in which a subject tries to make "contact" with an object that exists beside it. *Intentionality is what makes up the very subjectivity of subjects.*[4]

Sartre formulates this insight with the subtlety of the poet that rarely occurs to the psychologist:

> When I run after a streetcar, when I look at the time, when I am absorbed in contemplating a portrait, there is no *I*. There is [only] consciousness *of the streetcar-having-to-be overtaken*, etc. . . . In fact, I am then plunged into the world of objects; it is *they* which constitute the unity of my consciousness; it is *they* which present themselves with values, with attractive and repellent qualities—but *me*—I have disappeared; I have annihilated myself [in this moment of conscious apprehension].[5]

In other words, when I experience a rock, a tree, a feeling of sadness, I experience it just where it is: beside a hill, in the meadow, in relation

to myself and my beloved. Consciousness and the object of consciousness are given with one stroke. The things which I perceive constitute
my consciousness of them, just as I constitute their existence as things
through that act in which I perceive them and give them a name. And
since naming things is a purely human activity, it is obvious that things
do not exist as trees, rocks, or emotions in the absence of a human
consciousness which is capable of noticing them and apprehending
them through the constitutive power of language.

Thus, consciousness has no inside. It is, as Heidegger says, being
there, beyond itself. It is an absolute flight, by virtue of its refusal to be
the same thing that it sees. This movement of immanence and transcendence virtually throws us into the world in the midst of danger because
being in the world turns us inside out as our perceptions dictate that we
leap from isolation in order to burst onto the stage, through a dispossession of ourselves.

Moreover, consciousness of things is not limited to knowledge of
them, since my knowing, for instance, a woman is only one of the many
possible forms my consciousness can take of her. I can also love her, hate
her, fear her, and if I choose, refuse her, ignore her, deny her. And this
surpassing of consciousness through my apprehension of others discovers its subjectivity in love, hate, fear, denial. Nowhere in psychoanalysis is this multiplicity of consciousness accounted for.

Fearing another human being is merely one of the ways I am capable
of moving toward him and finding myself confronted by another human creature in whom I discover my fear, my hatred, myself, and my
desires. Suddenly love, hatred, and desire are torn from the depths of
consciousness as it becomes inscribed in those things and qualities
which constitute my world and situate the material expression of my
unadmitted desires and intentionality. Thus consciousness could never
be a mere "receptacle" in which representational images of things are
intuited because consciousness is nothing without an object of consciousness through which it discovers its own foundation. There are no
contents in consciousness per se; rather we are subjected to objects of
consciousness which situate our subjectivity in objectives of desire. The
subject is not the source of consciousness, for we discover our subjectivity and consciousness outside ourselves, in the world of our experiences.

My self-absorbed identity disappears in the act of consciousness
wherein I lose myself in the objects I perceive. It is only on reflection
that I gain access to myself and my desires by turning my back on the

world and poisoning the purity of my consciousness of others, by entering into a dialogue with myself. Thus, according to Sartre,

> Reflection poisons desire. On the unreflected level I bring Peter help because Peter is "having to be helped." But if my state is suddenly transformed into a *reflected* state, where I am watching "myself" act, in the sense in which one says of someone that he listens to himself talk. It is no longer *Peter* who attracts me, it is *my* helpful consciousness which appears to me as having to be perpetuated.[6]

However, the act of reflection is the only means we have of discovering the peculiar structure of our subjectivity, appraising ourselves of the situation we are in, and affecting a judgment about a situation in order to gain access to knowledge about our experiences. Through reflection we make objects of ourselves by a life-and-death struggle with the other (e.g., Hegel's master-slave dialectic). My acts and words take me out of myself by etching my intention onto the world where I realize the expression of my subjectivity through the other's recognition of it. I am recognized by others by turning myself over to them. Their response returns me to myself after transforming me with their reply. So by talking about my acts I make objects of them in order to gain knowledge about myself.

Since my consciousness of things is always situated in the world, I have no direct access to my subjectivity. I am always unconscious of myself as a subject. When I reflect on my acts by talking to myself, I become conscious of myself indirectly because my acts of reflection are always directed to another, even when this other is my ego. Thus, I am subject to two differing structures of consciousness. In one my unconscious desires are situated in the world of others to whom I surrender myself and in another I turn away from the world in order to reflect on the dialectical signification of my subjectivity.

Insofar as it is discourse which is the medium of the subject's realization of desire, the subject is recognized in his desire by virtue of that dialectic through which desire constitutes his world. Thus, the subject does not begin with subjectivity. He comes to discover his subjectivity after he reappropriates the signification of his desires by virtue of the other's recognition of them.

At the heart of subjectivity we discover a drama in which the subject submits his fate to discourse with others in order that his consciousness of self is realizable, so that his subjectivity can be returned to him in an authenticated, or recognized, form. Ultimately, it makes no real differ-

ence whether an actual other or the subject himself reveals the significance of his acts. Even when the subject discovers a truth about himself
by talking to himself, this very process has been made possible in the
first place by virtue of others (i.e., the psychoanalyst) who have enabled
him to become a subject to himself by becoming an other to his desire.
What is basically required is that discourses occur so that the subject
can place into question that reflective reappropriation of himself which
in turn makes self-consciousness desirable to the subject and recognizable to an other. Thus discourse moves the subject from self-consciousness in order to deepen his awareness of the intersubjective foundation
of his desires.[7]

It now becomes evident that the unconscious of Freud is that part of
discourse which refuses to return to the subject, a subject who has
become neurotically incapable of reestablishing himself in the intersubjective discourse of the spoken word. He keeps everything to himself. In
other words, the unconscious is the unspeakable. This is why the individual as an individual is merely a myth because the subject, in order to
be a subject, needs discourses with others in order to reappropriate a
truth which—while hidden to himself—is always evident to others.
Thus consciousness of self depends on the other's recognition (apprehension) of the unconscious desires I utter.

Moreover, these two structures of consciousness—the subject's apprehension of objects of consciousness and the reappropriation of his
subjectivity through acts of reflection—are translated by psychoanalysis
into two distinctive domains of experience: the unconscious and the
conscious. But, if consciousness is a structure of intentionality, then
what is the unconscious according to a phenomenological mode of
enquiry? And what is the relation between desire and consciousness?

The subject is subjected to his unconscious desires. He apprehends
objects of consciousness, which, in turn, appropriate his subjectivity,
then return him (his desires) to himself by the other's reply through
speech and acts of reflection. While consciousness takes as its ob-
ject(ive) any state, quality, affect, or idea which exists in the world,
desire is always directed to another subjectivity: the one that is capable
of understanding me. Consciousness is directed to objects of consciousness, while desire is directed to the other's recognition of my poten-
tialities as being desirable.

Thus, desire is never conscious of itself, any more than consciousness
is conscious of itself. The realization of desire is mediated by an other
and through an other, while it is deepening its participation in the

world by finding itself in the other's recognition of my appeal for recognition.

The Freudian unconscious refers to those desires which have yet to be recognized by others. The self-centered discourse of the neurotic, which hides in its own enclosed speech, has never been heard, understood, or responded to. The neurotic forfeits his subjectivity due to his reluctance to speak without equivocation. He becomes absorbed in himself by talking to himself, but no one listens because he talks to no one.

This theory of consciousness led Sartre to conclude that consciousness is not located in an ego, or a self, or even in itself, but rather, following Hegel, is a sort of transparency, which, ". . . is a *nothing,* since all physical, psychophysical, and psychic objects, all truths, all values are outside it; since my *me* (e.g., ego) has ceased to be any part of it. But this nothing is *all* since it is *consciousness of* all these objects. There is no "inner life" because there is no longer anything which is an *object* (inside me). . . . Doubts, remorse, or so-called 'mental crises of consciousness,' etc.—in short, all the content of intimate diaries—becomes sheer *performance.*"[8]

Sartre's conception of consciousness—though he himself apparently missed it—closely approximates what Freud always alluded to as the unconscious life of the individual outside the realm of egoic experience. While Sartre resisted calling this "pre-reflective cogito" an unconscious for reasons which are easy to appreciate, Lacan has taken this paradigm to mean the Freudian unconscious itself. Though Lacan has attacked phenomenology in general, and Sartre in particular, for advocating a theory of consciousness rooted in the notion of transparency, it is difficult to see how, in linking the unconscious dimension to the linguistic order, he has himself overcome this criticism. Just as Sartre uses his concept of consciousness to point to something other than what it is, Lacan—as we shall see in our concluding chapter—uses language to say something other than what it says. According to Fredrick Jameson, "The Lacanian unconscious is therefore not so much that dark inner reservoir of desire and instinct which used to be our image of the Freudian id, rather it is an absolute transparency, an order which is unconscious simply because it is infinitely vaster than our individual minds, and because they owe their development to their positions within it."[9]

We turn to the statement of Jameson only to show how similar, in certain respects, the views of Sartre and Lacan indeed are, though

Lacan, being a psychoanalyst himself, chose to retain the Freudian terminology, while altering his definition of the unconscious in a way that bears a similarity to Sartre's conception of (pre-reflected) consciousness. We shall see later how Lacan's adoption of Saussurian linguistics, Lévi-Strauss's structuralism, and Heidegger's ontology produce an interpretation of Freud that is vastly more complicated—and sophisticated—than Sartre had imagined. Suffice it to say for the time being that Sartre and Lacan shared similar views on the nature of the ego and the intentional—and dialectical—structure or desire. Each in his own way questioned Freud's conception of a conscious unconscious. The notion of an unconscious consciousness only makes sense if we perceive it as a prereflected mode of knowing and experiencing which is barred to reflection. It is not that we fail to know what we are doing when doing so unconsciously as much as not knowing that we are doing that which we most vigorously deny. The Freudian unconscious does not merely allude to this unformulated knowing, which is subjectivity itself, but to those acts we repeat unknowingly, and the circumstances in our history and in our everyday lives which guide us this way or that, whether for the sake of repressing a forbidden desire or in disavowing the consequences of our indirection. The ego is not a subject—whether known or unknown—but more likely that censor, to which Freud referred, of the subject's emergence into full expression of his unformulated (unconscious) desire. If the ego is an identity which stands in place of our unbeknownst subjectivity, all the so-called "mechanisms" which Freud attributed to its domain are nothing but substitutive ways of inhabiting our world which belie the other's recognition. The ego can never become recognized, since it is already an objectified form of knowing which we use as a password to mirror ourselves in the other's gaze. We are not conscious of pursuing this folly to the extent that we fail to question it. It is this questioning on which psychoanalysis is properly founded.

Apart from conceiving the unconscious as a metaphor for the unreflected subject, we can construct many metaphors which illustrate the multiplicity of Freud's ambiguous expression. The unconscious can be shown to be (1) my desire to be recognized as someone other than an ego; (2) my words which convey my desire which I speak without thinking; (3) my errors, slips, and other parapraxes which, committed unreflectedly, betray the truth of my desire; (4) my body, in both the preverbal history of my infantile conception, as well as my hysterical symptoms which symbolize my diverted desires; (5) my sexuality which, in pursuit of a pleasurable experience, expresses in a materialized form the ambivalences and dilemmas contained and retained in the abandonment of my mother's body; (6) my childhood memories, remembered, forgotten, and distorted; (7) my personality, or character, or ego, in a word, my false self; (8) my history, or rather the legends which comprise my history as told, hidden, surmized, and fantasized by myself and others, and the myths of my primal omnipotence, which in turn structure my egoic privilege; (9) my amnesia, which is both retrievable and lost forever; (10) my defenses, which merely mask my primal impotence; (11) and finally, language itself, which both reveals and conceals my desire, as well as all those things I care, or dare, not to know. This list, while not exhaustive, measures a world which, for me, is beyond my experience while, alternatively, the abode of all my possibilities toward experiencing what indeed has been lost.

The Phenomenology of the Other

Heidegger has proposed that our freedom to inhabit the world is limited because we are thrown into a world which is already there and which imposes on us the values and desires of others in circumstances so discreet and complex that we are hardly aware of their presence. This world, which is already given as a background, is the habitat of my desires. Yet, it remains always transcendent to my knowledge of its role in the realization of my subjectivity.

It has been suggested that the unconscious is like a city. We are familiar with some of its cafes and bars, the markets and shops where we conduct our business, while other sectors are forbidden and risky. Yet, it is not the forbidden sectors which represent the unconscious, but the city itself, the source of all our experiences, whether good or bad, terrifying or sublime. The truth of the city is my unconscious desire, while the city is that world which occupies the source of desire and the arena of its possible realization. Thus, the subject of desire inhabits an unconscious sector of his experience which intersects with the unconscious desires of others. Thus, it is the subject himself, the one who inhabits the city, who constitutes its significance and builds its avenues, who is in reality the unconscious id, since it is the subject of desire who has always to search in the absence of his own foundation.

In this respect, the concept of repression refers to an avoidance of a trauma or situation that we do not want to accept as our own. The repressed idea does not come to us because we are unable to disclose its significance to ourselves. Yet, this disclosure becomes a possibility in the presence of an other, for only he can hope to recognize the gaps in dialogue which point to the formative structure of what I cannot even admit to myself: my unspeakable desires and the snares they are trapped inside of.

Thus, the obsessional is a person who cannot afford to consider other possibilities than the one which makes him a prisoner: his devotion to the satisfaction of his mother's desire. The result is an obsession with her satisfaction and the re-creation of the perfect bliss which her body had once bequeathed him. What he cannot, must not face is the look of disappointment on her face should he forsake her demand for satisfaction. Yet he is not, strictly speaking, unconscious of this fact. Indeed, he knows the facts only too well. What he cannot, ever, admit is that this very devotion should be the occasion of his misery. Thus, it is the consequence of his desire that he fails to recognize and which the mother is unable to recognize.

Neurotic desire is not an unconsciousness at work despite itself, but rather a most peculiar consciousness which merely touches its objects while eluding them. It takes account of them as a blind man takes account of obstacles. While he fails to recognize his true motives, he is just as unsuccessful in disavowing them. Moreover, this unconscious constitutes avoidance because desire is not the intellectual possession of what we hope to acquire but rather a dispossession of ourselves in favor of our ultimate disclosure. The neurotic's dilemma is that he is always the last one to know himself.

In other words, what we call the unconscious is a perceiving consciousness that operates through a logic of implication, following a path that leads to a destination we cannot see clearly and which must be uttered in order to be admitted to our world.[10] To admit a truth is simply our way of opening ourselves to it. Like mistakes, the symptom is full of immanent truths which move through a network of relations equivalent to a truth which it lacks possession of, yet takes into account by virtue of its symbolic disavowal of them.

Indeed, it is often a matter of surprise that the neurotic or the madman can put up with himself. Such people are never, strictly speaking, in their identities, emotionally crippled or crazy. No matter how hard we might try to establish our true identity, any such notion of ourselves eludes us in the face of the realization that we are ultimately incapable of fixing our personalities this way or that. It is inescapably the situation which determines our relation to ourselves and which situates the structure of our desires. And it is in response to the situation that we ultimately discover ourselves. Consciousness does not simply define itself as neurotic or crazy. My consciousness of things requires that I recognize in my perception of things a reflection of intentional structures that are ultimately my own creations.

Precisely who or what I am is never entirely clear. And because of this I tend to chase after myself as I run away from myself while seeking the recognition of others. Though the demands of the present may demand that I act expeditiously, I can also choose to ignore this or that transformative act and cling to whatever hope of escape may remain. But I am never entirely alone even in these private deliberations. Even if I complain about my character or personality, I can do so only by comparing myself with others. Such complaints are never really truthful, for when I pause to question my true motives for being this way or that I cannot help but feel beyond my limitations by resigning myself to them. Even in solitude I experience the presence of others, since I experience myself as an other to myself.

Everything that I am, by virtue of choice or circumstance, I am never completely for myself. If I am hated or avoided by others, I can still seek their recognition as a creature who is suffered or avoided. And though I cannot compel others to like me, this is ultimately unimportant because all that really matters to me is that they take notice of me. If I should feel powerless to transform this particular identity for another, it is because I choose this identity above all the others, and lose myself in this identity.

If we should say that my temperament inclines me this way or that, it is still only a manner of speaking, since my temperament exists only through an order of knowing what I learn about myself when I see myself as others see me. Insofar as I recognize what others see, I place value on it and, in that sense, choose it. What misleads us in these considerations is that we often look for desire in the willful deliberations which look at one motive and then another, opting in the end for the one which is the most compelling. In reality, this kind of deliberation follows my desires, which in turn bring my choices into the open. Only by seeing myself as some sort of thing can I possibly cling to a specific definition of myself. What ultimately matters to me is what others think of me. However, I cannot even know for sure what it is they are thinking. Even if I am envious, kind, cruel, or self-serving, it is always in relation to others that I am all these things for myself.

We sometimes hear the weakness of the will offered as evidence of the ultimate helplessness of desire. But it is foolish to look for desire in any act of will, since we have recourse to acts of will only in order to go against our desires and for the purpose of demonstrating the utter futility of denying our interdependency on others. Even what we call obstacles to desire are in fact employed by it. This is why an unclimbable rock face has no meaning for someone unless he wants to climb it. Thus, nothing sets limits to desire other than those limits that desire itself sets in the form of our various initiatives.

In other words, if we claim that a hill is unclimbable, this distinction can be conferred upon it only through my desire to climb it, so that desire brings forth obstacles to itself by setting itself against itself. Only by virtue of my desire to do the impossible does the impossible occur to me. As a result, it is precisely in these deliberations that I encounter what merely appear to be obstacles.

The very notion of desire demands that my decisions should plunge into the world, that something should be accomplished by them, what Sartre calls a "performance." This is how desire is sometimes confused with those abstract deliberations by which we merely look for excuses to mask our impotence. Such deliberations are, in reality, lies to themselves while harboring the most hostile motivations. But this is not to say that desire contrives that this way be an obstacle and that way a way through. My desires arrange for there to be obstacles and ways through in general. Desires are apprehended in our encounter with those limits which serve to identify the dynamic structure of our possibilities.

Thus, there are no obstacles in themselves. Pain and fatigue do not prevent my desire to achieve a particular objective. I give up climbing this mountain because I dislike it, because I have already committed myself to a different style of existence. Having captured my life on the spear of an obsessive attitude that has endured for many years, it is not probable that I shall ever choose to give it up because it is only with great difficulty that I could ever undertake to destroy an attitude I have made mine.

My encounter with others does not inhibit my desire, since desire gears itself to the situation, supports it, and in the face of all opposition confers upon that situation the instruments of its perpetuation. But this

is not to say that I willingly choose myself or my situation, since desire
is never an unconditional desire. On the contrary, I am what I am on the
basis of a situation which I have no control over; but, it is a situation,
nonetheless, which I can transform by taking it up and being it.

The world I encounter is already constituted but never entirely constituted because my part in it spontaneously confers upon it new possibilities which, in turn, contribute to a new composition of the situation. This is why I can never be sure precisely what share I contribute to
the situation and what share is contributed by the situation. I choose
the world and it chooses me. Together we struggle to confirm the
destiny of each.

Thus, all my actions stand in relation to a manner of being, a style. It
is by being unreservedly what I am that I have the chance to be recognized. Only through being with others can I ultimately discover myself.
Yet nothing determines me, not because nothing acts on me, but because I am, from the start, outside myself. Moreover, I need not fear
that my choices restrict my freedom, since choice and action alone cut
me loose from my self-indulgence.

What is finally most interesting in Freud is not a second, or even
third, "I think," which could know what I do not know about myself,
but rather the discovery of a primordial desire which is always symbolic, encountered in a world which withholds the promise of its deliv-
ery while requiring that others, by virtue of their desire, too, recognize
the interdependence of the boundaries and frontiers of their embodied
world. This world is not merely the source of all my conceptions and
misconceptions about myself and others but, even more significantly, it
is the habitation of my unformulated thoughts and expectations, and
the abyss of my unconscious, or rather, my unspoken, destiny. The
specific formulations that desire structures in this destiny, its failings,
and its objectives, will now be examined.

CHAPTER THREE
THE LOST OBJECT
OF DESIRE

Desire is the search for a symbolic repetition of a satisfaction whose completion has become impossible. This impossible desire arose from the gratification which was initially provided at the mother's breast. It is not a return to the breast which the subject of desire is seeking, but rather that peculiar gratification which was once afforded.

The child's earliest relations with others are dominated by a dialectical drama between his needs and the emerging desires which demand and then betray his inarticulate appeals for love. At birth the helpless infant is incapable of assuming command of a language which might enable him to engage in a conversation with those who provide for his welfare. Thus, he is dependent in two ways: not only on the biological needs which insure his survival, but on the social organization which anticipates his needs while remaining outside the sphere of his direct participation. While capable of making known—through gesture and sound—the presence of an agitation which signals the urgency of a response, he lacks the sophisticated mode of communication which can pinpoint the specific need in question.

Language is in the possession of the other, while the child remains outside articulated speech, capable only of making known a general appeal for the mother's presence. The mother's response contains the contradictions and the prototype of what will come to define the peculiar structure of the child's desire. Her gestures of response and regard for the child's needs contain more specifically her dutiful care for his welfare while simultaneously conveying the expression of her maternal love. While attending to his needs, the very success of her response also serves to crush his plea by silencing his only means of establishing a communicative relation with her, since the satisfaction she provides renders his appeal obsolete, producing a desire for her "presence" which transcends his biological needs.

The coming and going of the mother's breast serves a double purpose. While providing for the sustenance of his bodily hunger, the breast even more significantly represents that part of himself the child loses at birth, thus symbolizing the return of that most profound lost object he once enjoyed inside the mother's body.

The relationship of the mouth to the breast is especially significant because it serves to particularize in a ritualistic mode of expression the child's generalized appeals for love. While the biological cries of hunger are regularly satisfied through the intervention of the breast, the child's desire for the mother steadily increases, since the culmination of the nurturing act coincides with the removal of the breast and with it the object of his desire. Thus need and desire diverge in different directions, since the satisfaction of need prompts desire all the more forcefully.[1]

The removal of the breast evokes that primordial separation from the mother's body, increasing the child's desire for the lost object, then splitting off in all directions and seeking its impossible satisfaction in anything that pertains to the mother.

Thus, the lost object of desire is the totality of the completeness the subject has enjoyed while incarnated as an embryo inside the uterus of its mother. This series of linkages—fetus to placenta; placenta to uterine wall; uterus to the inside of the mother's body; blood passing into and out of the fetus, bringing nourishment from the mother's body and out again, conveying the refuse from the manufacture of its body—comprises for the fetus a rather cozy arrangement in which everything happens automatically. The disruption of birth which results in the loss of these primordial linkages ordains for the newborn child the birth of desire: the desire to be at one with an other.

It is no wonder that the mother's breast is such a comfort and satisfaction in this moment of the infant's uncertainty. This structure of bondage symbolizes the mediating influence the mother brings to bear on her efforts to usher the child back into an arrangement which has been lost but which must be reenacted if survival is to prevail. Thus, the infant's linkage to the mother's body becomes the first object of desire for the human infant, a desire which is born from the lack which his initiation into the world insists upon.

We might question in this regard Melanie Klein's suggestion that the significance of the breast comes from the assumption that the infant fantasizes its detachment from the mother's body through his idea that the breast is a part of himself.[2] On the contrary, the breast comes to signify the pure loss that is commensurate with living because in the midst of the infant's extrauterine existence comes to life a separation from the breast which serves as that first experience which recapitulates the loss of a part of itself at birth. Indeed, what is crucial is the separation of the breast from the infant, which occurs intermittently between each feeding, and permanently with weaning. Thus, the breast is not merely a partial object, but more significantly the infant's first object of desire.[3]

The desire which is born from the infant's separation at birth is thus of a different order from that which the infant is prone to experiencing after his assumption of language and his egoic incarnation. During the first six months the infant, still ensconced in a preverbal and pre-egoic apprehension of his environment, experiences his desire both physically and sexually. Apart from his need for nourishment, the child experiences nursing and touching in general in terms of an eroticized desire which Freud used as the foundation for libido. Still barred from insertion into a symbolic order which language will eventually ordain, the infant fantasizes a sort of union with the mother which sexual pleasure epitomizes, per se. After the formation of the ego—which Lacan refers to as the mirror stage—the child's desire will become more specifically narcissistic than erotic, as he becomes captivated no longer by the mother's body but with his identity as perceived, as the imaginary complement of his lack.

Thus, in the midst of this drama, about six months after birth, the child encounters what Lacan has already drawn our attention to: the recognition of his own image in the mirror, forming for the first time a sense of wholeness and completeness in himself (rather than in his symbiotic maternal relation).[4] It is at this point that his desire becomes imaginary as well as erotic. This apprehension of his own body image is astounding in the effect it has on the child, on his relation with himself, and on his relation with others. While previously it was his mother who occupied the seat of his idolatrous fascination, now his own reflected image gives the appearance of a revelatory discovery of uncontrollable ecstasy, since this image holds the suggestion of fulfilling the place of his lost object in the form of that narcissistic captivation of his own appearance. This new-found sense of wholeness derives from his discovery that he is an individual creature in his own right, with a similar appearance that others have. Yet this image of his body in the mirror, while formalizing for the first time his sense of selfhood, ushers into the world through an entirely imaginary structure the child's experience of selfhood.

While seeming to integrate his world, this very integration is realized at the expense of a mistaken recognition. He takes this egoic image in the looking glass to be himself, while in reality this reflection and the creature whose significance it implies is merely the image of his appearance.

Understandably, the child's response to this discovery is one of rapture, since he does not realize that he has, in effect, become captured by this fixed image of his bodily organization. All he knows is that this image (while gazing at it, clutched in his daddy's or mommy's arms, in the mirror) responds immediately and faithfully to each of his cues, creating the illusion of communion with himself, evoking the communal sensibility he once enjoyed inside his mother's body.[5] It is not difficult to imagine the sense of power and omnipotence he must feel at having done this magic all by himself.

Yet this very moment whereby the child magically becomes his reflected image ushers into his world a misalliance with that illusion through which he fixes onto himself a specular image of himself which only serves to alienate him from himself. The important point to emphasize is that this transformation points the agency of the ego in a mythical direction, creating an internal conflict between the ego and the subject who created it, polarizing forever into two opposite and opposing directions the omnipotent and narcissistic tendencies of the egoic organization on the one hand, and the never-ending quest for the realization of the subject's desire on the other.

Out of this conflict emerges the child's tendency towards competitiveness and aggression. As he strives to be this ego he takes himself to be, he is haunted by a nagging sense of failure and unease as he tries to bind the chasm between the lost object of his desire and the egoic directive which alienates him from himself. The frustration yields to new demands upon the parents whose responsiveness and gratification he turns to for confirmation and reassurance.

But there is more at stake here than an urge to complete a self which is thus divided. The mirror reflects more than just his own image. He notes that this image is surrounded by other objects as well. They, too, enter into a silent collusion with him as participants in the illusory support of his own completion. Thus the world of objects and things outside the mirror become symbols of his fragile integration, and the responsiveness of the parent who hands him objects and toys coincides with the responsiveness of his image in the mirror.

He now experiences objects in the same loving way that he experiences the narcissistic component of himself. When a child demands objects or toys, he is actually demanding signs of love from those very people whose task it is to provide them.

But eventually he comes to realize that his parents are not entirely responsive to his still inarticulate demands. Thus he begins to appropriate language to resolve the frustration that arises because he cannot make himself understood. With the acquisition of language a new transformation occurs. Once he is able to say what he wants, he discovers that having got it he no longer wants it. The appropriation of the objects he adores betrays the fact that once needs are satisfied they tend to evaporate. Love is no longer enough to satisfy him, and he crosses that threshold into the world of desire as a speaking subject, where the object of his desire must be uttered in order to be realized.

The whole point of speech is that it is addressed to an Other, not just an other who I speak *to* as an object of my desire, but a "desiring" Other who *listens* to my appeal, who is capable of recognizing the utterance of my desire in the myriad ways it conforms to the rules of the game we play together. In a word, through his capacity to recognize my desire, the Other is the only one who can understand me.

I distinguish between "Other" with a capital "O" and "other" with a small "o" to define the Other as a subject who is capable of recognizing my appeals of desire, and that other who, in failing to recognize them, inserts instead an objectified ego (my ego) in its place, so that the desires he is satisfying are merely his own in projected form. (This usage should not be confused with Lacan's, which more specifically designates the Other as the unconscious, ruled by the signifiers of Saussurian linguistics.)

At this point it is the word instead of the child's image of himself which dominates his struggle to become recognizable. While his demands for satisfaction once required that he possess those objects which served to confirm the love of those who provided them, his investment in language and that society of others who articulate its dimensions and govern its laws serves to mediate the expression of a desire which is always directed to an Other who listens. As the magic of the mirror phase loses its dominating influence, the child begins to realize that he must depend upon some other subject who desires to hear his words and who wants to understand him.

Language symbolizes the child's desire and place of privilege because words serve to mediate the child's relation with things, so that the things themselves are replaced by the linguistic symbols which families—each in its own specific way—use to indicate the context of meanings, including rules, values, and prohibitions, into which the child has been, and continues to be, initiated. This ordering of linguistic symbols is societal in its more magnified form, but it is also specifically "familial" in that it is from the child's own family that he is indoctrinated into his mother tongue. The helpless child is thus dependent on the existing order for his livelihood. It is for this reason crucial to distinguish between the signifiers (words) with which the child becomes indoctrinatd and the signified (meaning) these words are presumed to convey in the particular family he has been born into. The child is indoctrinated not so much by a signified ordering of linguistic meanings ordained by the reality of an absolute societal configuration as much as by the signifiers of his family's universe, the one which his family imposes upon him and the one he himself must master. His mother tongue reproduces his family's reality but not necessarily a reality beyond theirs. More generally speaking—and of equal significance—language never yields the precise reality to which it refers; it can only approximate it according to the people who happen to be using it in addressing one another.

In this respect, language mirrors the nature of desire itself. Just as the child will never again be at one with his or her mother, the signifiers of language will never link us to the specific reality to which they refer. In naming an experience and conceptualizing it, the subject achieves some distance from the experience itself and can, in turn, reflect upon it. This achievement bears a certain price, however, because the distance achieved by entering into the symbolic dimension of language constitutes the unbridgeable gap between the word and the thing. Just as our ability to reflect upon our experiences with words can increase our understanding of the experience itself, it can also result in our misunderstanding those experiences, and, in turn, experiencing those experiences based on these misunderstandings. Further, we do not need to take the time to reflect in order to conceive our experience in an aberrated way, since our knowledge of language shapes the signified we in turn give to experience. All experience thus becomes mediated through the symbolic references of our own unique insertion into language. The child's exposure to words occasions the way he will learn to experience his reality, which, in turn, will serve to both articulate and structure his desire.

In naming the child, the child becomes established as a separate entity. Other words symbolize his reality by replacing it with signifiers through which he situates himself as a subject distinct from his environment. Subject becomes distinctively separated from others. While Lacan conceives the effect of language as itself constitutive of subjectivity, it is more accurate to say that language serves to conceptualize the subject as a subjectivity and as a means through which he attempts to discover his subjectivity which is primary to his constitution as an ego. But language also serves to solidify the child as an ego, which the child assumes as himself. His awareness serves to split him into an I (subject) and a me (ego). It is a confusion between the two which constitutes the child's experience of alienation and selfhood generally.

In addition to appropriation and utterance of words, the child expresses his desire through identification and substitution. Essentially, the child wants to be the object of his mother's desire. When he sees that the mother wants other objects, the child in turn will want to become that object, in the same way that he became his own image. For example, he will want to become his (or her) father, the primordial object of the mother's desire. Thus, he substitutes the father as object for himself. And when the child sees the mother fondle an object, such as a cigarette, a magazine, a cup of coffee, he, too, will desire that object as he identifies with the objects of his mother's desire. As we have seen, these things are already charged with significance because they evoke the remembrance of that choreographic structure of his image in the mirror surrounded by other objects, objects which confirm the illusion of a perfect harmonious communion in which the child occupies the pivot.

Thus, the child fancies himself as the center of his mother's world, the apple of her eye. And since he wants to be the total object of the mother's desire, he feels himself to be in competition with the others who are rivals for her attention, a competitive intuition he is already familiar with in regard to himself. Inevitably, the father occupies the dominant position of ultimate rival, and this holds true for the daughter's experience of her father as well as for the son. The child realizes that from the start his (or her) father occupies a privileged position in relation to the mother: He preceded the child's assumption of time. At first, the position of the father is conceived as a support to his—that is, the child's—relation with the mother, as an extension of her being, as it were. This is why, as every parent notices, the father's desire is also accounted for and valued by the child. Anything in which the father takes an interest is prized as an object of desire, but not because the child identifies with the father and the objects he desires, but because through the child's desire for the mother he has already substituted himself in the place of the father vis-à-vis the mother's desire for him (that is, for the father). The significance of this distinction will become more evident when we examine the chronology of the Oedipal phase.

These acts of appropriation through which the boy or girl strives to become the mother's (and vicariously, the father's) object of desire, is the basis of the formation of the child's unconscious desire. These appropriations serve to stretch the horizon of the child's world and releases him from the bondage of the mirror phase as the desire for the mother takes on a new dimension. The mother's world and the complex structure of her own desire for other things and people become the field of the child's apprehension of the world.

The child realizes that he must compete for the mother's attention. And this realization serves to initiate the Oedipal drama in which he discovers the traumatic experience that he must share his mother's love, which means to abandon his desire. The individual never entirely escapes this trauma; indeed, he becomes the trauma.[6] In fact, this Oedipal drama of competing with rivals for the mother's desire can only be conceived if the way has been prepared for it through that primary identification in the mirror phase which structured the child's existence as a rival with himself (i.e., his ego).

The Oedipal drama initiates an evolution that substitutes the mother as the central and primordial reference of the child's desire for the father, who becomes the principle and ultimate reference, as symbol to the limits of desire.

While the child identified totally with the mother's desire, he was unable to grasp the complexity of his situation. Thus, he reduces this drama to: "In order to please mother, I must become what she wants."

But the child comes to realize that his solution does not in itself satisfy the mother because his attempt to become the father tends to omit the position of the father as the mother's reference point, which the mother will resist while unconsciously insisting on. This points to an ambivalence in the mother's desire both to satisfy the needs of her child by holding on, and simultaneously attempting to satisfy her own desire to be everything for the child. While the child's needs are perceived by the mother to be that of maturation and then separation from her embrace, the child's desires are unconsciously conceived as maintaining that symbiotic linkage which is the fantasy she shares with her child. Thus the mother is not merely the source of omnipotent satisfaction to the child's impossible demands. She is also the captivating agent whose spell the child must break free of in order to experience—in a realized form—the sublimated destiny of his desire. The ambivalence of this symbiotic expression epitomizes the maternal identification. The reality of this situation points him in another direction, towards the father, releasing him from his maternal identification and initiating the second phase of the Oedipal drama.

Thus, the father, as a so-called "third person," enters this drama as the liberator of the child's maternal identification. When the child comes to realize that he cannot maintain his dubious position as ultimate reference of his mother's happiness, since he cannot destroy the privileged position of the father without remaining enslaved to the mother's satisfaction, the child is left no choice but to submit to the father's prohibition, that primordial source of a "reality" which governs the limits of omnipotence and the utterance of desire. In effect, the child adopts a strategy both to identify with and love his rival in order to appropriate a communal triumph which will deliver the best of both worlds: the mother who the father possesses and the emancipation the father enjoys.

It is not merely the father as person with whom the child seeks to identify, but rather that symbolic dimension which inhabits the father as the eternal source of a hidden agenda which contains the unspoken herald of the child's unrealized desires. Thus the father is the source of an unrealized myth which is the unfathomed suggestion of an awaited reply who occupies the place of (1) the mother's satisfaction; (2) the unknown author of the child's conception; and (3) the source of the possibility for the child's emancipation from maternal bondage. Thus, the father represents—but does not ordain—the law of the land, the source of the word, and the ultimate freeing of the child's identification with his mother's desire.

Finally, it is not by virtue of the father's direct participation with his child that this freedom is achieved but through the mother's recognition of the father, who as a metaphor for the social dimension, is object of that desire by which she is willing (and able) to surrender the child from the bosom of her omnipotent control, to the father's law and the primal loss which results.

Thus, the mother plays a crucial role in her surrender to the father's social dimension, since without her compliance, insistence, and exercise of the mediating influence at her command, the law of the father would ultimately be rejected by the child (through his identification with the mother's omnipotence) and the emancipation from his maternal identification would remain deferred. It is now possible to conceive how this failure would occur if the mother is unhappy with or envious of the father's place in the social dimension and refuses to let go of her embryonic possession, or if the father is himself so castrated and alienated that he has no recognizable role for the child to follow, thus barring the child's accession to the real. Instead of initiating the child into submitting to his desire, the father assumes a position of abusive neglect which places the child in a situation where he finds himself at odds with his social calling and retreats to the mother's protective embrace.

The Oedipal drama is eventually resolved when (and if) the father indeed replaces the mother as principle signifier of the child's desire through his recognition of the child's urgency to assume his place in the social dimension.

To summarize, upon entering the Oedipal knot, the child is initially fused in its relationship with the mother. He wants to be everything to her, to be what the mother desires and, in effect, to become indispensible to her desire. This coincides with the mirror phase in which the child, in becoming a mirror image of his form, conforms his desire to that of the mother. He becomes what she sees, merges with the object of her desire, and behaves—as in the womb he was—as her appendage in symbolized form. Apart from this identification, his subjectivity is unknown save for those moments when he refuses the mother's demands, when he plays at negation. His state of wanting, which comprises his subjectivity, is hidden to the extent that his (imaginary) union with his mother fills his primal lack.

But with the advent of language the father enters the picture. Just as words institute the gap between signifier and signified, the father represents the gap between mother and child. If the mother indicates to the child that he can indeed satisfy her, can indeed be everything to her, his omnipotent fusion with the mother will remain unresolved. But if the mother indicates—not through a sign or a gesture—but merely in the way she perceives her child and through her relationship with the father (or, in the father's absence, with others) that to be everything for her is not her desire, then the child will move squarely into the Oedipal triangle. Though the father in question may be a personal one, his role is primarily symbolic in terms of the Oedipal resolution. His function, like that of language, is to introduce mediation and limit into the life of the child so that the child sublimates his unrealized desires into the social dimension itself, which does not exist in order to yield to his omnipotent demands, but rather to await his performance, one that will be recognized as his and thus desirable. The function of the Oedipal drama is to effect the child's sublimation into the social order by renouncing his omnipotence and identifying with the father who appears both to satisfy and symbolize the mother's desire. By placing his (or her) desire for the mother in abeyance—through a most painful and difficult repression—the child figuratively accepts desire into his life rather than its death in the form of omnipotent satisfaction.

Finally, the Oedipal drama can be said to be resolved when the child has submitted to his symbolic castration, which is the effect of his maternal separation. He passes from being what the mother wants to wanting what he lacks. By accepting the limits of his omnipotent demands, he is born into his desire for recognition in magnified form. Thus, desire in its most articulated form follows not the lack he was born with, but rather the lack experienced in his separation from the mother. Of course, the child's desire to be at one with the mother, not literally abandoned, is indeed merely repressed. Only the destiny that awaits him in the remainder of his childhood will fully indoctrinate him into the social order, where his desire will become fully articulated. Not that the child's passage through the various stages of Oedipal development will ever occur in such a linear progression—each family institutes its own constellation of events, confrontations, and resolutions. The end result, however, must effect a blow to omnipotence if the child is to achieve his desire to become a being of desire and not the being of another.

A failure at any one of the three phases of Oedipal transformation can precipitate any number of pathological directives, either of a neurotic or psychotic orientation. Though psychotic directives are often already formulated before the Oedipal phase as a result of the child's failure to form a liberatory identification with the mother, we shall see later that this is often a mere simplification.

The neurotic is a person who most likely succeeded in realizing a maternal identification and went on to encounter the Oedipal drama as an accomplice to the mother's desire. However, he failed to free himself from this identification by remaining stuck with the mother's demands for satisfaction. As a consequence, he actively seeks to avoid encounters with the Real: the social dimension. Instead, he promotes the symptom, which takes the place of her demands and inhabits his method of communication. So his social destiny is subverted in favor of his imaginary productions of symptom formation.

The hysterical symptom, by taking the place of a forbidden word (mommy "hates" daddy), has as its function the maintenance of a conversation which is supposed to be taking place. Thus, the symptom speaks a reply that the hysteric cannot reveal, for fear of the mother's death (separation). Thus, the destiny of the neurotic is to keep the mother alive inside in somaticized and projected form.

As for the obsessional, he is most likely nostalgic for a return to the first phase of the Oedipal drama, where he maintains a dream he cannot get rid of. In most cases, he was his mother's favorite child. He maintains and nourishes, despite all the difficulties of his existence, an unshakeable—yet private—self-confidence. And this is precisely the cause of his downfall. Serge Leclaire has described his predicament in a way which is suggestive of the nuances of the web that contains the obsessional's desire:

> This is the Eden of some of his fantasies, the wonderous garden of imaginary voyages, the sanctuary in the middle of multiple fortifications. Anyone who violates this place is threatened with death. This is the nostalgia of an unspeakable happiness, of an exceptional and perfect joy. If today he is banished forever from this universe that lies at the heart of the mythical rose, then he must have committed some crime.[7]

At the heart of the obsessional's guilt is a desiring mother, the treasure of a "perfect" world which he is always and desperately trying to re-create in his frantic and cautious activities. Thus, he is marked by his

mother's unrecognized desire. He retains the fondest and deepest memories from that first phase of Oedipal discovery when he (and only he)
was the total object of his mother's desire. He can still remember when
he was satisfied beyond all measure in the warm glow of his mother's
unrelenting devotion, and he cannot and will not forget it, as is evidenced in its symbolized and repetitive manifestations.

Thus he is still "mama's little boy." Instead of encountering the
mother's disinterest at the second Oedipal juncture, he encounters his
mother's satisfaction. He fails to participate in, nor is he ever subjected
to, a truly social dimension because the mother's unrecognized desire is
shifted to the child, making it *his* task to perennially satisfy her: "It is as
though she had found in me the satisfaction that she did not find in my
father."[8]

The obsessional dwells in a prison of a mother's desperate love. As a
result, she remains the permanent goal and object of desire, closing a
circle on the half-journeyed loop of the child's unquestioned subser-
vience. Thus his desire is trapped inside of this privileged, magical
world. Having answered his unspoken quest with the seal of her unre-
quited demand, the mother continues and nourishes a situation in
which the unformulated desire of the child remains disengaged, confirmed, and satisfied.[9]

And as a testament to his own capacity for devotional servitude, the
obsessional forsakes other worlds for the sake of a most privileged
world which tragically seals his fate as a substitute for the lost object of
the mother's desire. For him the lost object is a false shadow of a
fantastic gratification which necessarily subverts the possibility of his
ever becoming recognized. Fearful of betraying his mother's desire, he
betrays the very possibility of his own desire, replacing one goal for
another in the heat of a merely anticipated bliss.

The two poles of neurotic conflict—obsessional on the one extreme
and hysterical on the other—are two extremes of the spectrum of possible behavior resulting from an alternative of mastery or submission in
the face of the mother's death. Hegel's master-slave dialectic epitomizes
the plight of the neurotic in that the obsessional, who experienced the
"death" of his mother but wants her back again, controls in his endless
journey to the promised land of his lost Nirvana every detail of his
eventual victory. Step by step, he is prepared to suffer whatever injustice is necessary to achieve his inevitably delayed and endlessly deferred reward. Of course, this reward never arrives, since it is the mere

anticipation of this gain that he lives—or rather, dies—for. Aloof from
the pleasures of the masses, he appears to exemplify that most controlled of all aristocrats, shielded from the frantic concern of the ordinary. He may achieve the successes others envy, but for him these
successes are empty, since they are only *one more* step of his prolonged
journey to his Shangri-La: death and its final release. He must maintain control of every detail, for to fall but for a moment would destroy
his perfect ascent.

The hysteric is almost precisely the opposite of the obsessional. The
hysteric, too, is consumed with mastery, but more generally with the
mastery of another, that Prince Charming who will perpetuate the myth
that the mother has never died but is only momentarily out of sight.
The hysteric keeps the mother alive in fantasies that, in a symbolized
form, will rescue him from his frustrated desire—which he finds intolerable. He falls in love or idolizes others easily, only to be disappointed
when the illusionary ecstasy eventually evaporates. No matter, the hysteric will quickly replace the one with another, only to be disappointed
again. Whereas the obsessional has to be the master, the hysteric needs a
master to submit to, only to tear him down in order to preserve his
unfulfilled dreams. Each is in search of an alter ego that will complement the image of their own. In their vain search for satisfaction, they
will only be looking for themselves. So insistent are they on the rewards of a fleeting satisfaction, they fail to apprehend their desire.

The neurotic is essentially incapable of facing the reality of his desire.
The guilt of the obsessive and the envy of the hysteric determine the
fixations around which the object of their desire is constructed. Since
their egos bar their ascent toward another, their neurosis is essentially
narcissistic.

Narcissism, which delays the encounter with the real, is more emphatically constructed in what has recently—especially in America—
been termed "narcissistic disorders," categories of a newer pathology
noted in numerous works by Otto Kernberg and Heinz Kohut. Situating this idea of a pathological narcissism between the neurotic and
psychotic predispositions, it is in reality a neurosis of a most complicated form which contains the compulsive qualities of the obsessive and
the envious disposition of the hysteric, rooted in flagrantly paranoid
features. No better term than "grandiosity" could hope to characterize
the extraordinary self-reference through which they encounter others.
Consumed by an unremitting demand to achieve love and admiration,

their inflated concept of themselves is only exceeded by the extreme tributes they require in order to keep their omnipotence alive. While affecting great interest and concern for the object of their attention, their only real interest is in the tributes which support their enterprise. Underneath their concern lurks the contempt that maintains their supposed superior status. Their envy eventually destroys the good services of their benefactors, whom they exploit, suck dry, and then abandon before the other has a chance to abandon them, which their paranoid inclination feeds upon. Like the obsessive, the so-called "narcissistic type" enjoys nothing save the glorification of his identity, which, of course, is dependent on others for confirmation. Incapable of mourning the loss of his mother, he in fact keeps her alive by making himself indispensable—a trait not uncommon in the hysteric.

The man of resentment par excellence, if you disappoint him he will never feel genuine sadness or, as in the obsessive, guilt. Instead, he will be consumed by a seething anger which is occasioned by vengeful fantasies. These feelings are capable of being replaced by a melancholic depression which only serves to perpetuate his grandiosity. It is at these moments, of course, that these people get a glimpse of the profound insecurity and impotence which lies beneath their omnipotent posture. We would concur with Kernberg's assessment that,

> Narcissistic patients characteristically adapt themselves to the moral demands of their environment because they are afraid of the attacks to which they would be subjected if they do not conform, and because this submission seems to be the price they have to pay for glory and admiration.[10]

Like all neurotics, but perhaps in his case even more so, the narcissistic type is essentially a conformist. He conforms, not to the other's expectation of him, but to his ego which relies on the other to perpetuate this image. And this is what lies at the heart of his resentment and his downfall, for the admiration of others is precisely what perpetuates his unholy course in keeping his mother alive, and subverting his never-glimpsed emancipation. Locked in the prison of his maternal bondage, the narcissist perpetuates the omnipotent fantasy of being the phallus for his mother by projecting his wounded grandiosity onto all of his relations and sublimations, so that the debt for his aborted freedom need never be acknowledged or paid. The bastard son of his obsessive and hysteric ancestors, the narcissist is certainly superior, if only in the relentless zeal with which he orchestrates his neurotic destiny. A neurotic's neurotic, he is admired and envied by those even more perversely neurotic than he is, since what they themselves admire is the voyeuristic spectacle of his folly—a folly which they need only admire, but which he must endlessly pursue. No friend of desire, what all these neurotics share in common is the dread with which they keep their desires at bay.

In its fully articulated (sublimated) form, desire is the desire to be recognized by another subject of desire who desires the same thing. This dialectical structure of recognition comes to dominate the articulation of desire through the subject's use of that language which ushers him further into a discourse in which his ceaseless desire for dominance and completion can be realized. Once this gratification was evoked in his bodily integration inside the mother's body. Then he attempted to reestablish it through his intermittent encounter with the breast. And then an imaginary communion with self was formulated at the hands of an egoic structure the creations of which merely served to alienate him from himself. By means of language a new dominant experience is constructed, that is, a drama which relies on another subject of desire to be the slave to his ceaseless demands. And it is through this dialectical structure that he establishes a system of reciprocity which serves to recapitulate the attentive love of the mother's gaze upon greeting his birth into the world.

But his quest for communion is not merely a demand for completion (which is the alienating directive of the ego grasping at straws). The speaking subject encounters an open-ended world of possibilities in which his desire can never be satisfied or completed. Indeed, the recognition by another does not recognize his subjectivity as an entity in its own right. Rather, the other recognizes in the subject's appeal only what that appeal means to the one who listens to it: a recognition which depends on the other's desire.

The problem with the neurotic is that his speech is not directed to another subject, but rather to himself. In other words, his discourse serves to uphold that alienation within his egoic personality which symbolizes that which he takes himself to be. He tries to measure up to his own expectations and in doing so completes the circle of his own egoic captivation. Thus, his speech is censored by his ego as it passes through the filter which stands between himself and the other (and between himself and the object of his desire).

Consequently, the other is apprehended as merely that confirmation of himself who does not need to listen to his words in order to comprehend the message of his demand. Instead, he is expected to nod his head in agreement, to be the slave to his blind demands. In the service of his own servitude, the subject seeks positive reinforcement—which is music to the ego's ears—for all manner of narcissistic and self-serving directives, whose only purpose is to maintain a dialogue with himself by trapping the truth of his desire in the web of the ego's unquenchable appetite for his death in the form of satisfaction.

When the discourse of the subject addresses his own ego, the effect is that he always talks to himself about others, or he talks to others about himself. Locked into his internal dialogue, he loses all capacity to understand the other's response because he is incapable of listening to the other's discourse as it is passed through the censoring directives of an ego which is only interested in upholding its own preconceptions.

While the neurotic is enslaved by an ego which seeks to bask in the glow of someone's adulation, the psychotic is virtually at war with his ego, which he has merged with. This can only lead to a primal confusion and paranoia which are so characteristic of the psychotic disposition. Unable to distinguish between his ego and his desire, he places his ego outside his desire so that it becomes incarnated via substitution in a paranoic apprehension which locates his worst fears in culturally acceptable mythologies of betrayal, i.e., the CIA is after him; bugs are planted inside his brain; he is subjected to poisonous food; etc. While the real source of betrayal remains anonymous, all of us are implicated as coconspirators. Thus the paranoiac who hears voices in reality overhears a discourse he is having with himself. These messages appear as tormenting, dangerous, or suggestive and confirm his vague intuition that someone (in fact, himself) is out to get him. But failing to recognize the source of this tormenting dialogue, he ultimately betrays himself in his desperate cause to strengthen that very aspect of himself which upholds his devastation.[11]

Finally, language itself becomes enclosed on itself, repeating the same arguments and rationalizations, upholding the same circular logic, and wishing that someone might hear an inverted message whose discourse is turned inside out. Thus, the subject's desire for recognition by an other is lost in a desire (language) which has been foreclosed in order to maintain the omnipotent thrust of his imaginary discourse with himself.

Thus, if language is an expression of desire, then speech is the medium of its truth. As the child begins to express his desire by means of language in search of his own truth, he becomes subject to the social dimension and its world where the object of the child's desire is destined to be realized. Since man's relation to man is lived out in his everyday intercourse with others, the crucial issue of his life is the place the other comes to occupy in the dialectical structure of his desire for recognition.

Desire discovers its signification in the desire of the Other, not because the Other holds the key to the object desired, but because the real object of desire is to be recognized as desirable. Desire is not the appropriation of an object but rather a *dispossession* of ourselves in favor of the other's recognition.

As we have seen, according to Hegel in *The Phenomenology of Mind*,[12] the other's recognition is articulated by the other's desire of *my* desire. I apprehend his recognition as his desire to understand me. In other words, he must desire my desire in order to recognize me. And vice versa. When I address my words to another, the secret appeal contained in the fabric of my words is that the Other *understand* what I say.[13] This message is never explicit. Rather, it is implied in everything I may utter to another. By speaking I subject myself to my own truth through the medium of the Other's response. In order that I may discover the truth, I must await the Other's reply. But the Other's reply does not contain an "answer" to my question. Rather, it is a response which deepens its appeal. The function of language is not simply to inform, but to constitute a dialectic in which the speaker's appeal contains its own truth.

In the appeals I address to someone else, no matter how trivial or mundane, the Other becomes transfixed within the dialectical structure of my desire. While he is free to accept or reject me, he is not at liberty to disregard me. If he chooses to ignore me, he can do so only by assuming a posture of indifference towards me. His reality is nonetheless transformed—whether dramatically or imperceptibly—in my invocation of his response. He has no choice but either to listen to my appeal or to objectify me in his disregard. Either way, he must live with the consequences of whatever form his response may take, just as I must live with mine. In speech I impress myself on the other by etching onto my environment the material expression of my desire in order that I may be recognized by others and be desired by them in turn. Thus, I turn myself over to them so that they can give me back to myself, authenticated and understood. This seriality of exchanges is transformative in that I lose something (my appeal) in order to get something (a reply) in exchange.

The effect is that, through speech, the subject is removed from the center of his internal dialogue with himself by his appeal to another who, in taking up this message, returns it in the form of his reply, transforming the original question through the intersubjective link of his desire. And it is in this dialogue with another that the subject comes to encounter the limits of his omnipotence "through" the recognition of his desire. Moreover, even the "unconscious" is a shared dimension, since it occupies the locus of the subject's unspeakable desires: They cannot be spoken to, but through.

But if language has the power to disclose the realization of desires, it can also be used in order to conceal the truth of its realizations. When the participants in the Oedipal drama fail to recognize the child, he remains outside the periphery of the social dimension. As a result, he has no choice but to remain under the spell of the transfixing gaze of the mother's unsatisfied desire. He turns to her for the recognition which has already been foreclosed, encountering instead his incarnation as a substitute for his mother's unsatisfied desires. Child and mother work together to construct his egoic personality within the imaginary structure of his impossible desire which is contained in the mother's demand that he replace the lost (abdicated?) position of the father's response. Thus, the child is expected to overcome his mother's dissatisfaction. In other words, it becomes imperative that he become what she is not. And in order to achieve this task, it is ordained that he become that omnipotent creature who is the Frankenstein monster of an ego in the throes of a mother's bewildering gaze.

Everything the child then says is in the service of an egoic construction whose function is to keep the mother satisfied. And by this very endeavor in which he strives to construct himself for an other, he deepens even further that alienation which separates him from the locus of his desire. The more sophisticated his egoic strategies become, the more his paranoia constructs the dread of possible exposure.

The ego's captivating influence is marked by a compromise which determines its own foundation. The more the child succeeds in gaining the support of the others, the more disappointed he feels. This structure of alienation, which becomes elaborated in the marginal apprehension of his reflected self and his absorption into the false discourse of his ego, finds its resonance in all spheres of psychopathology—the egoic defense mechanisms, per se.

The psychotic is inserted into a language without dialectic because he no longer tries to make himself understood. He no longer wants to be recognized as something he is not. This is the paradigmatic universe of the incomprehensible utterances of the schizophrenic. However, the neurotic completely surrenders himself to his ego's demands for gratification, in alliance with the collusive structure of the mother's unrecognized desire. Whereas the psychotic is acutely aware of his alienation and is always at odds with himself, the neurotic desperately wants his ego to be supported and confirmed by others, while subverting the possibility of his recognition. By substituting the omnipotence of his imaginary ego for the ambiguity of recognition, and by insisting that his ego communicate in his behalf, the neurotic obscures the distinction between his biological and archaic needs and his desire for emancipation. He is essentially a conformist. Thus the ego acquires a certain invulnerability by the deadening of his desire. He gradually adapts himself to his lost reprieve. When you knock on his door, it is the ego that answers. But since the ego is a construct in the imaginary, it cannot hear the question. His desire goes unanswered and his discourse is silenced by the emptiness of a missing word. He resorts to the secrecy of denial, resistance, resentment, and lies, since he cannot admit to others what he cannot admit to himself. If he has nothing to say, it is because he is afraid that you might hear him. The loss of his voice parallels the loss of his desire.

Ultimately it is the neurotic's unsatisfied hunger for gratification—an unseemly lure—which compels him to acknowledge the limits of his failed omnipotence. The reply of the psychoanalyst reaches beyond the patient's ego in order that he might recognize his evasive appeals for recognition. If the therapist is to accomplish his goal, he must first recognize the specific position that the ego occupies, the position through whom the subject poses his question. Thus, it is through the patient's ego that the therapist addresses his reply. In order to hear to whom and through whom the patient's question is uttered, the therapist allows himself to become the object of the subject's egoic aggression. He needs to ask himself Who is it that the patient wants a reply from? And what is it that he wants to hear? In other words, whose recognition does the Other desire? And who or what is it that the patient wants to be recognized as?[14]

Even so, the therapist is not necessarily at liberty to reveal the truths that the neurotic fails to obscure. The subject of desire must discover them for himself if he is ever to take them seriously. The central purpose of the psychoanalyst is to suspend the patient's certitudes which uphold the dominance of the ego, until all of his omnipotent fantasies have, as Lacan would say, been consumed. By this method he avoids engaging in a battle, the outcome of which would merely humiliate the subject and strengthen his omnipotent resolve. Instead he concentrates on an elusive path of indirection, by reducing the power of the ego and introducing the subject to the dialectic of his unrecognized desire. By withholding any pretense of support or sympathy for the patient's demands for self-satisfaction, the therapist reduces the subject to that infantile drama in which, as a child, he was a slave to his parents' incomprehension. In assuming the position of the father's law, and by recognizing this singular quest for recognition, the therapist returns to the subject that desire which was lost to the captivation of an ego in alliance with the betrayal of his parents' best intentions. As to the consequences of the subject's failure to achieve this recognition, we shall now turn.

CHAPTER FOUR

THE SUBVERSION OF DESIRE IN THE APPREHENSION OF THE OTHER

Psychology is a discipline which claims to be scientific. Psychologists attempt to confront their human subjects in a manner not unlike the physicist or the biologist confronts his. The notion of man that psychology adopts is thus empirical: All over the world there are human creatures who share certain experiences in a manner somewhat similar to some and somewhat different from others. By subjecting police officers from Minnesota or taxi drivers from New York to arbitrary trials of investigation, and comparing the results to a group of schizophrenics from Pennsylvania, they proceed to determine the average—or "normal"—response of each group. We are told that these rituals of investigation provide us with scientific data with which to measure the appropriateness of this or that emotionally disturbed individual, thus establishing the boundaries of psychopathology. It is somewhat amusing that the psychologist—in order to remain objective—strictly forbids himself to consider that the men around him are men like himself.

If we were to apply this method of investigation to a particular human activity, such as, human emotions, we would have to do so from a perspective that would continue to place ourselves outside the object of our study. Emotion would then be approached in accordance to our stated task of isolating it from all the other phenomena of our experience in order to see it all the more clearly. Yet, if you were to ask a psychologist how it is he knows that emotions exist, he would willingly admit that he knows this from personal experience. But if you were to suggest to him that this question deserves a more rigorous answer, that it is necessary to examine the conditions under which the manifestation of emotions is made possible, he would say that such a study is both needless and absurd. Why question its possibility if it manifestly exists?

It is not surprising, then, that psychologists, for the most part, fail to question the very purpose of certain emotions that arise in everyday life. We hear the terms "mental illness" and "emotional disturbance" spoken matter of factly by psychologists and psychiatrists as popular and readily available expressions to denote psychopathology generally. It is implicit that a mentally disturbed individual suffers also from emotional disturbances and vice versa. However, the very origin of these emotions is deemed irrelevant. The emotions of the mentally disturbed individual (such as anger, rage, or sorrow) are, first of all, unpleasant, and, second, they have got him into trouble. That is the central issue. Our task is just to get rid of them. That emotions may convey a specific purpose is virtually incomprehensible to the psychologist because he views them primarily as a byproduct of miserable states (that is to say, they are pathological); and if these emotions are pleasant, then why question them in the first place?

For the most part, psychologists tend to view emotions as a set of tensions being somehow discharged from inside the body, so that they occupy a physical location. We often hear people say: "He's got his anger bottled up inside of him." The fact that a person may be fearful of declaring his feelings to an other person is immediately translated from a failure of communication (linguistics) to the encapsulation of quantifiable material (physics). Many therapists today simply suggest to their patients to go ahead and get their feelings "out in the open." If this individual does not seem to be particularly angry or upset, the therapist may encourage him to go ahead and get angry, or, perhaps, may deliberately provoke him into a fit of rage to prove his point. While psychiatrists are prone to prescribing drugs to control or alter the client's feelings, the psychologist considers himself somewhat more enlightened because he advocates getting the feelings out into the open, in a manner not dissimilar to that of exorcism.

Psychoanalysis has come a long way in explaining how human behavior is not merely orchestrated by random events, but rather that actions always have a motive, an intent, a specific end. Indeed, psychoanalysts were the first to emphasize the signification of psychic phenomena, that this particular thought or act usually stands for something else. Thus, the child who steals is only trying to reclaim his mother's love. A girl who faints at the sight of parsley cannot bring herself to face the memory of an earlier childhood incident that the parsley would otherwise remind her of. And yet, for the most part, the psychoanalytic interpretation tends to look for causal antecedents to the structure of our present behavior. Naturally, our history plays a tremendously important part in all our lives, and this is especially problematical for persons suffering from crippling emotional disturbance. Thus, I can project onto all women the quality of evil because my mother was cruel to me in childhood: I could not conceive of hating my mother, but I cannot forget the hurt I carry with me. Every time I feel fondness for a woman, I find myself consumed with feelings of anger and hatred. And so on.

Things are not always so simple however. The fact remains that these are real others with whom I am presently engaged, with thoughts, emotions, and histories of their own. The more I examine my situation, the more I begin to realize that I may have good reason to hate this person who reminds me of my mother. I discover that more than one of the friends I frequent are indeed despicable people; I seek out these very people to be with. Why on earth would I do that? Freud's theory of the repetition compulsion describes the phenomenon, but it does not give us insight into its underlying structure.

Sartre has suggested that the emotion is our way of magically transforming a situation we cannot bear.

> When the paths before us become too difficult, or when we cannot see our way, we can no longer put up with such an exacting and difficult world. All ways are barred and nevertheless we must act. So then we try to change the world; that is, to live it as though the relation between things and their potentialities were not governed by deterministic processes but by magic.[1]

Thus the woman who faints at the sight of her attacker does so, not because it reminds her of some previous event, but because it removes her—albeit magically—from the present situation. She no longer has to face the immediate danger she is in. But this is not to say that she willfully faints with self-conscious awareness. It is rather that she is seized by the situation, a situation which suddenly makes demands upon her. The impossibility of finding a solution to the problem demands that she create a solution. If she cannot take flight in reality, at least she can do so emotionally, or magically.

Yet an emotional response is not simply a substitute for other forms of action because, says Sartre, it is not effectual. It does not act upon the world but merely changes one's perception of it:

Emotional behavior seeks by itself, and without modifying the structure of the object, to confer another quality upon it, a lesser existence or a lesser presence.[2]

But emotions are not simply a magical way of taking flight from a situation we find dangerous. More fundamentally, the emotion is a structure of desire. Specifically, it is a way of coping with a desire we are unable to fulfill. Thus, the person in danger wants to be somewhere else, so the fainting magically fulfills this wish. Similarly, if I want something I cannot have, the emotion can serve to remove the desire itself, thereby magically resolving what would otherwise be an unbearable disappointment. Sour grapes is probably the most common rationalization.

I lift my hand to pluck a bunch of grapes. I cannot do so; they are beyond my reach; so I shrug my shoulders, muttering: "they are too green" and go on my way. . . . this little comedy that I play under the grapes, thereby confering this quality of being "too green" upon them, serves as a substitute for the action I cannot complete. . . . I confer the required quality upon the grapes magically.[3]

Max Scheler's classic study of "ressentiment" shows most clearly the intentional structure of the emotions and how they can be used in order to restructure what would otherwise be an unbearable world into one which is, perhaps, just bearable.[4]

Resentment and Revenge

Scheler's description of resentment—borrowed from Nietzsche—is liable to remind us of the complexes in Freud. In other words, Scheler approaches resentment as a structure of behavior which is beyond the subject's ability to grasp or resist. Desire for revenge, hatred, and envy may give rise to resentment when they are not satisfied and when they clash head on with the unconscious intentionality of a markedly impotent sensibility. The resentful person dreads each act, attitude, or word in which his hatred is manifest due to the power it has over him. It is this dreadful apprehension of the hated object that engenders a dictatorial anxiety over his interpersonal relations generally.

Unlike ordinary hatred which passes with time, resentful hatred exists for its own sake, completely detached from the particular situation and hiding in the repressed abyss of its own forgotten rationale. Consequently, it cannot possibly be satisfied. Resentment desires nothing because its aim is to destroy all desires. Thus, it accomplishes nothing in its triumph.

Anger, perhaps the most complex of the emotions, occupies a singular position in the life of the individual because it is probably the most commonly experienced while remaining by far the most overtly destructive. While anger does not prompt the development of resentment, surely, it occasions the experience of resentment, occurring, as it does, at those moments when our desire has not met its mark, moments when we clearly experience the other as a deliberate impediment to its realization. That this impediment to my desire can often—indeed, frequently—be experienced in respect to myself is merely one more support for the profuse evidence which indicates the ego is an other, a foil, to my desire. Anger is especially destructive because, in becoming angry, I wish to destroy both the object of my desire and my desire itself: It is a wish to annihilate the world.

But there is more. Anger is not content with mere destruction; its ultimate aim is to reconstitute the world, a world more acceptable to my demands. Everyone fears anger; no one finds it particularly pleasant, though some may be intrigued by it or captivated by it, like the addict hooked to his fix. What makes anger particularly insidious is that in becoming angry, we wish to mask the impotence that prompts it by putting forward a forceful appearance in order to persuade the other, through intimidation, to see things our way. What is so incredibly amazing in this play is that it often works.

I appeal to the other to please see things my way, to reciprocate and give in. No reply. I plead some more, this time becoming more insistent, my voice rising, the urgency showing on my face. Still no reply. Now I become demanding. After all, I have a right to my request. No is not good enough an answer. I now demand, with greater force, that surely I cannot be denied. Words pass between us. The other is protesting that he can understand my position, but he still cannot be moved to relent. Finally, in a burst of anger, I appear all powerful—indeed, a force to be reckoned with. Suddenly, I become transformed, I am no longer the same person. While previously I was merely a human making a request, now I am a giant of a man, whose demand carries the implicit threat of annihilation. The other shrugs his shoulders, moves as if to say "I see" and gives in.

This little play, with which all of us are familiar, has many variations

THE SUBVERSION OF DESIRE

and not always predictable results. The other may become angry, too, and escalate the game to an impossible resolution. Furthermore, anger, while allowing me to appear more powerful, more forceful, more sure, more "right," also subverts the very desire which prompted the anger in the first place. Often, when the other relents, I no longer want what I was fighting for. I withdraw, go into a pout, a sulk, and say "Forget it— you can have it," and stalk away, with my secret little triumph under my hat to deny him the pleasure of satisfying me.

Anger only means one thing, that we have basically lost control of the situation and are prepared to lash out, with tongue or other means, to destroy what stands in our way—even if it kills us! Of course, consciously suppressing anger, or even unconsciously repressing it, so that we do not even know that we are angry, are not viable alternatives. What is at issue is not merely the expression of anger, or the checking of anger, but rather a tendency toward anger, which is indicative of a voracious demand and an omnipotent sensibility that lies in waiting to do its deed, no matter what we do with the anger itself. Anger, which has long been associated with the psychotic madman, is omnipotence in its pure essence, an omnipotence that lies at the heart of all psychotic states as well as the so-called "narcissistic ones."

Anger is something that we could all do without. Perhaps this is why that in the present era, particularly in American culture, it has escalated to a romanticized level of heroic proportions: the so-called "angry rebel." This is due to a certain myth that proposes that the angry man is, indeed, a potent man. This, of course, is simply not true. Anger is the simplest and most straightforward expression of impotence there is, since it only arises when we are not being particularly effective or successful in having it our way, of being seen, heard, or recognized. Anger may not be resentment, per se, but the feeling of impotence which causes it certainly relates them.

While the expression of anger may be a valiant effort to behave potently—with erratic, and sometimes successful, results—resentment is bred from those occasions when anger dare not be expressed, when it was too dangerous to show one's hand, to make one's case. Resentment lies in waiting, for the right time, and the right place, to strike. The man of the resentful attitude must use circular means to weave his way round to where he started, as secretly and furtively as he can.

Subterfuge is the cornerstone of the resentful attitude. Thus, many allegedly generous acts are in fact just the opposite. Beneath an apparent state of serenity—chit-chat, work, a friendship of long duration—lurks the heart of a traitor. Perhaps the con artist or psychopath comes to mind, but resentment can be discerned in virtually all forms of human misery and psychopathology, in cripples as well as psychotics. This animosity, which is basically homicidal, eventually turns against itself, effectively taking vengeance upon itself. Even the body, in mirroring the anguish of the heart, comes to reflect and then join the sense of incompletion, loss, and interior emptiness which characterize *l'homme du ressentiment*. The physical and the mental become indistinguishable as the desire of the resentful person gradually consumes itself in its death wish to destroy the cause of its suffering: the impossibility of desire.

Thus, resentment is a self-poisoning of desire, prompted by emotional endeavors in cahoots with the misfortunes of its repeated failures. Revenge, hatred, malice, envy, and spite are specifically the emotions Scheler mentions as being associated with the formation of resentful suffering.[5]

Thirst for revenge is at the heart of resentment, being distinguished by two essential characteristics. (1) The immediate response to a slight or disappointment is temporarily checked for fear that an overt reaction would lead to greater harm. This dread is in turn characterized by a profound sense of impotence when the individual entertaining thoughts of revenge is confronted by anyone more powerful than himself. Thus, vengeance has to be taken at a later time and on a more suitable occasion. (2) It is of the essence of revenge that it contains the consciousness of tit for tat, so that it is never merely an emotional reaction.

According to Scheler, resentment need not be felt by the person who actually succeeds in avenging himself.[6] Seeds of resentment tend to flower in situations where the individual's aggressive emotions are especially powerful. However, they must be checked for fear that disaster would result if the feeling was discovered. The resentful sensibility is formalized in childhood, ultimately within the family context. While there is at least some resentment in us all, what concerns us here are the ways in which resentment can breed the most profound pathological results.

Scheler does not imply that vengeance is in itself the best or most effective response to each and every injury that a child may suffer. But the nature of revenge in childhood is such that the child is placed in an inherently powerless position. Should his trust for authority (the father's law) wane, the child has little choice but to conform to the status quo (the maternal identification) through the most expedient, and sometimes devious, means available.

From the perspective of the child, every disappointment or injury is experienced as a failure of recognition. An act of vengeance merely serves to direct the other person's attention to that desire which the injury subverted. The mother who, preoccupied, ignores her child at a time it is in some measure of distress, may discover that his discomfort is soon transformed into a tantrum. The child throws something at her, or breaks an object. It is an obvious act of revenge. The mother is usually aware that he did this in order to get her attention. If she comforts the child and he gets what he wanted in the first place, then his act of revenge has succeeded. His desire has been recognized. In other words, the motive of an act of revenge is always to have a desire recognized. It is expressed in a hostile guise in order to arrest attention. What the vengeful person is really saying is, "Look how hurt I am; can't you see?" Beneath this hateful exterior there is always concealed a failure—and desire—for recognition. But if the mother, angry, responds to the child's ploy with punishment, and if this should become her customary response, the result will be a child who—like a horse—becomes effectively "broken." While his behavior might become more controlled, his desires will become a danger to his survival.

While aggression arises in the life of the infant as a consequence of the fixations of his ego, resentment is a product of the child's encounter with others who fail to recognize his demands for recognition and his awesome need for their attention. If his acts of vengeance suffer repeated failure, he will gradually learn to place his desire for revenge in suspension. But in doing so, the original intent of his vengeance (recognition) is repressed and only the masquerade of the manifest hostility remains. It is this movement that ushers into being the foundation of a resentful attitude.

The repression of desire inevitably results in feelings of hatred. If the child is perceived as hateful, he will begin to feel hateful himself. But internalized hatred can sometimes lead to dangerous consequences. Joan Riviere has commented on the disastrous effects of subverted desire and the tortuous maneuvers a person may subject himself to when retaliation *must* find expression.

> The most impressive evidence of this may be seen when such a reaction leads to suicide—when disappointment and the fury of revenge engender such hatred and contempt for life and all it offers that life itself is finally rejected and destroyed.[7]

As hateful revenge becomes repressed, the attitude of envy begins to emerge. The envious person, by definition, suffers from impotence due to his desire to possess another's possession: the object of the other's desire. Yet, the mere tension between desire and its failure does not automatically lead to envy unless the owner of the coveted object is held to be the cause of the subject's privation. Hence, my inability to acquire another's possession is interpreted by me as the other's decision to prevent the realization of my desire, as symbolized by the desired object. The purpose of this delusion is to deny the sense of impotence that becomes associated with my failure to acquire what I want. But this strategy merely serves to further confirm the inadequacy that causes my delusion in the first place. The experience of impotence—the subversion of desire—which coincides with my tendency to blame others for my lack of power—is the essential precondition to envy.[8] While I may be free to court a coveted object or to let go, envy develops when I am unable to do either, an inability which is rooted in a paranoic apprehension which is capable of transforming those who have what I want into witnesses who then remind me of my impoverishment.

In examining the relation between envy and greed, Riviere concludes that greed

> . . . represents an aspect of the desire to live, one which is mingled and fused at the outset of life with the impulse to turn aggression and destructiveness *outside* ourselves against others, and as such persists unconsciously throughout life. And being a form of the impulse to live, it ceases only with death.[9]

More specifically, greed can be directed towards virtually any type of object, whether its realization is impossible or readily available. For the child with a fondness for stealing, his thefts signify a coordinated attempt to retrieve that initial lost object of desire which was taken at the hands of another. While Riviere pays considerable attention to the subject's innate feelings of greed, she tends to avoid the place of greed in the individual's relations with others.[10] Yet she does not fail to recognize the relation between privation and the more general projection onto another as the source of the individual's feeling of lack:

> One great reason why a *loss* of any kind can be so painful is that unconsciously it represents the converse idea, that we are being exposed as *unworthy* of good things, and so our deepest fears are realized. When a person, whose sense of security is largely based on his greed sees that

someone else has more than he, it upsets this self-protective edifice of security; he feels reduced to poverty, he feels in phantasy as if the others who have more must have actually *robbed* him of what had made him feel secure, which is now gone. That is why the feeling of envy is so exceedingly poignant and bitter to those who experience it. They feel they are being forced to submit to robbery and persecution![11]

The point that Riviere misses is that the greedy and envious person may indeed have been subjected to persecution and that the consequence of this experience leads to a tendency to perceive others more fortunate as being implicated in the construction of his meager world.

Thus, revenge and envy are directed toward specific objects of desire and may be satisfied if those objects can be possessed. But repeated failures of desire can lead to an impulse to disparage the object or objective, an even more destructive force than envy since it is never directed toward a specific object or objective. Without an object, there is not even the possibility of satisfaction, let alone recognition.[12] On the contrary, the impulse to disparage something or someone causes one to seek out those negative or undesirable characteristics of others which one likes to disparage, so that detraction becomes pleasurable in itself, a pleasure that can only be described as perverse.

The furtive aim of detraction or disparagement is to relieve the frustration of impotent desire. Detraction is commonly used by those who feel powerless and inferior in the company of others. They tell themselves that all people are so useless and unloveable that they (the others) are unworthy of their regard. In a similar manner, the spiteful person takes such pleasure in hating others that he may pretend to be a close friend of someone while secretly conspiring to bring about the supposed friend's downfall. He is essentially a betrayer.

Revenge, envy, disparagement, and spite lead to resentment only if the individual's desire is repeatedly unfulfilled, while the other is held responsible for his privation. Relinquishing responsibility for his own feelings serves to exacerbate even further the person's feeling of impotence and fuels all the more his conviction that the other is to blame. We shall now examine how resentment appears through the culmination of a progression of maneuvers the ultimate intention of which is relief from frustration through the death of one's own desire.

Resentment is born out of a set of circumstances of prolonged duration in which feelings of bitterness and hostility begin to feed on themselves, establishing their own survival. We would concur with Scheler's suggestion that

74 THE DEATH OF DESIRE

> Impulses of revenge lead to resentment the more they change into actual
> *vindictiveness,* the more their direction shifts toward indeterminate groups
> of objects which need share only one common characteristic, and the less
> they are satisfied by vengeance taken on a specific object.[13]

Thus the vindictive person is instinctively and unconsciously drawn
towards those events which he hopes will give rise to vengefulness. As a
result, he sees injurious intentions in all sorts of perfectly innocent
actions and remarks of others. "Touchiness" is the most common symptom of the vindictive person.

Moreover, the vindictive person is always in search of situations
which he can interpret as injurious so he can pretend he is wreaking
vengeance (in its purely hostile manifestation) against those who are in
fact not implicated in his impotence. By displacing the true authorhood
of previous injuries onto those who are innocent, he strives to
strengthen all the more his egoic pride and self-esteem through an
expression of aggressive motives which merely reinforce his alienation
because they are aimed ultimately at himself.[14] As the original object of
his vengeance remains untouched, his blind aggression betrays even
further the measure of his impotence because it is aimed in futility.
Thus, the act of illusory revenge is at the heart of the resentful attitude
and is a major component of the projective process.

The emergence of resentment coincides with that phase in the child's
development when the ego identifies with the mother's failure to recognize his desire. Thus, the child experiences an injustice which is formalized by the failure of his desire for the mother's love. The result is
the denial of his desire for the mother's recognition. He substitutes,
instead, the rapture of narcissistic omnipotence. Instead of transcending narcissism, he commits himself to it. As the ego becomes identified
with that image of the child who is unworthy of love, the subject
assumes this identification, confers value upon it, and, in that sense,
becomes it. Searching for the support of his own existence, the child
identifies with what he takes to be the mother's desire. If she sees him as
repugnant or a brat, he assumes this quality of repugnance or brattiness
and perpetuates it faithfully. The more the mother reacts against it, the
more his ego finds support in it.

The specifically resentful aspect of his world arises when this identification fails to procure the ultimate treasure he expected from it: his
emancipation. Moreover, his retreat into narcissism merely serves to
alienate him even more from his desire to be recognized by someone

else. Thus is born a situation in which the subject seeks his power in an imaginary salvation which is but an illusory reflection of true potency. This results in a conflict between the child's desire for a lost object and his omnipotent enslavement to his ego, which now becomes the foundation for that ambivalent aggressivity which inhabits his relations with others.

Thus resentment is encapsulated in the formations of the ego which is resentment, per se. The ego's defense mechanisms have no other purpose than to eliminate the frustration of desire, by no other recourse than to deny desires or by disparaging the desired object. Thus, the emotions are essentially "defense mechanisms" with the purpose of magically transforming desire by destroying it, in the negative sense by denying it, in the positive sense by fulfilling it. The unrealistic joy of the hysteric or the manic defense are merely the more obvious examples of this fact. Revenge is the omnipotence of the ego in its aggressive form, the "mastery" of desire in Hegel's master-slave dialectic, nowhere more tellingly exemplified than in all the complex manifestations—and repressions—of anger. Since resentment is coincidental with the subject's unbearable experience of impotence, the ego, omnipotence incarnate, is impotence in its most essential quality.

Contrary to the view of ego psychologists who suggest that strengthening the ego (or self) leads to health, it is precisely this shoring up of the ego, when the subject of desire is in retreat, which results in intensified alienation and is commensurate with the emergence of pathological countermeasures.[15] Omnipotence implies there is something (the ego) worthy of defending from others, that salvation lies within. By placing the ego at center stage, it takes precedence over the other, who is now apprehended with trepidation. The more importance is granted the ego to protect himself from the other, the more there is to protect. This is the illusion of self-esteem in its most retaliatory aspect.

The more the illusion of omnipotence, independence, or mastery is invested in the ego, the more alienated the subject of desire becomes, and the more dangerous the other appears. Yet, it is not others who are the real danger, but the ego which continues to dominate the subject's existence and the structure of his intersubjective world. The subject fails to recognize that his desires are not at the service of his ego (which is incarnated in his pride), so he displaces onto others the authorhood of his ego's fixation by means of projection. Thus the omnipotent structure of the ego is constantly imperiled due to the extraordinary responsibility it is now expected to assume.

His relation with others now becomes characterized by impotence and paranoia, increasing further his tendency to identify with others in order to obscure the enormous gap between them. The more he surrenders his desire to the dominating fixations of his ego, the less likely his desires will be recognized by others because the first thing they would recognize is his need to manipulate them. He simply cannot trust them for fear of this exposure. His world now becomes dominated by a soft paranoia which apprehends each encounter as a threat to his survival.

We have seen how the emotion is used magically to transform a reality which the subject cannot contend with. We will now examine how resentment is used to magically restructure the subject's values so that the very nature of his desire is transformed.

Distortion through Subversion of Values

The healthy person possesses a naive and nonreflective awareness of his own value which permits him to acknowledge the merits of others without the need to begrudge them. Indeed, he rejoices in their virtues since he derives from them their recognition of himself. The resentful person constantly compares himself with others and consequently experiences his own value by pitting himself against them, while perceiving only those qualities which constitute possible differences. While the healthy person experiences his value without making comparisons, the resentful person seeks to determine his value by means of such comparisons. Thus, his defensive capacity to identify with others in order to obscure those differences is itself jeopardized due to his need to downgrade the value of those persons he needs to identify with. Consequently, he feels incapable of rising to the other's level. This merely serves to increase his sense of inadequacy and the anxiety associated with it. Yet, this anxiety demands relief. Consequently, the resentful person devalues the other's virtues by blinding himself to those qualities. In other words, he strives to falsify the other's virtues which remind him of his own inferior status.

Since the resentful person is unable to realize the object of his desire, he tends to diminish the value of that object so that it is no longer desirable. He tells himself that he no longer desires what he does. The effect is to subvert his desire by denying the value of its object.[16] He subverts the value of desire by denying that desire is valuable.[17] Following this, his resentment radiates in all directions. Desire begins to vanish altogether, as it is substituted by a more-general negative attitude: a seemingly unsystematic rejection of all things, people, and situations whose loose connection with the original injury is all but lost.

By telling himself that all objects or objectives of value are unworthy, the resentful person finally subverts his own capacity to judge reality. By subverting the foundation of his own desire, he promotes a sense of newfound power on a purely illusory basis. He tells himself, "I don't need anybody," when in reality he is saying, "I don't want anybody to recognize my impotence." That this strategy is a lie does not deny its power to prolong this deception because his capacity to judge has been impaired.[18] Those who suffer are now more "authentic" than those who are happy. The effect is a falsification of his world view. He turns away from those things which represent positive (desirable) values and adopts instead negative (undesirable) ones. He develops the urge to scold and belittle whatever he sees. He slanders the world in order to justify his failure to inhabit it. If he cannot appropriate the "good life," at least he can appropriate a bad one, and he can then make it good by making it his. What was previously held in abeyance due to intact reaction formations, is dropped as hatred becomes manifest in a new form.

Salvation lies in the opposite direction. Poverty, suffering illness, and even death become desirable. Impulses of revenge against those who are more fortunate become diminished through the systematic avoidance of those who are a testament to a desirable world. Neurosis and psychosis become good. Life in a mental hospital or a miserable marriage takes on a compelling justification all its own because it helps to justify his impoverished existence. Thus, resentment brings deliverance from a conflict between impotence and desire by effectively subverting desire altogether. Now the resentful person has finally achieved his goal: He is effectively beyond hope, since hope has become fulfilled in the very satisfaction of his inverted desire.

Psychopathology

We are now in a position to see how the structures of psychopathology are determined by emotional and mental operations the purpose of which is none other than the deadening of one's desire for recognition

as an object of the other's desire. Emotions, which are frequently confused with desires (in the former's seemingly positive aspect), seize the
subject's experience of the situation he is in for the desired effect of
having himself appear more potent than he is and less impotent than he
is perceived. But what of the so-called "positive emotions"? If everyone
can agree that negative emotions are undesirable (though we may pretend they are, on occasion, justified), surely the positive experiences of
joy, gladness, exuberance, contentment, among others are precisely the
reverse of the negative ones in the sense that we can embrace them as
the pivot of our desires, as the very fulfillment of a particular longed-for
desire for satisfaction. This is difficult to untangle since what frequently
passes for positive emotions are not really emotions at all. Rather, they
arise from an experience of recognition, realization, or well-being
which, while experienced as fortunate or desirable, are in fact devoid of
the more-illusory manifestations of passion. Let us take for an example
the feeling of joy.

In joy, the subject contains no hostile motives (unless, of course, they
are experienced in an inverted form which lies at the foundation of
perversions, which we shall turn to later), no hatred of self or other.
Contentment has finally been achieved and with it release from
the unbearable frustration of unrecognized desirability. Returning to
Sartre, we find there is no such call to rejoice as might appear to the
unwary eye:

> Joy, on closer consideration, is characterized by a certain impatience. We
> mean by this that the joyful subject is behaving very much like a man in a
> state of impatience. He cannot keep still, makes innumerable plans, begins
> to do things which he immediately abandons, etc. For in fact this joy has
> been called up by an apparition of the object of his desires.[19]

Sartre points to the phenomenon of anticipation as the basis of the
joyful emotion, which he takes pains to distinguish from the so-called
"joy" we attribute to equilibrium, which is not an emotion at all. We all
know of these experiences. Some have suffered unemployment, when
frustration is the rule of the day and the relief of obtaining a job will
bring with it the rewards of security, a means to survival, new possibilities, and so on. The longed-for, hoped-for job finally materializes, and
in the midst of his relief from the thought of annihilation he celebrates.
Satisfaction has finally arrived, and his desire has apparently been fulfilled. But on reporting for the job his first day, he finds himself, on the

one hand, still anticipating the rewards that his new job will bring—
they are not, in fact, experienced—and, on the other hand, he is concerned with a new apprehensiveness: Will he perform adequately? Will
he measure up to the task handed him? Will he be fired anew? Will he,
in fact, now that he has his new job, like it? The experience of joy which
occasions his newfound hope for salvation is purely illusory, intangible,
always and inevitably in abeyance. What he has, in fact, achieved is not a
satisfaction so much as a new lease on hope, an achievement that momentarily has released him from the uncertainty of everyday living with
an exaggerated sense of a salvation already achieved. It is his experience
of joy and not the situation itself that brings home this experience of
salvation. This leads Sartre to conclude that

> Joy is magical behavior which tries, by incantation, to realize the posses-
> sion of the desired object as an instantaneous totality. This behavior is
> accompanied by certainty that possession will be realized sooner or later,
> but it seeks to anticipate that possession. The various activities expressive
> of joy . . . are animated and transcended by an intention which envisages
> the world through them.[20]

Just as the man who, finally finding the job that saves him from his
unemployment, will momentarily deny his new responsibilities and the
tasks which occasion them through his joyful exuberance, the isolated
or unhappy individual will do the same in his encounter with the
woman who has suddenly come into his life:

> It is thus, for example, that a man to whom a woman has just said that she
> loves him may begin to dance and sing. In so doing he turns his mind
> away from the prudent and difficult behavior he will have to maintain if he
> is to deserve this love and increase it, to gain possession of it through
> countless details (smiles, little attentions, etc.). He turns away even from
> the woman herself as the living reality representative of all those delicate
> procedures. Those he will attend to later; he is now giving himself a rest.
> For the moment, he is possessing the object by magic; the dance mimes
> his possession of it.[21]

The notion of giving ourselves a rest is indeed the basis of all the so-
called "positive emotions," which, in innocent form, is nothing to be
disparaged. Freud was careful to distinguish between the coping mechanisms of defense—the purpose of which was to achieve a respite on the
relentless path of our desire—and those same mechanisms of defense
which, in becoming a substitute for our encounter with everyday living,

become the bedrock of psychopathology. Emotions, too, can offer a momentary reprieve from the frustrations of life when they have become especially problematical.

But a reprieve is not of the same order as an escape, and taking refuge in the fantasy of manic or illusory satisfactions can be just as destructive in the subject's quest for recognition as the hateful, vengeful emotions. The incipiently happy psychotic is just as out of touch with his desires and the realities of their possible realization as the psychotic who is absorbed in anger, hatred, and malice. It may be more pleasant for those of us who are the recipients of this behavior to encounter the pleasant rather than the unpleasant manifestations of emotion. Perhaps for the subject, himself, one could say that a happy dreamworld is preferable to a nightmarish one. However, the experience of intolerable frustration is more likely to lead to emancipatory action that the giddy illusion of a dream fulfilled, which is, in reality, a dream foreclosed and destroyed.

The experience of love itself finds expression in numerous states which include what can only be referred to as an emotional experience. What one experiences as love can, of course, be a reaction formation which masquerades the hatred and contempt underneath. What is this experience other than one emotion which hides another, both of which vie for ascendency in a desperate attempt to keep the frustration of desire at bay? However, as Melanie Klein has said, love is often a projection onto the love object of the primary maternal identification from which the subject has not successfully separated.[22] Only later, when his expectations have not, shall we say, "materialized," does the disillusionment set in and the illusory character of his experience of love show its face. These experiences of love contain a certain possessive, voracious quality which have illusion at their foundation. That is, they convey the illusion of having attained a release from frustration which, in fact, has not occurred. Yet, the emotional experience of love is so profound that the subject experiencing it cannot possibly be swayed from his conviction that he is indeed experiencing the real thing. Only later does the truth come out, and what he had believed to be love is now judged as a mere infatuation. Naturally, authentic, selfless experiences of love are indeed possible, but in such cases we are not speaking of a passionate, emotionally charged situation but rather one in which we place ourselves at the other's disposal, for no intrinsic or ulterior reward. Such experiences are indeed rare and are probably experienced by most of us only in regard to children—if then. In most cases, love is a subtle system of exchange.

In short, what we call emotions are often something else entirely. But, in most cases, an emotion is *just* an emotion, and an emotion is, in any case, however pleasant or piognant it may be, a substitute for the gap that desire demands to be reckoned with. We fill that gap at our own peril, while denying that gap is our privilege.

The psychoanalytic defense mechanisms, with which we are so very familiar, can also be conceived as this or that operation of the subject who, in encountering the frustration of desire negated, spontaneously and unconsciously relieves this frustration by positing in its stead, through the imaginary machinations of his egoic identity, a momentary and illusory salvation. Each and every defense mechanism—and if we really wanted to be inventive, we could probably conceive of hundreds—has in common with the others a singular objective. The objective is to eliminate frustrated desire, essentially by one of two means. It is done either by obliterating the desirability of the desired object, or, by fulfilling the desire on a purely illusory foundation. The repression of desire obviously, in following Freud, is the most important of all the so-called "defensive operations." A sort of amnesia is resorted to which serves to shrink one's world of possible desires to a tolerable fixed point. By abdicating the specificity of one's desires, the subject is rendered stupid, oblivious, or naïve in respect to regions of his experience which are central to his destiny. While the hysteric gets much of the blame, repression is a technique that none of us could readily do without.

Projection, which is commonly equated with psychotic and paranoiac personalities, is indeed as equally common as repression: The subject projects his desires or impediments to them onto others or projects previously introjected desirable qualities onto others. He then proceeds to fall in love with those qualities or identifies with others whom he takes to be desirable, or places his expectations of others onto others' expectations of himself and resists them in the name of his individuality. In effect, projections help to distort reality sufficiently to make it bearable, to make oneself more like those others whom one feels to be so inferior to, all to one's imagined benefit. One draws the line between everyday projections and hallucination very carefully. Like all defense mechanisms, projection is guided by the resentful urge to right an experienced imbalance between the desirability of the object desired, and the desirability of one's desire in the eyes of the desired object.

Reaction formations, so commonly equated with obsessionals, is indeed so coincidental with guilt—i.e., the unworthiness of one's desire—that we often forget what can happen when the reaction is expressed negatively. What is common to all its formations is disguised bitterness, inferiority, and contempt toward the object of desire, an object who must be secretly undermined in order to take one's sweet revenge against the other's audacious superiority. We are all familiar with the hysteric who, after this posture has all but failed, reveals her true colors in the form of a manic explosion which corrects the previous imbalance or injustice.

What could better characterize the phenomenon of splitting than the inherent split at the core of man's being. It is the split between desire and the ego who protects the subject from it, between the bearing of frustration, on the one hand, and its elimination through murder, on the other. That is, it is the split between life and death. In its more extreme form, we must inevitably reckon with psychosis. In everyday form, we merely approach the constitutional ambivalence of which we are all made.

As to the rest of the mechanisms, it is only too easy to recognize the lengths the subject of desire must go to relieve himself of the burden—yes—the weight, of desire. Whether he regresses magically to a time when his desires were materially present, or denies that he has any desires or frustrations at all, the subject of desire can always find a way to overcome his desire by imagining a solution, enacting it in the most skillful of performances, and then telling himself he never set foot in the theater.

The Negative Transference and the Therapeutic Encounter

Surely, the greatest problem arises for every psychoanalyst when he encounters the patient's aggressive tendencies, embodied in the alienating maneuvers of his imaginary ego. While the ego is the product of continuous identifications, the subject of desire is an ambiguous enactment of secret intentions which are expressive of a dialectical relation with the other's recognition of his desirability.

The ego is cherished by many as the very seat of personal identity, as a threatened residence of selfhood which requires continuous fortification against incursions by the id and the outside world. If the ego were indeed expressive of subjectivity, then the unconscious would remain inconceivable as a source of secret motivations. The ego is not a source of motives but simply the rationale for the deceitful motives of the subject. Thus, the ego is merely an obstacle to an unconscious desire whose purpose is to integrate the subject round a false impression of himself, an impression which is constantly threatened by the presence of conflicting desires.

When we are able to grasp that the ego merely obstructs the possibility of a discourse of desire, and that its role is to lure the psychotherapist into a collusive arrangement whereby its omnipotence is confirmed and supported, then we must realize that the ego is the very seat of all resistance to therapy. Thus, the role of the therapist is characterized by his refusal to offer any kind of support or to influence the patient in any particular direction. He disavows expressions of interest, reassurance, or reaction which might be expected of him. He adopts the position of the unknown and unknowable quantity. He remains steady in his refusal to provide the satisfaction for the demands of the patient's ego.[23] Most importantly, the therapist avoids direct conflict with the patient's ego by adopting the position of a third person whose task is to expose the conspiracies of an ego situated in the confirmation of its own illusory foundation.

Only by following the role described above can the therapist hope to avoid the trap of taking on the patient's illness—which is just what is expected of him, for it is participation in his illness that the patient demands.[24] But it is ultimately the patient's hostile reaction to the therapist's refusal to do so that guides him in his exposure of the patient's internal conflict with himself. It is precisely these hostile intentions which form the nucleus of the negative transference and the analytic drama. Once the therapist realizes that the patient's hostile feelings are disguised appeals for recognition, he is free to examine the patient's resistances to his forbidden desires.

What the therapist wants to avoid at all costs is to allow the other's aggressive intentions finding support in the patient's idea of the therapist. It is these intentions which prompt the subject to act with opposition, ostentation, lying, negation, and betrayal, and which characterize the ego in dialogue.[25] But since the ego is but a construct in the imaginary, that is, a fiction, it is incapable of speaking for itself because its speech is the product of those identifications to which it has become attached. Nor is the ego capable of hearing the discourse of the other. Its role is to screen the other's words through its own fixations. Clearly this is not the ego to which Freud refers in his metapsychology consisting of a so-called "perception-consciousness." Rather, the ego is a peripheral object of consciousness which is marked by self-satisfaction and bad faith and which serves to obstruct the realizations of the subject. Thus, the patient's aggressive intentions reveal the omnipotent directives of an ego which strives to perpetuate the subversion of the subject's desires. And it is the possibility of these realizations which the ego is structured to refuse through its omnipotent position in the negative transference, and which situates the patient's resentment toward the therapist who refuses to comply.

Thus, exposure of the ego's alienating function is at the heart of the analytic enterprise. It is for this reason that the therapist should avoid the temptation of providing answers to the subject's demands for omnipotent mastery. He would be advised to invert such questions onto themselves in order to reveal the lures for support which the questions imply. Thus, psychoanalysis is an encounter in which the patient analyzes not himself but rather his demands for support from the analyst. Since the tendency of the subject in psychotherapy is to say whatever it is he believes the therapist wants to hear, any expectations that the therapist indeed has are bound to result in the identification of the latter as substitute for the former's desires. It is by frustrating these expectations that the ego is eventually overcome and the desires of the subject can be revealed.

The psychoanalyst need not go out of his way to frustrate the patient's demands. Frustration is built into the therapeutic encounter. As the words of the subject reveal a truth he has long since denied, he gradually comes to realize that he is not in command of his choice of words. Rather, his words take on the appearance of possessing him. In effect, he discovers that he is expressing his unconscious desires. As he feels increasingly dispossessed by the words which reveal his repressed desires, he begins to recognize that he has never been anything more than a "construct in the imaginary," whose treacherous task has been to obstruct the realization of his hidden subjectivity.[26]

The ego, which psychoanalysts characterize by its capacity to bear frustration, is frustration itself. Yet this frustration is not the frustration of desiring but rather the frustration of attaining an object to which the ego has become attached and from which the subject has been alienated. The analyst supports the maneuvers of the ego at his peril. Indeed, the analyst's task is to disengage the ego in order to overcome its resistance to the cure. Thus, the unspoken truth of the subject will never be realized through the alluring notion that the therapist should form some sort of alliance with the ego, since the consequence of such a strategy would merely strengthen the ego's resolve and its repression of the unconscious. To the contrary, the goal of psychotherapy is to suspend the ego's certitudes until their mirages have been dispelled. It is through the disintegration of this imaginary unity, which is constitutive of the ego, that the subject eventually discovers his salvation.

The Death of the Ego and the End of Analysis

If *happiness* is defined as that state of unification, completion, wholeness, togetherness, and autonomy whose egoic integrity it presumably confirms, then this vision of happiness is clearly not the goal of a therapeutic endeavor whose aim is to engage the realities of ordinary living. Indeed, the neurotic is a person who believes that this particular definition of happiness is possible. On the contrary, the therapeutic relation should be structured in such a way that it promotes the inevitable discovery that this state of unification is a fiction, that it behooves us to surrender our egoic fixations in favor of our—necessarily—painful recognition of desire, and that the realization of an individual destiny is impossible without the shared realization of a mutual or collective destiny. The implications for the resolution of the transference relation are not insignificant. If the patient wants his desires recognized by the analyst, then what does the analyst want? What does he stand to gain by losing a patient? Until the patient is capable of asking these questions, he will stay trapped in the immediacy of his self-serving narcissistic haze.

Since the neurotic is someone who does not know what he wants, he structures his relation to the therapist around the image of an authority who does know and will tell him. He expects him to yield this information, and it is precisely this expectation that structures the transference relation, which in turn revolves round the narcissistic component of the subject's aggressive subjugation of his ego. Because of this dual character of the therapeutic drama, it is inevitable that the subject's narcissistic demands will be activated in his relation to an authority who refuses to comply.

Just as the infant recognizes himself in the image he beholds in the mirror, the patient in psychotherapy sees in his therapist someone who is essentially similar to himself; a friend. This positive component of the therapeutic drama situates the patient's experience of compassion for himself. Yet the therapist is also perceived as an alter ego, someone he hopes will confirm his false image of himself. In this expectation lies the thread of reversal which leads to hatred and disappointment at the hands of that inevitable disintegration he must endure.

As the infant sees a whole image of himself in the mirror, this totality is in direct contrast to that experience he has of his fragmented, disordered self. Compared with this sense of internal chaos, his reflection suggests an ideal—although impossible—unity. This idealization of the so-called "perfect other" becomes the analyst in psychotherapy: the authority who is "supposed to know."

Ultimately, the patient encounters through his desire for the psychotherapist his relation to his absolute master: death. Not the death of his own possibilities, but the death of a lifetime of deceit for which the purpose has been the support for his own alienation. As Lacan said:

> What is an Ego, if not something that the subject at first experiences as foreign to him but "inside" him? It is in an *other*, more advanced, more perfect than he, that the subject first sees himself.
>
> Specifically, he sees his own image in the mirror at a time when he is capable of perceiving the image as a totality, but when he does not feel "himself" as such, but as living rather in that primal incoherence. . . . Thus the subject always has an anticipatory relationship to his own realization which in turn throws him back onto the level of a profound insufficiency and betokens a rift in him; a primal sundering, a *thrownness,* to use the Heideggerian term.
>
> It is in this sense that what is revealed in all imaginary relationships is an experience of *death:* an experience doubtless inherent in all manifestations of the human condition, but especially in the life of the neurotic.[27]

Thus the silence of the therapist correlates to that silence of the image in the mirror which refuses to correspond. Because the therapist remains silent and refuses to say what is expected, he evokes the patient's sense of his emptiness and lack which is derivative from his identification with his ego. Since the formalization of the "person" is realized through this dialectic of death and desire (ego and subject), death is an imaginary presence in all our dealings with our desires and other people.

The analytic cure is impossible without the presence of the patient's aggression and hostility, since his resistance to analysis is evocative of that aggressive component of the ego which structures his personal identity. Moreover, the formation of the ego is a strategy of defense which is intended to block the anxiety which results in the lack of a concrete self with which to negotiate the world.

And just as the form of the imaginary ego undergoes continuous transformations in childhood, the neurotic patient in psychotherapy produces successive apsects of his ego in response to the pressures of his encounter with an analyst who represents the death of the ego's domination. Frustrated in his repeated failures to persuade the therapist to confirm his identifications with the multiple images he has of himself, the patient gradually comes to realize that his ego represents a symptom which is formulated for another but stands between himself and the object of his desire. Thus,

> . . . the patient and analyst both come to their encounter with the faith that the willingness to confront one's own annihilation without fear is the only means of achieving freedom from psychic bondage.[28]

Finally, the death of the patient's ego nullifies the subversion of his own truth, which has been sustained in his resentful hostility towards another, who, in the end, he comes to realize is merely a creature of his imagination. Once the patient's demands for self-gratification have been consumed by the analyst's refusal to sustain them, the analyst becomes the total object of the patient's desire, who, ultimately, serves no other purpose than to be abandoned.

CHAPTER FIVE
ONCE REMOVED TO THE SECOND POWER: PSYCHOSIS

We are all familiar with the two avenues of thought which derive from Freud's thinking on psychoanalysis: a search for meaning, on the one hand, and a search for mechanism, on the other. There are those who would affect a convenient cleavage between Freud's theory and his clinical practice, suggesting that we dismiss his mechanistic metaphors and simply pay allegiance to the case studies and the theory of man which they imply.[1]

It is true that in 1900 Freud sought a new level of meaning in what his patients said and did. Freud was convinced that the psychical manifestations of his patients were essentially linguistic. But after the initial headiness of playing the part of a revolutionary in the face of conventional psychiatric practice, Freud apparently wanted to transform the establishment and make it his own. It became necessary that psychoanalysis achieve respectability and wear the cloak of a science.

However, Freud was less concerned with the elaboration of his talking cure than with creating a psychological program that would make everything perfectly clear. He spoke in terms of psychical mechanisms made up of id, ego, superego, which now join, then resist, drives, instincts, and censors which secretly determine the fate of the individual. The message is nothing if not clear. We have only to make these mechanisms comprehensible in order to interpret their crippling power and escape from neurotic bondage.

There are those who believe this later, psychological path was more precise and scientific. Others saw it as the death blow to Freud's true genius. The shift in strategy from meaning to mechanism led many practitioners to seek an alliance with behavioral psychologists while—paradoxically—concerning themselves more and more with the whereabouts of psychical activities, the very existence of which always had been in doubt. This turning led to the notion of the so-called "autonomous ego," that presumably willful aspect of the psyche which defends its constituent from the dangers of the id and the outside world in the service of psychical cohesion.

Freud gradually shifted his emphasis from the mysterious unconscious to the adaptive faculties of the ego's struggle with society. Now the ego emerges as a sort of heroic warrior which faces the rigors of reality by keeping the instincts at bay. Ego psychologists went so far as to claim for the ego a privileged aspect which was immune from the betrayal of neurotic forces. Their conception was that of a potentially autonomous agent free of social constraints. The analyst merely had to ally himself to the patient's healthy ego as it struggled to conquer the wiles of irrationality.

There are those who have criticized the hypothesis of an autonomous "aspect" of the ego.[2] Which part, exactly, is said to be autonomous? Who is to make this decision? Presumably the analyst is so equipped because of his superior understanding of psychological knowledge. There are those who have suggested that the analyst, on the contrary, should place himself in a position of radical self-doubt and questioning in order to resist his definition of reality from becoming the measure of the patient's destiny. Moreover, he should be on guard against the ego's influence (including his own), since it is unable to distinguish between the subject's unconscious desires and the demands of others. In other words, this ego of adaptation is never autonomous but rather alienated from the subject's relations with others, while remaining helplessly attached to their support. The ego is indeed an instrument of adaptation, but it is precisely this adaptation to an arbitrary social order which helps to subvert the realization of unrecognized desires.

It was due to Hegel's dialectic that deviance was no longer situated in the proprietorship of any one individual, because actions were comprehended from within a context of relations between social reality and private experience, between self as viewed by others and self experienced by self, between others as conceived by others and others as recognized by self, and so on. Linking individual consciousness to a deeper historical consciousness and to a broader social dimension challenged the traditional view of man as a being who could be situated abstractly outside of society, while at the same time challenging the notion that man could ever be a mere product of society, or a mindless agent for society. Irrational behavior, which was previously conceived as individual deviance, could now be understood as the occasion of an interrelationship between man, his environment, his history, and his self-conception.

The dialectical structure of the subject's interpersonal relations determines that society does not merely influence the individual but that it helps to structure his subjectivity as well. Since man becomes social with the appropriation of language, language constitutes man as an individual. Alienation is not merely psychological or social, it is both because man discovers himself in a world that does not constitute his desire as much as it *situates* it.

Man's desire is realized precisely through that act in which he engages those who are capable of recognizing it. The elaboration of his subjectivity in this engagement in turn reveals the world he inhabits. Thus, the nature of his world is defined by his intentions which go beyond the act itself toward an aim to be realized: a chosen end. The chosen end reveals what we, as subjects of desire, want and expect from others. Moreover, the world we live in reflects our desires, so if we find ourselves in a situation from which we want to escape, the world becomes constricting. My experience of myself and my experience of my world are inextricably entangled. Thus the San Franciscos of a frustrated attorney, a successful intellectual, a contented young mother, or a chronic schizophrenic are all the same in a certain sense. Equally obviously, they are different. They are different in the significant system of relations and the respective structures of desire which characterize the world of each.

This structure is not extended in merely one direction; it is reciprocal. An act can only exist if there is a correlate, or object, to this act. Thus, every act stems from a subject and every correlate belongs to a world. The way we account for our objects of desire and their realization is merely abstract until they are recognized as part of our world; that is, until we assume them. The neurotic is unable to inhabit certain acts since his execution of them is removed from his field of desire (i.e., unconscious acts). Thus, the respective objects, or correlates, to his desire are not a recognized part of his world. The psychotic disavows his acts as his own because he has abandoned his experience due to his profound denial of himself as a subject.

To understand the other as a subject of desire is not merely to gain awareness of the acts he performs but to gain access to the world he inhabits, a world which reveals the unconscious structure of his desire for my recognition. One single concrete act of a person contains what uniquely belongs to this person and only this person. At the heart of the other person we discover the heart of his world, so that the other person is understood as an unformulated intentionality in relation to that pregnancy of meaning which serves to structure his desires. Thus, the problem with many people diagnosed as mentally ill is not an "illness" in one person, but rather a rupture in the structure of reciprocity in which that person lives: his or her reality. This means that it is not merely a question of what is the matter, but also of where something is the matter that has disturbed one or more of the people in a given situation, thus disturbing the situation and, in turn, all of the people who comprise it. This disturbance is not only located in the behavior of one individual. We are faced, rather, with a complex disordering of a social order which includes the behavior of the people who are part of it and the reciprocal desires which determine it.

Traditional medical and psychological views of mental disorder attribute it primarily to an undiscovered physical or psychical cause. If the social context is considered at all, it is merely in order to define this or that so-called "psychosocial stressor" which is said to contribute to a pathological illness already in place. While physical and psychical alterations do correlate with different forms of experience, it is simplistic to reduce complex sets of relations to a technically sophisticated set of theories which take little, if any, account of social structures and intersubjectivity.

Psychoanalytic intervention is best conceived as a science of knowledge and, alternately, ignorance rather than a "cure" for disorders of the mind.[3] Psychoanalysis is essentially a logical science rather than, strictly speaking, a psychological one. Yet our concern is not merely with observing the mind and its functions but with paying attention to the development of a situation and recognizing how to judge and respond appropriately to it. The context of a social field immediately requires our attentiveness to the actions which occur between those people who are a part of it, so that the other person is recognized as the agent of his actions and not merely the proprietor of some anonymous behavior that is derived from the laws of social or psychological conditioning. Since our relation to society is reciprocal, our responsibility rests on the ways in which we respond to the situations we encounter.

Nowhere is this dialectic of responsibility and its failure more self-evident than in the social institution of the family, a truth at the heart of Freud's conception of neurosis that was derived from the vicissitudes of the Oedipal drama. Freud conceived every analytic intervention as resulting in an interaction within the subject's family as well, since, as we have noted, transformations occurring in the individual restructure the situation the individual inhabits and the people in it. Considerable research over the last 30 years into families has resulted in numerous theories concerning the interpersonal structure of the so-called "dynamics" involved, especially in reference to the etiology of psychosis. In America, where family therapy has become an institution with its own theories, biases, and methods, authors influenced by psychoanalysis, as well as those opposed to it, have developed theoretical positions regarding schizophrenia, generally focused on the mother's relationship with her child and often rooted in the defense mechanism of projection. Perhaps the most interesting contribution in this field was made by the anthropologist, Gregory Bateson, in collaboration with a number of colleagues loosely referred to as the Palo Alto group. Bateson's research into communication patterns in families of schizophrenics revealed that a logically impossible command could be issued to a child by others in the family. This would result in a psychotic experience which was perceived by Bateson as a metaphorical expression of the psychotic's dilemma.

R. D. Laing was more concerned with the exchange of identities which occurred in families of schizophrenics in the context of the child's enormous vulnerability to the way he was perceived by the parents. Following Hegel's notions of alienation and objectification as presented in the master-slave dialectic, Laing adopted a concept from Marx called "mystification," a term which alludes to unrecognized contradictions in families, not unlike the logically impossible commands Bateson observed.

Marx used the concept of mystification to describe a sort of power employed by one class of society to subjugate another class. By passing off forms of exploitation as acts of benevolence, the exploiter bemuses the exploited into feeling at one with him. In effect, the exploited class feel grateful for being exploited, since they do not perceive it as such.

The concept of mystification can mean both the act of mystifying someone and the state of being mystified by someone. I would like to show how acts of mystification are used to disavow the other's experience so that he no longer "knows" what he is experiencing, ultimately losing his sense of reality in favor of someone else's, leading to psychotic breakdown.

Laing employed Marx's theory of mystification between classes in society to his study of interpersonal relations between two or more members of families of schizophrenics.[4] According to Laing,

> In the active sense, to mystify is to befuddle, obscure, or mask what is going on between two or more people. In this sense mystification leads to *confusion*, since the person being mystified fails to see what is being done to him, and he is unable to distinguish the *real* issues involved.[5]

It is essential to the state of being mystified that the passive participant does not necessarily realize the confusion he is being subjected to, so that he may take it to be an act of benevolence, appreciation, or love. That is, the mystified person is, by definition, confused. But he may not feel confused. If we detect mystification being employed, whether in a family, a group, or between another person and ourselves, we are immediately alerted to the presence of a conflict of some kind that is being systematically avoided.

One of the primary purposes of mystification is to avoid authentic conflict. Although the effect of mystification may not avoid conflict altogether, its aim is at least to obscure what the conflict is really about.[6]

A certain amount of mystification occurs in everyday life. A girl becomes jealous when she sees her boyfriend making eyes at another girl. Angry, she confronts him. He says, "Don't be silly, it's only your imagination." He says this in order to avoid a conflict, which is accomplished by describing her perception as her imagination. What she says is discounted; she's just imagining it. She is being mystified by her boyfriend, but she may prefer this mystification to the reality that her lover is interested in someone else. She feels relieved to be told that what she thought was real was only her fantasy. There is always an element of collusion between the mystifier and the mystified.

Mystification typically begins in families, where it occurs most frequently between parents and children. A child is being noisy and generally a nuisance to his mother who would like him to go to bed so she can have some peace and quiet. A perfectly straightforward remark might be: "I'm tired and I want you to go to bed." A mystifying way of *inducing* the child to go to bed might be: "You're feeling tired, darling, you want to go to bed, don't you?"

What is ostensibly an affirmation of how the child feels is really a command: "Go to bed." But it is not stated as such. The child is told that he feels tired, when in fact it is the mother who feels tired. If the child does not happen to feel tired and says so, the mother may continue her mystifying ploy by saying "Mother knows best." The child is now made to feel that he is either unaware of what his true feelings are, or that his mother is not being honest with him. He will most likely prefer to believe that his mother, whom he loves, is telling him the truth. Therefore, he must be tired if she says so, although he does not feel tired.

This kind of deception and manipulation is common, and in itself would probably not cause any particular harm to the child if the basic structure of trust and reciprocity in the family remained intact. But we shall see how mystification can be employed in a systematic fashion with the consequence of driving the child crazy.

June is a 15-year-old girl whose mother went to see Laing, complaining about a change in her daughter which began six months previously.[7] This change began after June had returned from a holiday camp—the first time she had ever been away from home. According to her mother, June had always confided in her but after returning from holiday, June stopped.

Before she went away, June went everywhere with her mother. Now June prefers to be by herself most of the time. Before, June used to go swimming and cycling. Now she prefers to read. Before, June was sensible. Now her mind is "filled with boys." June's mother ascribed this change in her to an illness: "She's no longer 'June'; that's not *my* little girl." June's mother also believed that this change in her was an expression of evil. "A good girl wouldn't do these things."

What June's mother perceived as signs of illness and evil, Laing perceived as normal maturational expressions of growing up and achieving greater independence. However, in six months time, June had become completely mystified. Although she was becoming more independent, June still loved and trusted her mother. As her mother continued to insist that these signs of independence were expressions of illness and evil, June began to feel ill and evil. June is beginning to lose her sense of agency in her own experience and is adopting the experience which her mother attributes to her.

We must wonder how June's mother is capable of such power over June's own experience. We can easily imagine how other girls in June's place might choose to disagree and argue with their mothers. Yet June does not agree or disagree with her. She simply adopts as her experience the experience which her mother attributes to her.

Indeed, June loves her mother and begs forgiveness for being such a bad daughter. She cannot help the way she feels, but promises to get well. By this time June is complaining that "Hitler's soldiers are after her."

But not once does June's mother make observations about her other than to attack her for the very processes of development which are perfectly normal. Due to the mystification that June has been relentlessly subjected to by her mother—through which her experience of desire was consistently discounted—she begins to display signs of a psychotic breakdown. This, however, goes completely unnoticed by her mother.

As June gradually began to recover from her psychotic breakdown and loss of reality, her mother became more and more alarmed that June was getting worse. As she began to recover her sense of agency and subjectivity, her mother saw intensified evidence of evil.

Mystification can only occur within a context in which the person who is perpetrating the mystification is concerned with avoiding his or her rigid preconceptions of the world, the realization of which are aroused by the person who is the object of mystification. In other words, the former blames the latter for upsetting the status quo, for acknowledging that a conflict exists. He then mystifies that person into believing that a conflict does not exist. If the mystifier wants to avoid a conflict by pretending it does not exist, it is not enough for him to deny it. He cannot and must not allow the other person to remind him of it. In addition to self-denial, the mystifier must make the other person deny it as well. He maintains a kind of security blanket over his own defenses by immobilizing any possible opposition from the other person, thereby obscuring any conflicts which may arise.

Laing's use of mystification in his own work and Bateson's theory each allude to, but do not develop, the failure of desire in the child who turns to the parental structure for his initiation into the world and is refused. Through the state of being mystified the desire of the child is

subverted by the parent who defines the development of his individuality as a destructive or unholy force. Thus, the child who is indeed the
victim of unremitting mystification becomes psychotic by the family's
(often unwitting) betrayal. Since the real conflict between June and her
mother was systematically avoided, she was placed in an untenable situation. She was encouraged to retreat into herself (her attachment to her
mother's image of her) at the expense of her desire for recognition. By
condemning June's desire as evidence of illness and evil, she was denied
the reality of her own experience of the world, so that her desires became
psychotic through her personification of her mother's alienation.

Thus, the purpose of mystification is to maintain the status quo. It is
employed when one or more members of a family (or group) threaten
the status quo of the others, usually the parents. They struggle to
preserve their own fragile foothold on reality by maintaining their
neurotically rigid preconceptions about who they or their children
ought to be. Consequently, they remain impervious to the maturational
needs and desires of their children which threaten to disrupt their preconceived scheme. And because of their helpless attachment to their
parents, these mystified children are virtually incapable of rebelling
against—or even placing into question—the parental structure that
they so desperately depend upon.

This is not to say that mystifying ploys occurring as late as adolescence are in themselves sufficient to lead to psychosis. Normally, the
child would remain resilient enough to discount, evade, or rebel against
these ploys by relying on his or her own subjective experience of reality.
What is needed for psychosis to occur is an entire lifetime of mystified
encounters which result in an experience of subjectivity so fragile that,
by adolescence or even adulthood, the subject cannot bring himself to
separate from the family structure without regressing into the helpless
child he truly is.

It is the structure of the family's mystified alienation which symbolizes the ego of the child in question. This structure is not merely comprised of the rules, premises, and prohibitions so central to the family
order, but more significantly consists in the reciprocal structuring of
desire which inhabits the discourse and the silences passed among its
members. But this field of desire the child is born into is not of the
same order as Freud's primordial, impersonal, and instinctual drives for
"satisfaction," on the one hand, or the achievement of a safe-enough
environment, or good-enough mother, or intact-enough reality, on the
other.

The British school, due largely to the development of the object-relations theories of Fairbairn, Klein, Winnicott, Guntrip, and others, and the adaptation of ego psychology into object-relations theory by Mahler, Hartmann, Rapaport, Kernberg, and Masterson, among others, have tended to discount Freud's emphatic attentiveness to the conception and prevalence of desire in the life of the child in favor of a behavioral-social theory which views the child's survival and unimpeded chronological development as central to its emergence as a well-adjusted, or healthy, adult or, conversely, a psychopathological one.

Object relations theorists, taking their lead from Melanie Klein in Great Britain and Margaret Mahler in the United States, tend to view psychosis as a regression to a pre-Oedipal stage of development, which is perfectly normal for the infant but highly problematical for the adult. Each have their own terminology. Klein refers to the paranoid-schizoid position; Mahler talks about the autistic and symbiotic phases. Both, however, see psychosis as a reenactment of an early developmental phase which, due to the failure of either the environment or of the child, or both, the child entered and then excited the Oedipal drama incapable of integrating reality sufficiently to keep up its doomed performance. As the child grows older, and increasing demands for increasingly sophisticated responses to the social order grow stronger, this individual is more or less destined, sooner or later, to break down under the weight of a world it is haphazardly prepared for. When the dreadful occurs, the adult will withdraw into the particular style of psychosis which is ordained from the precise moment in its childhood that he failed to take to his environment.

This view of psychosis is not unlike that of a ticking time bomb, waiting to go off at that moment when external pressure is sufficient to trigger the inevitable explosion. The bomb is defused, according to these developmental theorists, by what they call "re-mothering." Accordingly, one could prevent an explosion by providing whatever nourishment and love the child/adult had been lacking to begin with. Thus psychosis is conceived as being induced during the first year or so of life—back, as it were, to the scene of maternal failure.

Everyone since Freud has been concerned with distinguishing the difference between neurosis and psychosis. A notion of psychosis in terms of the ego's relation to reality has emerged. Thus, the psychotic, in regressing to an infantile stage so early and so extreme, is said to mirror that earlier withdrawal from reality in order to invest his desire in himself, narcissistically. Thus the notion of the psychotic as that individual who withdraws from an unbearable world, which occasions a commensurate loss of reality, is the hallmark of post-Freudian psychoanalysis. This, of course, raises difficulties in the psychoanalytic treatment of psychotics since, according to this view, any loss of reality makes the establishment of a transference relation—the capacity for which the neurotic is not only capable of making but virtually condemned to make—impossible.

The relation between the psychotic and reality is, of course, central to any endeavor to understand psychosis, but the problem in clarifying this question lies in our chosen understanding of reality itself. What's more, in respect to the psychotic individual and his falling out with reality, whose reality is it we are speaking about? Freud, himself, distinguished between neurosis and psychosis in 1924 by emphasizing the crucial issue of world, or environment, concerning the genesis of psychosis:

> Neurosis is the result of a conflict between the ego and its id, whereas psychosis is the analogous outcome of a similar disturbance in the relations between the ego and the external world.[8]

At first, this statement appears to be ambiguous and even confusing. Since psychoanalysis stands on the prevalence of what is called "endo-psychic conflict" for all psychopathological states, it would seem that Freud was attributing psychosis to a conflict between the personality and the environment. However, Freud makes it abundantly clear in numerous other passages that this is not his intent. His formula for psychosis does, however, in pointing to the psychotic's hostility to reality and his conflict with it, help us take note of the one element within the endo-psychic conflict which, in Freud's view, determines the psychosis. Having established the psychotic's relation to reality as central—in contradistinction to neurosis—to the etiology of psychosis, what is to be said of this reality?

For one thing, we have seen that Laing gives extraordinary importance to the social—or intersubjective—dimension in his treatment of schizophrenia, in a manner totally unlike the object-relations theorists. Nowhere does Laing give the impression that psychosis is the result of momentary rupture. On the contrary, the impression conveyed is the relentless nature, over great gulfs of time, of the maddening and mystifying engagements and disengagements throughout the lifetime of a childhood which are required to produce a psychotic individual. While Laing is not suggesting that psychosis can be created instantaneously at any time or place that mystification is engaged in, neither is he suggesting it is ordained by the failure to pass from one developmental stage to the next. Rather, he suggests that there is an array of exchanges between parent and child, parent and parent, child and parent, whose quality never wavers or varies from its inception: the total domination of the mind and life of this impressionable individual subject.

The question of mystification to which Laing refers in his explanation of the exchange that constitutes schizophrenia is not limited to this particular psychosis but rather to all its forms, save for those of obviously organic or drug-induced origins. Laing tends to favor schizophrenia as the paradigm for all the psychoses, i.e., a state of confusion. That schizophrenia is by far the most common of the psychoses has led many to accept this emphasis. However, Lacan has favored the state of paranoia as the paradigmatic center for the psychotic personality, i.e., a state of *suspiciousness,* concerning himself especially with the phenomenon of auditory hallucination. Not surprisingly, it is this aspect of psychosis which alludes specifically to the verbal—or linguistic—dimension that Lacan is so very taken with.

Since everyone who has attempted to contribute to our understanding of psychosis has had a hand at improving on Freud's exposition of the Schreber case, including Lacan, we shall turn to this case briefly in order to compare Freud's concept of psychosis with one which relies on the phenomenology of mystification as the paradigm of the psychoses.

As we know, Freud based his understanding of paranoia on the memoirs of Daniel Paul Schreber, a German judge. Schreber became a mental patient at the ago of 42 and spent 13 years in mental asylums, where he published a book, *Memoirs of My Nervous Illness,* which describe his psychotic experiences in extraordinary detail.[9] Freud's analysis of Schreber is unique in that we have at our disposal other data about Schreber's childhood in the form of 18 books published by Schreber's father, a pedagogue who was a popular specialist in raising children. Many of his books recount his methods of child rearing—methods he applied to his own children. Freud never read the books which were readily available, despite his knowledge of the father's work. This is somewhat surprising, given Freud's conviction that the psychotic's conflict with the outer world distinguishes the genesis of his pathology from that of the neurotic. One would have thought that, rather than confusing Schreber's account of his illness by contrasting it with other information, insights might well have been conceived in exploring other sources. As we shall see, had Freud done so, his theory of paranoia could have possibly been altered.

Basing his assessment of Schreber's paranoia on a homosexual phantasy, Freud explains in his paper on Schreber that the paranoid male contradicts his love for a man by hating him and then replacing his internal perceptions with external perceptions:

> Consequently the proposition "I hate him" becomes transformed by *projection* into another one: "*He hates* (persecutes) *me,* which will justify me in hating him." And thus the impelling unconscious feeling makes its appearance as though it were the consequence of an external perception: "I do no *love*—I *hate* him, because *he persecutes me.*"[10]

Thus, according to Freud, if a man loves another man (such as his father), but believes, for whatever reason, that this love is forbidden, he then denies it and reverses it: "I love him" is transformed into "I hate him." But if his hatred is also forbidden, he projects his hatred onto the love object: "I hate him" becomes "He hates me." His love for a man is transformed into his persecution by a man through denial, reversal, and then projection. But the crucial step which is then taken is repression, in order to remove all traces of his supposed crime. He is thus unconscious of loving a man and equally unconscious of the steps he has taken to keep it unconscious.

Schreber's account of his illness is filled with detailed descriptions of tormenting daily abuses to his body which he insisted were wracked upon him by God's miracles. Schreber never reported any hatred for his father, and the ambiguous relationship he had with a God who was intent on persecuting him (why not the devil?) struck Freud as an obvious allusion to the incompatible feelings of love and hatred he must have had for his father. Thus Schreber's repressed love/hate relation with his father reemerged in symbolic form late in life as miraculous persecutions. What Freud did not know was that homosexual feelings were hardly necessary to account for Schreber's psychosis because his father's physical treatment and, more importantly, his conceptions about children and child rearing were more than sufficient to account for his persecutory delusions.

William Niederland has pointed out some striking similarities between Schreber's experiences and his father's child-rearing techniques, though he does so in an attempt to confirm Freud's thesis about the etiology of Schreber's paranoia, himself failing to realize the full import of his findings. Morton Schatzman, a student of R. D. Laing in the late of 1960s, published a book[11] based in part on some lectures delivered by Laing at Kingsley Hall, outlining the efficacy of the Schreber case for his concept of mystification, and partly on Niederland's findings.

Niederland goes to great lengths to compare passages from Schreber's memoirs with those from his father's publications, showing the alarming similarity between them. After his breakdown, Schreber describes a variety of experiences of persecution which he suffers at the hand of his merciless God. "Miracles of heat and cold," says Schreber, "were and still are daily enacted against me. . . . From youth accustomed to enduring heat and cold, these miracles troubled me little. I myself have often been forced to seek heat and cold."[12]

Niederland compares this passage with one taken from one of his father's publications: ". . . starting from about three months after birth cleansing of the infant's skin should be by cold ablutions only, . . . in order to physically toughen up the child."[13] While Schreber remembered these baths from his childhood, he made no connection between his having endured them as a child and his seeking them out as an adult.

In another passage Schreber describes "the so-called coccyx miracle" which he suffers at the hand of God:

Its purpose was to make sitting and even lying down impossible. Altogether I was not allowed to remain for long in one and the same position or at the same occupation: When I was walking one [of the "miracles"] attempted to force me to lie down, and when I was lying down one wanted to chase me off my bed.[14]

Again, on comparing Schreber's experiences with the pedagogic admonitions of his father, one finds Schreber's father warning parents to fight against the child's tendency toward laziness and awkward sitting postures to prevent the deformation of their backbones:

Half resting in lying or wallowing positions should not be allowed: if children are awake they should be alert and hold themselves in straight, active positions and be busy; in general each thing which could lead towards laziness and softness (for example the sofa in the children's room) should be kept away.[15]

Schreber describes other miracles which can be directly attributed to devices his father invented for the purpose of keeping the posture of the child erect in order to counteract the child's natural predisposition toward weakness and laziness. According to Schreber, "One of the most horrifying miracles was the so-called *compression-of-the-chest-miracle* . . . ; it consisted in the *whole chest wall being compressed,* so that the state of oppression caused by the lack of breath was transmitted to my whole body."[16] Again, the father invented a "straightholder" which compelled children to sit upright while studying at a desk—whether at home or at school. (Schreber's father's techniques were so popular that school teachers cooperated with parents in making their children use these devices in the classroom as well.) This device consisted of an iron cross bar which, fastened to the desk, pressed against the child's collarbone to prevent him from slouching forward. The cross bar discouraged the child from leaning forward, "Because of the *pressure* of the hard object against the bones and the consequent *discomfort.*"[17] Dr. Schreber points out that, having tested this device on his own children, he became convinced that its effects were not merely physical, but *moral* as well.

Schreber suffered numerous other miracles that Niederland compares with various practices and devices used by his father which clearly point to the sources in childhood of Schreber's tormenting experiences. What is more remarkable in this evidence is Schreber's amnesia, his inability to remember his having been subjected to these practices despite the fact that many of them were carried out well into his adolescence. Schatzman concludes that,

> It is as if Schreber is forbidden by a rule to see the role his father has played in his suffering, and is forbidden by another rule to see there is anything he does not see, and as if a rule forbids him to see that rule, or *that* a rule might exist. For instance, he never says he cannot find what his experiences mean, and that he cannot because a rule stops him, or that he cannot, and does not know why he cannot. He is certain he knows what they mean; although he discussed their meaning in detail, he never connects them with his father.[18]

Of course, Schreber's certainty regarding the explanation of the facts is the hallmark of the paranoiac, a certainty which naturally precludes the sort of doubt and questioning which might lead one to put two and two together. For Schreber it is far more preferable to blame God than his father. How is it possible that he could not, would not, remember earlier experiences which he had apparently found intolerable? We know that physical abuse in childhood is not in itself sufficient to produce psychosis. It is more likely that the abused child will repeat these abuses on his own children or against society. What is necessary to induce psychosis and the specific amnesia which is so characteristic of the psychotic is that he not experience it as abuse at the time he is experiencing it. Only if he was forbidden to experience it as such could he fail to do so.

In examining Dr. Schreber's philosophy of child rearing we discover ample evidence of the sort characterized by Laing as the parents' mystification of the child. That is, the child must be made to experience the parents' behavior—no matter what it may be—as expressions of love, so that the child himself can learn to love, honor, and obey his parents willingly and without fear. Schreber's father taught parents it was crucial that their children not experience bitterness or anger towards them, even if these feelings were justified. It is in Schreber's conceptions regarding the proper mental attitude of the child that we will find the seeds of his son's psychosis and not in the abusive techniques themselves.

Dr. Schreber considered sensual desires to be bad and that bad elements of the mind needed to be expunged. For the sake of the child's mental and moral health it was crucial that the parents go to work on him from the start, to rescue him from his innate inclination toward heaven knows what, but apparently from what Schreber believed would be a life of crime, sin, and ill-health: "Suppress everything in the child, keep everything away from him which he should not make his own but guide him perseveringly towards everything to which he should habituate himself."[19]

As Schatzman points out, Dr. Schreber's intent was to instill self-determination, self-reliance, and free will into the life of the child through the most illogical of means. To learn self-determination the parent must exercise suppression. In order to learn the nature of free will, the child must be *forced* to be free. In order to achieve this,

> One must look at the moods of the little ones which are announced by screaming without reason and crying. . . . If one has convinced oneself that no real need, no disturbing or painful condition, no sickness is present, one can be assured that the screaming is only and simply the expression of a mood, a whim, the first appearance of self-will. . . . One has

to step forward in a positive manner: by quick distraction of attention,
stern words, threatening gestures, rapping against the bed . . . or when all
this is of no avail—be moderate, intermittent, bodily admonishments consistently repeated until the child calms down or falls asleep. . . .[20]

In other words, Dr. Schreber advised parents that the achievement of
mastery over the child was the crucial step necessary to insure a healthy,
well-balanced individual so that their command—in a word, their
"law"—should never again be questioned. "Such a procedure is necessary only once or at most twice and—one is *master* of the child *forever.*
From now on a glance, a word, a single threatening gesture is sufficient
to rule the child."[21]

But it is not enough that the child learn to obey out of fear, but rather
from the experience of fear masquerading as love: "One should keep in
mind that one shows the child the greatest kindness in this in that one
saves him from many hours of tension which hinder him from thriving
and also frees him from all those inner spirits of torment which very
easily grow up vigorously into more serious and insurmountable enemies of life."[22]

It is clear from a reading of Dr. Schreber's views on child rearing that
mastery, or control, over the child's behavior is merely incidental to
what he describes as "an intelligent pedagogic approach." What is more
crucial is to control the child's sentiments, motives, and even his heart.
Consistent with the philosophy and practice of mystification—which,
of course, must not be admitted to, experienced, or recognized as mystification—is the elimination of outer conflict, disagreement, a difference of opinion.

Dr. Schreber was so concerned that his children might learn to hate
him that he devised a system of indoctrination which was guaranteed to
prevent such a possibility. Since only a child with a mind of its own
could possibly assume the subjective position of hatred toward an other,
it was necessary to mystify the child into believing that, after having
been punished, it was he (the child) who must be recognized, in all
cases, as the object of contempt—even if the parent knew the child to be
in the right!

It is generally salutary for the sentiments if the child after each punishment, after he has recovered, is gently prodded (preferably by a third
person) to offer to shake the hand of the punisher as a sign of a plea for
forgiveness . . . After this prodding has occurred a few times the child,

feeling his duty, will freely approach the punisher. This assures against the possibility of residual, spiteful or bitter feelings and mediates the feeling of repentance . . . and generally gives the child the salutary impression that he still owes the punisher something, not the other way around, *even if maybe a word or a blow more than necessary should have befallen the child.*

. . . If one forgets about the repentance process here one risks always that a kernel of bitter feeling will stay stuck in the depths of children's hearts. If one were to omit this procedure altogether one would permit the punished child the right of anger against the punisher which is certainly not consistent with an intelligent pedagogic approach.[23]

Thus Dr. Schreber prescribes a "cure" for his conception of the sickness of being a child with a mind of its own. If the child learns his duty, his free choice will follow, as ordained by the law or commandment of the parent or God.

Schatzman lists numerous other examples clearly demonstrating the God-like position Dr. Schreber exercised over his son, in the form of principles and methods which, having been repressed for what they were, later reappeared in the form of miracles shortly after Dr. Schreber's death. While psychoanalysts rightly emphasize the presence of projection on the part of the psychotic's experience of persecution, one must also recognize the presence of projection at the time the mind of the young child is being stripped of his subjectivity. That is, one must see the projections of his parent while being subjected to the sort of mystification we see evidenced in Dr. Schreber's pedagogic approach.

Laing emphasizes that the goal of mystification is to preserve the preconceived scheme the parents feel they and their child *should* be. But in order to preserve this preconceived scheme, it is necessary to rid oneself of qualities one takes to be repugnant. The apparent sadistic impulses of Dr. Schreber, which were unknown to all who knew and followed him, were certainly inconsistent with the view he had of himself as an intelligent pedagogue. Dr. Schreber could not tolerate the "inner spirits of torment" he witnessed in the child who cried, which he viewed as "insurmountable enemies of life." This is why he had to save children who experienced these feelings. When Dr. Schreber saw no reason for a child of six months to cry out, he assumed that no reason existed. The inner spirits of torment he recognized in his children were actually his own repressed torment which, having been projected onto his children, he then felt he could save them from. He thought he wanted to master or control his children, when what he apparently was doing was mastering the bad parts of himself. In denying his child his own experience of reality, of his own subjectivity, Dr. Schreber carefully constructed for the child an identity or ego which the child assumed as his own. One form of this identity was to experience terror as love, slavery as free will, self-determination as willfulness, desires as evil, and his father's experience of reality as his own. With no mind of his own, young Schreber, through the relentless practices of his father, from birth through his adolescence, became what his father conceived him to be: the repressed projections of his own tormented mind, the sacrificial lamb who would insure for Dr. Schreber his own magnanimous image of himself—who would not dare utter even a word of this truth until after his father's death, and even then in the only manner that was left to his disposal: the ravings of a lunatic who could only utter his truth metaphorically.

Schatzman is quite right when he sums up Judge Schreber's delusional psychosis as the manifestation of reminiscences. Schreber did not remember being tormented or persecuted by his father, but his amnesia was in no way complete. His paranoid delusional system was a perfect play on his real-life experiences. The tormenting miracles his body was subjected to symbolized a geography of his historical pain:

> His body embodies his past. He retains memories of what his father did to him as a child; although part of his mind knows they are memories, "he" does not. He is considered insane not only because of the quality of his experiences but because he misconstrues their *mode:* he *remembers,* in some cases perfectly accurately, how his father treated him, but thinks he *perceives* events occurring in the present for which he *imagines* God, rays, little men, etc., are the agents.[24]

Judge Schreber's father was not only sadistic and cruel. One could also make a case for his having suffered from a markedly paranoid view of the world himself. While Judge Schreber is often referred to as paranoid, we know his diagnosis is more complicated than that, exhibiting as he does a clearly schizophrenic personality as well. His father, in contrast, was not apparently insane, though his rigid view of himself and of his children could hardly be regarded as merely neurotic. Otto Will, in a commentary on Schatzman's research, reported

> It is of particular interest to me to learn that Schreber's father considered children to be criminal or ill at their beginning, to be rescued from an evil fate only by proper training. This oversimplification of people—and be-

havior—into categories of "good" or "bad" is an aspect of the paranoid solution to living. Perhaps we must note an unpleasant possibility—that what we become is largely the result of what we are taught. The paranoid Schreber had the background to become paranoid, in that he could reduce the complexities of life to the dreadful simplicity of persecution, a device remarkably resistant to alteration.[25]

While no one is suggesting that Dr. Schreber's treatment of his son caused the latter's psychosis, the mystification the son was subjected to adds an element to young Schreber's experience of himself which, having assumed this identity, became bound to it and, for all practical purposes, enslaved to his "evil" experience of himself. The function Dr. Schreber served in his son's upbringing was not merely—as Lacan would say—symbolic, but all too real as well. It is precisely to this dimension of the real that Freud referred when he distinguished between neurosis and psychosis. It is this dimension for which Lacan's treatment of the Schreber case fails to account adequately. But at the same time Lacan does provide insight into the position of the father in the genesis of psychosis, one that adds further weight to our thesis that the father can constitute the environmental structure of a future psychosis just as adequately as the mother.

After the insistence of many years of psychoanalytic theorizing—especially from the object relations viewpoint—that the failure of mothering is the explanation for the genesis of psychosis, it is refreshing to see the emergence of a theory which takes equal account of the role of the father. It is surprising that Laing himself has failed to develop this position since his concept of mystification in the etiology of the psychoses is equally relevant to both parents. His studies, thus far, have been largely devoted to mothers and daughters. While Lacan takes emphatic account of the mother's place in the Oedipal drama, he ascribes psychosis to the failure of the paternal metaphor, or of the child's accession to the father's law. The way to this accession, however, is rooted in the child's total dependence upon the mother figure. As we have stated earlier, the child wants to be everything for its mother, to be the total object of her desire, while struggling against its own total dependence on the mother. It struggles against knowledge of this dependence due to what Melanie Klein has described as the child's fear that, if the mother is not dependent on it, the child risks the danger of the mother's abandonment.

Thus the child resists the dawning realization that the father will beckon the mother's desire, so much so that it is typical of the young child to resent the parents even talking to each other, manifested in its attempts to disturb them. It is this realization that constitutes the child's accession to the Oedipal drama. The child attempts to hold on to its omnipotent fantasy by denying any significant reference to the position of the father as primordial object to the mother's desire, as exemplified in her recognition of him as desirable.

Lacan rightly emphasizes that it is not important for the father to be present or even alive for this drama to occur, since the father is remembered by the mother as the child's father. Further, the father also symbolizes any other that the mother recognizes as a desirable object. In this respect, the father symbolizes the social dimension from which the mother is born, in which she is inserted, and to which the child must inevitably accede in order to achieve emancipation from its maternal identification and its birth as a subject—and not merely an object—of desire.

Lacan pays particular emphasis to the mother's recognition of the father in terms of her respect for his name, which Lacan designates "name-of-the-father." According to Lacan, the child, too, must learn to recognize and submit to the name of the father in order to break free of its maternal bondage. The child's failure to do so occasions, according to Lacan, the origin of schizophrenia. In other words, by maintaining its omnipotent fantasy that *it* can be the phallus—or object of desire— for the mother, the child fails to become a subject and remains rooted in a fantasy world which ordains a future psychosis. In Winnicott's terms, the child would thus refuse to substitute for the mother other objects for its desire and then fail to situate its own subjective reality in the form of symbolic play. Lacan explains the child's failure to achieve this symbolic initiation as one of foreclosure, a concept which is for the psychotic what repression is for the neurotic. While the future neurotic represses his desire for the mother and the yearn for her return, the future psychotic forecloses the very possibility of his desire ever being born.

While placing emphasis on the symbolic importance of the father as initiator of the child's emancipatory desire, it still falls squarely on the shoulders of the mother the eventual fate of the child's failure, since, in order for the child to recognize the father, the way must first be prepared by the mother's recognition of and respect for the father's name, or law.

To be sure, we know that the mother's position is most important in the child's ability to separate from her and to discover his own desire. In

Alphonse de Waelhens's study of Lacan's conception of psychosis, he maintains that it is first necessary for the child's emancipation that the mother indicate that his destiny lies elsewhere.[26] In spurning the father's privilege, his place, his role, his name, his law, the mother effectively becomes a law unto herself. In quoting the work of Mme. Piera Aulangnier-Spairano, Waelhens pays particular attention to research on the mothers of psychotics who demonstrate omnipotent fantasies of their own: "For the subjects of whom I speak, i.e., the mothers of psychotics, things are of an altogether different order: the rules of the game have never been accepted, or, what is more serious, understood; one could say that the only game they know is 'solitaire,' a game without partners and without stakes, except for those that confirm an autistic omnipotence."[27]

Waelhens qualifies Lacan's seemingly total reliance on the paternal metaphor as his exclusive explanation for the etiology of psychosis. The point is a difficult one, for if the mother is herself insistent on remaining the total object of her child's desire, how can the child then accede to the father's dimension? Indeed, such a mother, given the opportunity to perpetuate her hold on the child's desire, would appear to be in an impregnable position.

> If, clinically, they (the mothers of psychotics) are not psychotics, if their defenses permit them a kind of superficial adaptation to the real, it is nevertheless true that we find that their lives are always very ahistoric (i.e., they are poorly inserted into, if not excluded from, the order of the Law). Moreover, it is possible and probable that, in these cases, the child may be the factor which sets an abrupt breakdown of the defenses in motion. . . . However, at the same time, the child will also be that which permits these mothers to fill up the gap in the defense mechanism . . . which receives and holds back any irruption of poorly dammed-up repression.[28]

While invoking the paternal metaphor as central to the child's emancipation, Waelhens and Lacan do no abdicate the pivotal reference point of the mother—or maternal function—in providing the very possibility for the child's accession to or refusal of the social dimension. In fact, Lacan's acquiescence to the mother, at least in terms of psychosis, may be too extreme. One gets the impression that the only father present in the child's struggle is the one noted, recognized, or repudiated by the mother. In Wilfried Ver Eecke's introduction to Waelhen's study, he also raises doubts regarding the efficacy of Lacan's position.

In Lacan and de Waelhens, one has the impression that the cause for the foreclosure of the name-of-the-father is to be found in the mother who undermines the Word and the Law of the father; such a mother may even repress the sexual origin of her child which would remind her of her husband. De Waelhens seems to be aware that the mother's attitude towards the Word of the father cannot be the whole story. Indeed . . . the influence of the name-of-the-father is not solely determined by the mother's attitude, but by what the father himself is and how the child perceives the name-of-the-father in imagination.[29]

What Eecke refers to in this passage is a comment by Waelhens questioning Lacan's insistence on the mother's position as total arbiter of the child's accession to the social dimension.

According to Waelhens,

If the father is the caricatural personage so energetically ridiculed by Lacan when he describes Schreber's father for us, how will the mother transform the nonexistent into a presence, and how will this nonexistent be able to impose himself as the guardian and the guarantor of the law? And how can this nonexistence avoid stimulating the narcissism of the mother and child dyad?[30]

In other words, even if the mother wanted to surrender her child to the father's law, how is she to do so if the father's presence is experienced by all as a singular absence, a form of existence that, in describing Schreber's father, Lacan claims to be the case. Contrary to the view that Schreber's psychosis could have been occasioned by the nonexistence of his father at the moment of his accession to the law, Eecke adds a footnote to this passage, in support of Schatzman's study, which suggests that it was due to Dr. Schreber's all-too-real presence that accounts for this particular etiology of psychosis.

The book of Schatzman: *Soul Murder* . . . suggests that Schreber's father might not have been "inexistent" for his children. On the contrary, he might have been "brutally" present. Lacan's theory has a tendency to reduce the role of the father to that of a statue that the mother must respect. This respect she must communicate to the children, who then are capable of accepting the "name-of-the-father." . . . [Indeed] the acceptance of the "name-of-the-father" depends not only on the respect shown by the mother for the figure of the father, but also on the *father's presence to his children*. Furthermore, the respect of the mother for the figure of the father is not solely a function of the emotional maturity of the mother, it is also dependent on *who that father* shows himself to be.[31]

This leads us to the central difficulty—and failure—in Lacan's exposition of psychosis. Despite the value in Lacan's conception of the father's role in the genesis of psychosis, the father to which Lacan refers is limited to a symbolic function which, allowing for its undisputed merit, is not sufficient to account for a comprehensible theory of psychosis. What is lacking in Lacan's theory is the process of mystification whereby the subjectivity of the child is foreclosed in favor of an egoic identification which the child becomes "absorbed" by. Unlike the neurotic who is in love with his ego, is separated from it but endeavors to be it, the psychotic has no such privilege of distance which leads to the classical neurotic conflict. Having become his ego, the psychotic's conflict—as Freud understood—is with the real. And it is precisely at this dimension of the real that mystification occurs. What is crucial in the genesis of psychosis is not, strictly speaking, the child's accession to the symbolic order—this would remain equally true for neurosis—what is unique in psychosis is the child's merger into an egoic identity which has been presented to him as his own creation—and which the child has henceforth assumed, as his own. This ego, which does not belong to the child but "inhabits" the child, can be conceptualized and constituted by either the father or mother figure.

We have seen that, in the case of Schreber, the father was indeed very present in the family and that his law was strictly enforced. Schreber's father taught that striving for independence (i.e., subjectivity) in children should be suppressed. Dr. Schreber advised families to convene monthly sessions at which its members could account for the faults and merits of the children—and boasted of the results of such exercises on his own children. He would place his child on the lap of a nanny while the latter was to eat and drink, yet the child, who was forbidden to eat between meals, was compelled to watch.

Dr. Schreber was a powerful presence in the Germany of his day, a writer, lecturer, inventor, with millions of devotees. Thus Schreber Senior was anything but nonexistent to his son as Lacan would suggest. On the contrary, it was Schreber Senior's dominance of Schreber Junior which led to the latter's psychosis. While Waelhens, who follows Lacan, who in turn repudiates contemporary psychoanalysis, perceives Judge Schreber as a latent schizophrenic since childhood, Antoine Vergote recognizes—in keeping with Laing's thesis—a "network of real causes."[32] In citing his work, Eecke notes three relevant facts of the case:

Judge Schreber's illness erupted at about the age that his own father had died; at a time too when he saw himself deprived of normal paternity; and at a time finally when he was elevated to presiding Judge to a Court of Appeals, i.e., a function which is very paternal.[33]

These coincidental occurrences, which encroached upon Judge Schreber at the time of his first lapse into psychosis, relate to a loss of the Judge's real father, his wife's failure to bear him a child, and his assumption of a position of paternal authority he was incapable of assuming. Combined, they brought home to Judge Schreber the lack of assumption of his own phallus, a lack which he ultimately came to terms with in the assumption of a psychosis which ordained for him instead that bisexual metaphor which became symbolized in becoming for his father or God the metamorphosized body of a woman who could receive his father's semen in the form of his tormenting miracles.

According to Waelhens,

> What Schreber loves and wants to save is the persecuted creature, destined to shame and nothingness, which he keeps alive by his own word, insofar as he does not cease to respond to the divine challenge. . . . By unifying himself with the primordial object, Schreber identifies himself with his mother; he does so in order to become the spouse of the father, as symbolized by the hallucinatory God of his delirium, with whom, one day, he will unite himself.[34]

In Schreber's view of the family, the women apparently exert no singular influence. The dominance of the paternal metaphor is complete. Yet this does not prevent the son becoming psychotic—in fact, it ordains it. The issue central to psychosis in the familial order is the presence of a parental order, promulgated by either gender, which assumes for its privilege the necessity that the child embody the projected repressions of either parent in the service of the latter's fragile accession to the real.

What is at work here is a combination of exchanges which symbolize a structuring of reciprocal desires—and their failures—the singular purpose of which is to perpetuate the status quo instilling in the future psychotic the symbolic manifestation of a specific maternal or paternal alienation. The psychotic is always an ambiguously bisexualized or desexualized figure because it is his fate to freeze the passage of emancipatory desire at that junction where it is collectively denied.

Whenever the psychotherapist is called in to question the breakdown of a family structure, the communication which ensues involves the parents, the child, and the therapist. It is thus a collective process which is concentrated on the child's symptom. While the problem that is discussed is focused upon the child's symptom, the parents' complaint implicitly reveals the adult's conception of childhood. Maud Mannoni, the French psychoanalyst, believes

> It is the child's task to make good the parents' failures, to make their lost dreams come true. The complaints of parents about their offspring thus refer us first of all to their *own* problems. The same characteristic emerges in analysis when the adult tells us about his own past. What he describes is not so much a reality experienced as a dream betrayed.[35]

Thus, in reconstructing his childhood the subject in psychotherapy reorganizes the past according to his desire, like a child at play who reorganizes his world to make contact with an imaginary companion: the adult.

As therapist, Freud listened to what the symptom was telling him. He discovered that words, particularly lies, constituted the truth that was veiled. Childhood memories only made sense when they were situated in relation to the unconscious desires of the parent.

In his study of *Self and Others,* Laing describes the case of a four-year-old boy name Brian who was taken by his mother to a couple who were to adopt him.[36] The mother kisses Brian, bursts into tears, and then runs away, never to be seen again. Brian was utterly confused. His new parents tried to soothe him by saying, "You are our son." But Brian refused to accept it. He became a difficult child and, eventually, maladjusted.

Brian no longer knew who he was. No longer his mother's child, he lost his identity. He waited for her return so he could be who he was once more. Although he no longer knew who he was, he did know "what" he was: a wicked boy whose mother had got rid of him. It was on the basis of this conviction, explains Laing, that this traumatized child built his existence: "Since I am bad, there is nothing else to be but bad."[37]

Maud Mannoni criticizes Laing for not elaborating his critique of Brian according to the structure of desire that was inherent between Brian and his lost mother.[38]

> In the past which linked Brian to his mother, he had her words that defined him as her son. Although he had lost her, Brian retained in himself these past references which placed him in a specific line of descent. The

traumatic experience was the means by which the child found himself flung into another line of descent *without a word of explanation.* . . . He then had to build his life on the basis of words that had been foreclosed.[39]

Although his adopted parents claimed Brian as their own, his mother had failed to make this transition possible by indicating to him that he was no longer her child. All that his mother indicated—through her actions—was that Brian was no good. This was confirmed by his new parents who—unable to comprehend the complexities of his suffering—described Brian in terms of his bad behavior. Brian believed that he was a bad boy, an identity (ego) he inherited from his mother's desire that she get rid of him. This identity, also, was adopted by his new parents, so that Brian held onto the only thing which bridged his old life to the new: the implied reason for his mother's abandonment.

Thus, Brian did not know what was going on, and, in the absence of this knowledge, had no choice but to act on his mother's actions, adopting the veiled intent of her disappearance as the inheritance of her unspoken desire. In order to ease her own guilt concerning Brian's fate, it was necessary that she keep him in a state of unknowing. She could leave the scene and imagine that everything had worked out for the best, untroubled by the unspoken truth of the situation.

Mannoni explores the mystification of the child further in her examination of Freud's famous study of "Little Hans." Her interest is not so much the analysis of the case but the descriptions by the father of his son to Freud which occassion the parents' efforts to keep the child in a state of repression.[40] Freud relates that Han's disorder, a dread of horses, appeared at the age of four years and nine months.[41] It was initiated by the fear that his mother would go away.

Hans asks his mother: "Mummy, have you got a widler too?" This ambiguous term, which he inherited from his mother, designates both the urinary and sexual functions of his organ. His mother was careful not to use another term which might distinguish between her sexual organ and the one she lacked. Hans knew the differences between the sexes, but did not dare to exercise his right to this knowledge due to the implicit prohibition of his mother. When the mother replies "Of course. Why?" he is incapable of saying why. Instead, he says, "I was just thinking."

Thus Hans mystified himself whenever he came up against his mother's resistance to the truth of their respective sexualities. Hans was searching for the recognition of his own sexuality, but his task was made doubly difficult because his father consistently referred Han's quest to his wife for the answer. She regarded his sexual parts as "a pretty little machine." His organ could be looked at, but not touched; it was tolerated as a urinary organ but not as his seat of desire. Although his mother exhibited a fascination in looking at his organ—a fascination which was adopted by her son—he was told that he must not touch it: "That's dirty."

Hans's question to his mother ("Mummy, have you got a widler too?") implies a deeper quest. What is desirable? But her response makes it all the more ambiguous. In turning to his father, he confronts his unwillingness to encounter the implications of the mother's response. Thus, "His father condemned Hans to remain confronted by the meaninglessness of being merely a passive object loved by a mother who does not desire a man."[42] In other words, his mother's desire was that Hans not be the master of his own masculine desire.

Hans's sudden anxiety that his mother might leave him was embedded in his apprehension that his mother was repulsed by the masculine gender (like father, like son). She would not admit to him that she had no desire for her husband. And she disguised the truth of the danger of her leaving his father by clinging to her idea of her son as a nice little boy.

Thus his genitals belonged to his mother, to be looked at only by her: "He was walled in by his mother's desire of not desiring a man, and by his father's desire of seeing him conform to his mother's wishes."[43]

In effect, the parents were both voyeurs to their son's desire. Not only did they joke about his sexuality, it was the link between the father and Freud. The father did not discuss his own sexuality; he talked about his son's, or rather his own, lived through the sexuality and desire of his child. Since Hans lacked the support of his father, he was unable to transcend the situation in which his mother imprisoned him.

Thus Hans acted as a support for the sexual impasse the parents could not face. Though the father was ostensibly the patient, Freud used him as an intermediary in order to address the veiled desire of his boy. Hans discovered that he was able to discuss his sexual concerns with the maid, who was not nearly so sexually repressed as the mother. As Hans began to improve, the mother began to crumble under the weight of her lost position as the center of gravity for the family's sexual repression. She turned to her daughter for solace, though this was of little avail in preventing the end of the marriage. What was ultimately at issue was not so much the relation between Hans and each of his parents, as the structure of unconscious desire that inhabited the family constellation.

Laing and Mannoni would agree that it is the failure of the parents to understand and articulate what the child's symptoms signify in the family drama that promotes the symptom further and prohibits the recognition of its truth. At issue is a forbidden truth which the child's illness is meant to expose. Only by speaking this truth can the child be saved from his castration.

Melanie Klein has shown how the child feels exposed at a tender age to the threat of "interior" aggression, and how this hostility is in turn projected onto an external environment that becomes dangerous in phantasy. This is perceived by the Kleinian school as a normal operation of development, the result of which is the incorporation (introjection) of the threatening parental figure which, in turn, constitutes the acceptance of authority.

But if the parent proves to be dangerous in reality, the acceptance of authority would fail to develop, and the child is left with no alternative but to attack, either himself (the incorporated other) or his parent (the perceived threat). Thus, his concept of self becomes composed of a real danger that is constituted by a threat to his desire. His sense of alienation is then perpetuated by the demands of an authority who refuses to yield him the truth of his desire. With no alternative but to try to escape his alienated self, he attaches himself to a symptom which becomes the alienating directive of his subverted desire and the expression of a possible psychosis.

While the reality of the symptom is never underestimated in a psychosis, it is nevertheless very important to our task as psychotherapists to examine the situation that is lived by the subject and his family. It is the symbolic value which the subject attaches to the situation that points us toward its meaning. By focusing our concern round the manner in which the patient situates himself in relation to himself and his desire, we are able to grasp what is alienated and strange in his relations with others. Thus, the symptom is a sign through which the individual indicates via a tortuous path how he orients himself in relation to his unrecognized desires. In other words, the symptom is a substitute for the foreclosure of a forbidden desire.

If the child cannot gain the recognition of his parents as a subject who desires, he becomes alienated from a truth which must not be uttered. His relation with his mother remains colored by a desire that finds no expression but for the renewal of demands which continue to mask the truth while denying the assumption of his reality. When the mother demands that her child should be clean, he gives her his shit which he conceives as the object of her desire. But she is searching for her own desire, which she confuses for the object of her demands. The child wants to know what mother wants, but if she is incapable of knowing, how is she to tell him?

Thus the symptom of the disturbed child—especially the psychotic— is embedded in a conflict situation, a conflict between contradictory and mystified desires. The realization of the child's desire depends on the parents' desire to let him be born into a state of desiring. The child, in his attempt to establish himself as a subject, encounters his parents' unconscious obstruction to the realization of *their own* desires. He is incapable of engaging this drama without challenging the parents' attachment to his symptom, which is a substitute for their own despair.

In our encounter with the psychotic individual we find ourselves wrestling with the history and structure of an entire constellation of others, so our responses depend on our understanding of the situation and the suffering that the child inhabits. Although he is alienated in his desire for others, he does not come to us alone because we can never isolate him from the context of his world.

While the subject's words reveal a special kind of relation (either past or present) with the other, his illness is a mask for the other's anxiety. The value the parent places on a particular kind of psychosis transforms it into a currency of relation and a system of exchange that becomes a symbolic substitute for his own unfulfilled desire.

In psychotherapy the psychotic's quest for recognition ultimately reveals the manner in which his birth was awaited by the parents and what this birth represents for them in relation to their respective histories. Thus, his existence comes into conflict with the unconscious projections of his parents. This is precisely where all their misunderstandings arise. If the child finds that the way to his truth is barred, he can search for the possibility of its expression in an illness.

When parent and child are brought face to face with the problem of desire that is embedded in the relation that each of them (the parents) has toward the other's desire, they will be in a position to appraise themselves of its origin in their own histories, instead of the history of the child. To speak this truth is an unsettling experience. It is the therapist's task to help them utter it.

CHAPTER SIX
THE TEMPORALITY OF
THE SUBJECT

I am thrown into the world, and that world appears not only as outside me, it is also at the center of my life. In the eclipse of a moment that belongs to no one to speak of, reveries take hold of the present and open before me an enigma we call the "past." It is a foreign nation which, not coincidentally, occasioned my childhood. If I could actually take myself back to the horror and magic of those years, my naïvete then could not possibly explain the protective atmosphere of that environment. If things seemed so simple, and if events were also more fascinating, it is equally true that my memory of those experiences could never reveal a richer understanding of that landscape than it had of itself at the time that I lived it.

Today, my interpretations of these events are anchored in my current understanding. Tomorrow, with more knowledge, I may comprehend it differently and thus understand my past from yet another perspective. Moreover, I may go on to amend or disregard these interpretations, disclosing fresher revelations so that in order to intuit their meaning I will have to keep these earlier reveries in mind.

My hold on knowledge and my hold on my self are precarious because this latent subjectivity which hides itself from itself relies on a past and future which is always in abeyance. My possession of this moment, of this subjectivity, is always delayed until a time when I might finally realize its significance. But this final understanding is never attained, since its foundation relies in turn on further developments which have yet to be realized. Thus, my existence merges into other dimensions that continue to transform and delay its realization.

Since my life is never completely understandable, what I know now never really measures the grasp of my experience. As a result, I never can fully reconcile myself with the ambiguous texture of my life. The fact that my childhood lies behind me like a fog is not due to poor memory or a failure of recall but due to the fact that my destiny lies beyond me, in a dimension that has yet to be discovered.

Most classical attempts to account for the subject as a unity of experience have proceeded from the assumption that this unity is substantial, like a thing. There is a common belief among psychologists that subjectivity possesses the property of connecting, or binding together, those experiences to which the individual is "subjected" in his lifetime. Heidegger attempted to discover the definition of Being through man's power to understand himself and his capacity to encounter others in a way that would enliven his existence.[1] In his view, man projects a horizon for himself within which he encounters others and discovers his unfathomed desires. Though we are thrown into a world which is not of our own choosing, it is nonetheless up to us to decide what we shall do there and who we will become. I am responsible for choosing who I am and what I do, but only partly so. Since my existence is characterized by how it is I intend to act and what it is I aim to do, I am always in a state of flux and eternal survival. Further, I can never be sure of the precise consequences my actions will bring to bear. Since my intent inhabits all my actions, my subjectivity can only be discovered by acting and reflecting on the results.

Since I am thrown into this situation or that, I have to contend with the problem of situating myself to an historical context which has made my existence possible to begin with. If I reflect on this past with a certain dread, it is simply for the purpose of masking my uneasy apprehension of a future which is always in abeyance and oblique.

My past, which is symbolic of a specific history, suggests to me that my possibilities have certain limits which restrict promises of salvation and my adoption of false solutions. Between these two poles lies the present: myself. But this present has an unclear meaning. The fundamental mystery of my awareness of time is not located in the mere exchange between a past, a present, and a future, but is located in what Heidegger called my *presence* to time. This presence is constituted by my experience of a past, present, and future which I subjectively hold together. This presence is inhabited by me because I am this presence, which is a disclosing of my subjectivity.

Since the past is more readily available to investigation than the future, it is not surprising that this dimension of our experience has

captured the attention of psychologists. Talk of the future is often rele-
gated to good luck or the clergy. Freud's views about temporality also
favored a preoccupation with the past. This is evidenced most clearly in
his theories on transference and repetition. Further, he equated the
personal past with the subject's archeology, the chronological progression of his life's events. Accordingly, the neurotic's archaic fixations
were said to preclude his capacity to live in the present because he
remained attached to situations and relationships in childhood which
continued to determine, and undermine, his experience of the present.

Since even the neurotic's affection for the analyst was said to be
located in the past, Freud held that it was not the person of the analyst
whom the patient loved but his mother or father. It is thus clear that if
the past is really capable of yielding any knowledge about our relation
to ourselves and to our possibilities, we will first have to examine the
subject of temporality himself.

We like to say that the past was, the future will be, the present is now.
But what is this *now*? If *now* refers to an absolute knife-edge moment
which stands between the past and future, trailing behind itself a course
traveled while anticipating a future at each turn, then this moment can
presumably be divided further still, so that it is impossible to ever
reach, let alone grasp, the ultimate moment which might present to us
our experience of the present.[2] Thomas Reid has called this moment an
"invention of the philosophers."[3]

Reid suggests that most people "find it convenient to give the name
of the present to a position of time which extends more or less according to circumstances 'into' the past or the future."[4] The present becomes a "small portion of time which we call the present, [but] which
has a beginning, a middle, and an end."[5] This conception of the present
has been called the "specious present" and has been the focus of numerous phenomenological studies.[6]

Merleau-Ponty's famous meditation on temporality, which owes a
great deal to Heidegger, exposes the fiction we commonly assume when
we equate the "flow" of time to a river.[7] We sometimes say that time
"passes" or "flows by." But this often-repeated metaphor is extremely
confused. If the passage of time is indeed similar to the flow of a river,
then it would flow from the past to the present and from the present to
the future. The present would appear as the consequence of the past
and the future the consequence of the present.

The water we witness rolling by today comes from the mountains where it was melted from a glacier a few days ago. Tomorrow it will be further on its way, towards the sea into which it will eventually empty.[8]

Merleau-Ponty points out that the problem with this analogy is that we implicitly presuppose the existence of an observer who has witnessed the river originate at its course, and another witness who will see the water discharging into the ocean. But if we remain true to ourselves, which is to say to the world of our subjective experience, it is obvious that, for me, there is only one indivisible and changeless being in it. There are no events without someone for whom they happen. Time presupposes a view of them, so it could not be like a river, something that flows from an invisible past toward an invisible future.[9]

If we talk about the river discharging itself, we are simply describing a thing in itself, outside the realm of human subjectivity. However, as soon as we start to talk about an observer who experiences time, our relation to time shifts radically. In the first place, if the observer is on the river bank he sees the river moving by, but the river is not going into the future. It is sinking into the past. The source of the river represents the future, where the water is coming from. The future does not lie behind me but is like a "brooding presence moving to meet me, like a storm on the horizon."[10] However, if the observer is in a boat moving down the river, he is moving toward his future. But the future lies in the landscape rolling by and the course of time is no longer the river itself.

Thus, time is not a succession of events moving before me but something alive which comes from my relation to things. Future and past are in a kind of eternal state of preexistence and survival. Yet, the common definition of time regards it as a succession of instances of now. This is a nonhuman definition of time because the subjective involvement of the person is left out. By trying to make time objective, we destroy it.

This is the approach typically promoted by psychologists, and even Freud, who try to explain consciousness of the past in the terms of memories and consciousness of the future in terms of memories projected ahead of us.[11] This notion of memory traces represents a physiological assumption of memories being somehow stored in the body, a concept which has been refuted by Bergson.[12] In a similar manner the notion of psychological traces of memory embedded in an unconscious is equally untenable. The presence of a past in an unconscious still remains a factual presence, so that neither physiological nor psychological traces of the past make consciousness of the past comprehensible.

For instance, Merleau-Ponty points out that a table can bear traces of a man's past life. However, even if he previously carved his initials in it or spilt ink on it, these traces are not embedded in the past. They are present. If these traces represent signs of some previous event, it could only be because my sense of the past and the significance of these signs are carried with me in the here and now.[13] A preserved perception is still a perception, whether it is viewed as a physiological or psychological trace. And since it continues to exist in the present, it could not possibly open behind me a dimension of escape or absence called the past. However, a preserved fragment of the past can occasion a thinking of the past; but we do not go to the past in thinking of it, nor do we retrieve the past by remembering it. Recognition of the past always exists for me in the present situation.

But the present is not merely something we experience as slipping into the past. We also feel a pressure on the present of a future, intent on dispossessing it. In other words, the subject, who is always situated in the present, is also situated in his experience of a future which is coming toward him, of a desire seeking to be realized. Thus, the past and future exist for him not in their separate dimensions, but through his experience of time itself.

Time, which is alway present for me, is contemporary with all times. Thus, time is not a linking together of one instance of a present followed by another, but one single phenomenon of time running off on itself, comprising a trajectory of future to present to past which moves throughout its whole length.

Merleau-Ponty concludes that the past is not past and the future is not future. They exist only when a subject is present to give them a meaning and a reality, through the subject's realization of his place in time. Past and future spring to being when I reach out towards them. However, my experience of the present can only exist while including my experience of the breakfast I ate this morning, the appointment I will keep later this afternoon, the friends I plan to meet this evening, all of which bring themselves to me as part of my experience of this moment. All of these temporal experiences exist for me in the present because all of my present experiences include what has already passed and what lies ahead. The passage of time is not something which I merely see as an onlooker, since I am time. Time is not outside of me: It abides in my presence to the world. In other words, "The problem is how to make time, not an object of our knowledge, but a *dimension* of our being."[14] Thus, time is a cohesion which is the fabric of my life and exists for me only in the sense that I am situated in it. Time opens me to a future which is primordially implicated in the historical movement of my life.

The psychologist who fails to understand how our experience of time consists of a past and future embedded in a present will view consciousness as a series of psychic facts, amongst which he tries to establish causal relations. Following this example, Proust describes Swann's love for Odette, a love which is said to be the cause of his jealousy, which, in turn, increases Swann's love for her even further.[15] But Swann's jealousy is not aroused by his love for her, since his love is already of a kind in which its destiny is already determined. Swann is attracted to the spectacle of Odette's personality, which he experiences as a kind of fascination that shuts him out of her life. His love is only a wish to force his way in and take possession of her so no one else can have her.

Swann's love does not cause him to feel jealousy; it is jealousy already, as it has been from the start. His love was not transformed into jealousy because his attraction for her was just a pleasure in looking at her and in possessing her through his omnipotence, and being the only one to do so. If we were to examine Swann's behavior further, apart from his jealousy for Odette, we would find this possessive quality manifested throughout the existential structure of his personality. His jealousy is not caused by his love because his subjectivity is already possessed of a jealous regard which exists for him at all times.

Thus one event in a life does not in itself explain an attitude later on because time does not exist in a chronological series of events. By taking up a present, I draw together and transform my past, alter its meaning, and transcend its captivating power by freeing and detaching myself from it, by committing myself somewhere else. Swann chose not to do this. He chose, instead, to indulge himself with a possessiveness which was the instrument of his own downfall. His neurotic condition demanded satisfaction, and in so doing he foreclosed the future and the possibilities it might offer.

Each moment of experience is not merely an awareness of what is now, but contains also an awareness of what has passed and indicates a future. We are presently related to our past failures as well as to our undisclosed aspirations. The essential unity of time is the only way to explain how it is possible for a person to go through life as the same person and achieve any continuity from one moment of his existence to the next. This means that there is nothing which supports my existence, whether we call this support a substance, ego, self, or soul. I can know myself only on the basis through which I resolve to anticipate my possibilities in my encounter with others. I do this not by abandoning my past or seeking refuge in it, but by taking it up and realizing it.

Indeed, the relation between Freud's conception of the transference, the repetition compulsion, and temporality would appear to lie at the heart of psychoanalytical knowledge. Psychoanalysts have tended to reduce the concept of transference to behavior which is repeated by the patient with a therapist who takes over as the father. The analyst has his position, to be sure, but defining it is no easy matter. Freud believed that in transference the patient's forgotten feelings of love and hatred become manifest through his relation with the analyst.[16] In other words, the patient expresses in action and reproduces in the relationship with the analyst infantile feelings for his parents which have become re-pressed. He wants to act them out, onto the person of the analyst, while remaining unconscious of his desire to do so. This acting out is an indication that he resists consciousness of emotions he had for his parents in childhood. These repressed feelings are symbolized in his experience of the analyst. The patient, in turn, is encouraged to remem-ber feelings he had for his infantile love objects so that he will cease to act them out. In other words, the transference is eventually overcome by showing the patient that his feelings do not originate in the current situation and do not, in reality, concern the analyst. In this way, the repetition of ancient emotions is transformed by the recollection of the forgotten event. By refusing to passively comply with the acting out of the patient, he compels the patient to remember infantile love objects and to detach himself gradually from the transference situation.

Freud emphasized that overcoming resistance is merely a secondary means of eliciting recollections from the patient. The uncovering of the repressions surrounding the event which gave rise to the symptom was the primary aim of psychoanalysis because the cure for neurosis was held to be coincident with the elimination of pathogenic amnesia. The patient says what comes to mind, and the analyst interprets the patient's resistances. When these become clear to the patient, he "often relates to forgotten situations and connections without difficulty."[17] Freud goes on to say that, "The aim of these different techniques . . . is to fill in gaps in memory . . . [and] to overcome resistances to a repression."[18]

Although Freud modified his views on transference throughout the course of his career, he never gave up the proposition that true recollection constituted a cure.[19] The patient's compulsion to repeat his infantile neurosis was used by the analyst to indicate how the patient was acting out desires toward his parents rather than remembering them. For Freud, understanding the relationship between himself and the patient—while important—was subsidiary to remembering repressed events of the distant past.

Douglas Kirsner, in a study of Freud's concept of the transference, reports that

> Freud found to his chagrin that seeking the origin of the patient's repressions alone was not very productive. He had not tried to understand the dynamics of his relationship with Dora, as he pointed out himself, and we might add neither did he attempt to understand hers with himself. But even in his self-criticism Freud does not see the failure of the case as lying in his lack of understanding of the treatment as a whole in its inner structure as a transference relationship; rather he was concerned with particular *transferences* that Dora made to him during the treatment. His view of transferences was that they were new editions of old impulses made conscious from time to time during the course of the treatment, and that displacements were made from the parents on to the analyst who happened to be the object.[20]

Freud proposed in 1897 that his patients' recollections of seduction in early life were not based on fact but on the fantasies of the patient. Thus he refused to believe that his patients actually wanted to seduce *him*. Fantasies of seduction became a new object of interest. Yet, Freud failed to draw on the consequences of this discovery in 1901, as Kirsner has pointed out, when he was interested only in the reality of Dora's actual past. He resisted understanding her fantasy world adequately, which, not coincidentally, included the importance of her desires toward Freud. Like a detective on the scent of a crime, Freud was after the facts of the case. For Freud the main issue was, "How did these symptoms arise?" Therapy was not an interpersonal endeavor but a battle to uncover the truth. He even likened his investigations to archeological excavation.

But exploration of the patient's desires immediately leads the investigator from questioning what is the cause of a symptom—which always lies in the past—to asking what does this symptom mean? Where does it point to? What purpose does it serve? Although Freud talked about the meaning of a slip, dream, or symptom repeatedly, he seemed genu-

inely undecided about where it is that meanings lie. Freud insisted that
meanings were buried in the past and that it was his task to break
through the barrier of the present moment into the early life of the
patient where all the secrets lay buried.

Yet, it is one thing to suggest that transferences are based in the past
and another thing to propose that we attend to their origins. Freud
liked to think of the analyst as an archeologist who reconstructs an
actual building with what remains of its ruins. But this simply demon-
strates that he failed to distinguish vestiges from sources. In a phenomenological investigation of these terms, John Heaton holds that

> Vestiges are fragments of a past object that have survived and assist the
> reconstruction of the object of which they are a remnant. Sources on the
> other hand constitute a power, a tradition which opens up possibilities for
> the *future*. Thus Freud's own writings are the source of the psychoanalytic
> tradition. They are not mere vestiges of the past. Patients [in psycho-
> therapy] need to get in touch with their own sources with the aid of
> interpretations which enliven them and give them meaning rather than
> mechanically trying to reconstruct the past with vestiges in the present.[21]

Freud's insistence upon looking to the past for meaning persisted
even when he could no longer ignore the tremendous importance of
what was occurring in the present between himself and his patients.
This holds true even in his conception of the so-called "transference
neurosis." Freud saw this as a new, artificial neurosis which took the
place of the presenting neurosis in analysis. Memories now begin to
fade into the background. Thus,

> All the patient's symptoms have taken a new sense which lies in a relation
> to the transference. But the mastering of this new artificial neurosis coin-
> cides with getting rid of the illness which was originally brought to the
> accomplishment of our therapeutic task.[22]

We are now faced with an illness which exists in present context, the
roots of which are not anchored in the past but in the patient's relation
with his analyst. Although Freud began to emphasize the interpersonal
aspects of psychoanalysis, he continued to justify the use of transference neurosis in terms of its power to arouse latent memories. Concern with the patient's history begins to give way to the meaning of
actions, phantasies, and persons in relation to each other. The past is no
longer composed of archeological vestiges; it is a past that inhabits

intentional desires which, in turn, determine historical meanings as we recognize how our present relations dictate and influence our view of the past.

Today the emphasis on the transference relation and with the here and now is a considerable advance over Freud's investigations. Many analysts see their patients' discussions about their parents as displacements away from the analyst in order to avoid facing their relationship with the analyst:

> Thus the resolution of the transference neurosis is not necessarily involved with the repair of faulty memory as much as with coping with the fear of relationship.[23]

Freud thought of himself as an archeologist of the mind. He emphasized those aspects of our past relations which are indelibly stamped on the present context. But Freud failed to distinguish between events which occurred in a person's childhood and his past; that is, characteristics and attitudes that a person has learned in his childhood and which he retains in the present. A person's past still exists for him now, but it only has meaning for him if he is able to place it in the context of a desire which is struggling for recognition, symbolized in the neurotic conflicts that stand in the way.

Freud's emphasis on the diachronic, or vertical, dimension of the person's world view led him to an exaggerated concern with the actual cause of symptoms, the nature of which the transference would hopefully illuminate. Current structuralist and linguistic theories of meaning emphasize the synchronic, or horizontal, dimension of the person's world by seeking the meaning of a word, symptom, or other act in relation to the present structure of other elements in the subject's world. Ferdinand de Saussure distinguished between *langue* (language), the underlying structure of a language—much of which is unconscious— and *parole* (speech), the individual speech act. In his view language is a total system which is complete at every moment and has a valid existence distinct from its history, while adding another dimension to that history. It is constituted by the speech of the speakers in the present moment. In Kirsner's view

> Sassure compares language to a game of chess. To understand the rules of chess I do not investigate its history nor do I look into whether the chessmen are made of wood or ivory as these are external matters. In order

to understand the value of a piece and the way it moves, I must refer to the underlying system which governs the game. Outside the game a knight has no value for instance. It does not have a specific material make-up but only has value within the equilibrium of the system. The knight does not make sense as an item by itself nor is the history of the piece of intrinsic interest; it only acquires meaning in terms of its contrasting relations with other pieces which constitute the game of chess.[24]

The analysis of the patient's speech in therapy within the context of the transference neurosis depends on an adequate understanding of the structure of the patient's world view in the present context. The meaning of a word or remark makes sense in relation to other words or remarks in the so-called "signifying chain."[25] As in a game of chess, the patient's situation changes from one moment to the next, so that the meaning of his situation is discovered in the position he assumes within an ongoing system of relations—especially with the psychoanalyst—just as the value of a piece in chess is determined by its position on the board in relation to the other pieces.

While the patient is a history, this history can only be grasped by investigating the structure of the patient's symptoms as they are repeated in the present. Jonathan Culler states

> What is especially significant here is the move away from historical explanation. To explain social phenomena is not to discover temporal "antecedents" and to link them in a causal chain but to specify the place and function of the phenomena in a system. There is a move from the diachronic to the synchronic perspective. . . . Instead of conceiving of causation on a historical model, where temporal development makes something what it is, the historical results are "determporalized" and treated simply as a state, a condition.[26]

Properly speaking, psychoanalysis aims to uncover the present structure of relationships which comprise the patient's world. The interpersonal relation between patient and therapist intermeshes with the world of each. The elucidation of this present relationship is the object of psychoanalysis, which unveils the patient's desires and the history they are rooted in.

In fact, transferences do not transfer anything. Transference love and transference hate are aspects of a tortuous and ambivalent interpersonal relation which the patient experiences towards the therapist himself. If the patient behaves in an infantile manner and misjudges the situation he is in at the time, it does not follow that he is simply confusing the therapist with his parents. Freud admitted that "One has no right to dispute the genuine nature of the love which makes its appearance in the course of analytic treatment."[27] But he was never able to make an adequate distinction between transference love and genuine love, retreating instead into the questionable view that the patient's attempts to seduce the analyst were signs of transference love, while suggesting that the patient's willingness to accept the analyst's interpretations and his general improvement were signs of genuine love, an idiosyncratic distinction at best.

Obviously, our expectations of others are generally rooted in our historical experience of the world, including those prejudices that guide our behavior. Thus, the transference relation is structured by prejudices that interfere in our ability to judge the situation from a new perspective. Some prejudices we are perfectly aware of, while some prejudices we are not aware of as such. It is those prejudices we do not recognize as prejudices that constitute much of the transference phenomena.

Prejudices refer to value judgments and preconceptions which have been formalized in early life around the ego's imaginary attachments. Thus a hate transference emerges in relation to an other who—in refusing to agree to our demands—puts into question the foundation of the egocentric structuring of the subject's world. In this respect the purpose of the transference is to hold on to one's prejudices by deceiving this person who examines his beliefs. By obscuring the truth of the situation, the purpose of the transference is to prevent the truth from emerging. Rather than thinking for ourselves, we turn to our stock of prejudices to think for us. More to the point, the transference—whether positive or negative—engenders the maintenance of a situation in which the subject lets the ego think for it, which is not to think at all, maintaining his captivation by his egoic identifications.

When a transference structures a relationship, it is the fortifications of the ego that are in transference. In other words, the transference is characterized by the rigid fixations and prejudices of the imaginary ego which dictates the subject's responses to emotionally charged situations. The positive transference is a strategy of the ego whose purpose is to seduce the therapist in order to disclaim the real differences that exist between them. The negative transference emerges when the patient realizes that his familiar world is in the throes of catastrophic transformation. The natural response is hate and hostility, subterfuge and counterattack, to protect himself from the loss of his omnipotent fantasies.

Since negative transference is an expression of the subject's aggressiveness in relation to another from whom he expects a gift (i.e., his emancipation), its appearance in therapy is evocative of the subject's own internal struggle with an identity which is incapable of conforming to this desire. The analyst's refusal to comply with the demand that he effect this emancipation makes him the inevitable target of this aggressive expression. There is nothing particularly unique in the analyst's position, since his place can be assumed by anyone the subject has placed in the position of ultimate savior. It is this expectation, projected onto the analyst, that fuels much of the love felt toward him by the patient—and the disappointment which in turn fuels its retraction. What is transferred onto the analyst is not so much an imago or paternal metaphor—though the validity of these possible projections is unmistakable—so much as a chronic expectation that someone else release him from psychic bondage—an expectation which lies at the heart of this bondage. Naturally, this expectation can only have derived from a failure at the Oedipal juncture which is repeated each time the crisis of desire is made manifest. The repetition of this singular impasse inevitably points to a chronic conflict in the subject—a conflict which drives his compulsion to repeat this impasse with the analyst.

According to Laplanche and Pontalis,

> . . . the compulsion to repeat is an ungovernable process originating in the unconscious. As a result of its action, the subject deliberately places himself in distressing situations, thereby repeating an old experience, but he does not recall this prototype; on the contrary, he has the strong impression that the situation is fully determined by the circumstances of the moment[28]

Every psychotherapist knows that most symptoms—especially those which are obsessive in character—are repetitive to some degree. Indeed, one could readily agree with Laplanche and Pontalis that, "The defining property of the symptom is the very fact that it reproduces, in a more or less disguised way, certain elements of a past conflict."[29] Freud was so struck by the importance of this phenomenon that he insisted the whole aim of psychoanalysis was to help the patient to remember the traumatic conflicts which were said to be repressed in the unconscious. Thus, "The repressed seeks to 'return' in the present, whether in the form of dreams, symptoms or acting out."[30]

Freud put it more succinctly in saying that

> . . . a thing which has not been understood inevitably reappears; like an unlaid ghost, it cannot rest until the mystery has been solved and the spell broken.[31]

The question of transference is inevitably bound up with that of repetition since Freud came to view it as that situation in the psycho-analytic drama in which the patient reenacted his repressed, unresolved conflicts in his relationship with the analyst. The completion of analysis was said to occur when the patient realized that his conflict with the analyst was merely a repetition of his forgotten conflicts—a realization which coincided with his ability to remember the repressed material.

Yet, the question remains why should the subject have a compulsion to repeat unpleasant experiences, when the repetition of these experiences per se fails to emancipate the subject from the burden of these traumatic events? Indeed, although the repetition of these experiences is unquestioned in psychoanalysis, the rationale behind them remains one of the most problematic and unresolved theoretical issues before us. However we may choose to respond to or interpret repetition phenomena in the therapeutic situation, the very purpose of these phenomena remains to be solved.

The general approach to this problem appears to fall between two rather extreme alternatives. On the one hand, the purpose of repetition is said to reside in the service of the ego's attempt eventually to master the underlying tension that lies at the heart of the repressed conflict. On the other, more ominous vein, the repetition is in the service of the instincts which give rise to the conflict itself at the behest of the death instinct. In other words, the compulsion to repeat is reduced to a choice of perceiving it as either advantageous or detrimental in the context of the psychotherapeutic enterprise. That the repetition might serve the purpose of fulfilling a repressed wish is negated due to the unpleasant nature of the repetitions themselves.

Rather than reduce the question of repetition phenomena to amnesia buried somewhere in the patient's forgotten past, we might reformulate this question by approaching the repetition as being constitutive of a search for the realization of an unrecognized desire. What is absent in the neurotic is the very grounding of his possibilities, a ground which rests on the historical context into which he is born and which points him toward a future. The past is of significance only because it points to a forbidden future, while the repetition contains within itself a trauma that has left something to be desired.

Freud recognized that the repetition contained elements of a moral masochism ruled by the death instinct, that tendency in the individual to revert toward an inorganic state. This destructive instinct lures the subject into repeatedly placing himself in disadvantageous situations which were said to be reminiscent of earlier experiences. But what could be so compellingly destructive as to lure the subject into it? Freud advised that the solution to this mystery lay in discovering that pro-totypical experience the subject repeats in the course of the analysis itself, in the newly formed transference neurosis. What we discover in following this formulation is the limit, or death, of the subject's mater-nal bondage, which, if not inadvertently fueled by the analyst, will result in the birth of the patient's desire.

Freud's death instinct does not refer to a literal death of the subject so much as the subject's realization of his own limitations. This results in his freedom from the maternal identification which occasions his crip-pling narcissism—to reclaim a future which lies embedded in his his-tory. At the moment the child comes to realize his separateness from the mother he begins to engage in what Winnicott refers to as a "play with reality" in the form of symbolic games—such as Freud's "Fort!-Da!" reel game—which allow the child to gain mastery over his maternal rupture. The repetitive play of the young infant when he becomes transfixed in the loss and recapture of the prized object allows him to maintain the mother in symbolized form while accepting her absence. What struck Freud as most remarkable in this play was the child's rapture with that part of the game which symbolized the loss—not, as one might have expected, its capture. It is precisely this compulsion toward rupture which is so tellingly evident in the neurotic's compul-sion to repeat situations which are presumably to his detriment. This would certainly appear to be a sort of masochistic tendency if it were not for the fact that it is in his separation from the mother that the child will inevitably discover his emancipation. Despite his resistance to this emancipation, it is only in transcending his maternal need that the child will experience the lack at the heart of his being, a lack which will structure his desire. But this can only occur with the death of his maternal bondage, which will be replaced by a desire, first for the mother he has lost, and then for other objects. This desire is not mo-mentary, fleeting, or haphazardly available to accept or reject, but rather eternal—never to be consummated until his death. This destiny is precisely what the neurotic has failed to accept. The repetition compulsion drives the individual back to that rupture, that event, that place in time which will occasion yet another opportunity to take his destiny in his hands and to be born into the time of his timeless desire.

Further, it is not necessary—or even conceivable—that this subject could ever remember the nonoccurrence of this blessed event since this event is occurring for him at all times and in all situations of his daily existence. It is rather his realization that his emancipation has not occurred that will lead to the reversal of his primary maternal bondage. The analysis of the repetition is not so much concerned with the retrieval of a past as it is with the assumption of a history that points toward a future. It is the ambivalent dread and desire for this future that is at the heart of the transference situation.

In analysis, the patient's words indicate a peculiar logic in which we will discover the historical imperative to his present bondage. Relying on this logic, we can see where it is intended to lead him. Confronted with this logic, the patient is placed in a position either to resign himself to it, or revise it. As his fantasies and memories are put into words, they are revealed as the source of his alienation which is rooted in his enslavement to a false identity. Having lost his conflict with his mother who perpetuated this bondage, he perpetuates this conflict by projecting its essential structure onto the analyst who now becomes the authority who can release the patient from his servitude. He struggles to maintain his helpless position preceisely in order to be saved by the analyst. The analyst's refusal to do so structures the negative transference, leading to an unbearable situtation which the patient himself must resolve. As the patient comes to realize the source of his bondage, he discovers that it does not lie in a past he can do nothing to change, but rather in his expectation of a future salvation, which, in turn, maintains his helpless position.

Thus, the patient's neurotic bondage is not so much situated in a past forgotten as much as in a dream betrayed, a dream that can still be realized by taking his future in hand. If his emancipation implies an assumption of his history, this assumption does not suggest or involve a reevocation of events that actually happened but rather, in the telling of his history, a reordering of its significance by making them present and by indicating necessities to come. This history is not so much remembered as it is invented, according to the structure of his present malaise.

To sum up, the temporality of the subject is complex. It is not composed of events themselves but rather his understanding of these events, the reality of which contains no objective validation. The past is not so much forgotten as it is felt to be unreal. This unreality is not peculiar to his past but exists for him at *all* times, most significantly in his present deliberations. If we were to take an inventory of this temporal dimension and its relevance to the analytic setting, we could do so from any number of perspectives, but in order to locate the subject in the truth of this dimension we would have to keep in mind the totality of an expression which never abandons the source of that knowledge which can only be derived from the subject himself. The timeliness of these deliberations exists for the subject in the following.

1. He must have the ability to "delay" his gratification in order for his desire to emerge.

2. He must have the ability to remember, to learn, and to put things together.

3. He must desire to desire in general and, more specifically, to engage in actions and objectives which exemplify his desire and remain faithful to his desire.

4. He must inhabit a future in order to transcend his bondage.

5. He must inhabit his history in order to reclaim his destiny.

6. He must have a future that is primary, since that is where his desire points to. Yet without a history in which his possibilities are rooted, he will remain trapped in the perpetual abeyance of his desire which is so characteristic of the obsessive.

7. He must establish his desire in the desire of the other's desire; otherwise, he will retreat in the mesmerized haze of fantasized desires so characteristic of the hysteric.

8. He must submit to the timelessness of his desire in terms of the analysis itself, since the duration of his analysis can no more be predetermined than the duration of his own existence.

9. He must remember that his time is running out, a fact he is endlessly reminded of in the face of the clock which imposes its artificial reality upon the length of each session.

10. He must return to what Freud termed the "death instinct": that regressive tendency which has no other end than the destruction of all obstacles to desire, to a time before time to engage in the birth of all desires.

Thus if we are ever to succeed in discovering the timelessness of our subjectivity, it will not be realized through a hypothetical formulation but by looking for it.

> To analyze time is not to follow out the consequences of a pre-established conception of subjectivity; it is to gain access, *through* time, to its concrete structure.[32]

This structure will not be understood by analyzing the consequences of past events but by plunging into the heart of time itself, where all our desires are born. Time and subjectivity become present to me only from the perspective of desire. Since the world and desire are the linking together of perspectives, they exist only to the extent that they are lived by a subjectivity and followed wherever they may lead.

CHAPTER SEVEN
UNMASKING DESIRE OF ITS SEXED EXPRESSION: PERVERSION

A strong egoism is a protection against falling ill, but in the last resort we must begin to love in order not to fall ill, and we are bound to fall ill if, in consequence of frustration, we are unable to love.

—Sigmund Freud

That act of transcendence whereby we "throw open" our bodies to the world runs away with itself by losing itself in the discovery that we sometimes find ourselves again in the presence of others who do not have to be there in order to exist; in other words, in phantasy.

Psychoanalysis represents two trends of thought. On the one hand it emphasizes a sexual substructure which is linked to the root of all neurotic disorders; on the other hand it expands the notion of sexuality so far that it absorbs into itself the entirety of existence, so that precisely for this reason its conclusions remain ambiguous. If we insist that our sexual life can no longer be regarded as a mere function of genital organs, we must also avoid the declaration that all existence can be understood through sexual life, since the term "sexuality" would then retain no meaning of its own by becoming nothing more than a taut-alogical expression for existence itself.

If sexuality were a mere reflection of existence, we would be unable to account for the fact that impaired sexuality can account for activity in some sectors of life, such as artistic or religious endeavors. However, impaired sexuality can lead to grief and eventually to no other aim in life than to end it. Life is particularized into separate currents, so that what we call the sexual life is a sector of our existence which bears a special relation to the existence of sex. It is always tempting for the psychotherapist to allow sexuality to become lost in existence, especially when we see the evidence, over and over, that the sexual problems of neurotics are indeed an expression of their basic human drama in magnified form. Yet, it remains to be seen why the *sexual* expression of this drama is always more pathetic, more striking, and more frequent than the rest, and why sexuality is not merely a symptom but a very difficult one to pin down.

Freud recognized that underneath sexual activity existed an erotic desire which might be expressed in that activity. At the same time, he realized that desire can be concealed beneath inactivity through the repression of unconscious wishes. Freud conceived his use of the term "libido"—a Latin word meaning wish or desire—as the vital force of all sexuality. But Freud's energistic tendencies compelled him to view the libido as a kind of energy, sexual in nature, which would endow the concept of desire with an exclusively sexual thrust. In other words, the libido as not merely an expression of wanting, but an emphatically eroticized wanting that was then linked up to his conception of love. Freud said

> Libido is an expression taken from the theory of the emotions. We call by that name the *energy,* regarded as a quantitative magnitude (though not at present actually measurable) of those instincts which have to do with all that may be comprised under the word "love."[1]

Freud claims that even infantile sexuality is the love relationship in one of its varied forms. Yet, it is always in the form of desire that Freud identifies infantile sexuality. In contrast to love, desire is inherently unconscious and is a precondition of—and not synonymous with—love. While it must be admitted that the infant has sexual feelings for its mother, it must also be said that the infant desires more than sexual pleasure. It desires, for example, to be seen, to be paid attention, in other words, to be recognized.

It is not surprising that the religiously inspired Jung could not bring himself to embrace Freud's exclusively sexualized conception of the libido, though Jung made the mistake of conceiving the libido in purely psychical terms, approaching desire as a psychological force rather than an existential regard.

It would be useful to distinguish at this time between Freud's conception of eroticized desire and Hegel's concept of desire per se. According to the former, the person strives for satisfaction in his sexuality, whereas in the latter the person seeks to be recognized as a subject of desire. Sexual desire is, in the first place, at the heart of the relationship each person enjoys with his own body, so that it is possible to satisfy erotic desire and to do so independently of another body, as with masturbation and some of the other so-called "perversions." All that is required in such instances is the existence of an absent other who takes his or her place in the sexual drama in phantasy. It is enough that the subject grasp himself as a sexual creature in order to gain satisfaction of his erotic drives. This view of desire is not unlike a hunger that looks toward a definite aim: the discharge of tension which occasions frustrated gratification.

But with Hegel's desire—which is always the desire for recognition—satisfaction is not the ultimate goal; nor can it be since desire can never be satisfied.[2] Since recognition by another (as desiring subject) is the ultimate goal, the realization of this desire is afforded through a deepening of the dialectical embrace that upholds their respective centers of orientation. Unlike the orgasm, recognition is never realized in a specific moment. Rather, it is achieved dialectically, when it is rooted in the other's regard—not in his own body.

Certainly, a relation between eroticism and desire exists. Erotic satisfaction and desire for recognition find themselves enjoined in the spontaneous reciprocity of a certain relation between two respective desires, inside which physical, emotional, relational, sexual, and other dimensions of subjectivity can become recognized. Sex without the recognition of desire is merely perverse, a subject Freud found endlessly fascinating.

In his lecture on "The Sexual Life of Human Beings,"[3] Freud's opening remarks should not go unnoticed, not merely because of the humor with which he chooses to introduce the subject, but also because Freud uses these remarks to approach the subject of sexuality in general. The problematic to which Freud refers is the inherent difficulty in defining precisely what sex is—a problem that his lecture was intended to confront.

> One would certainly have supposed that there could be no doubt as to what is to be understood by "sexual." First and foremost, what is sexual is something improper, something one ought not to talk about. I have been told that pupils of a celebrated psychiatrist made an attempt once to convince their teacher of how frequently the symptoms of hysterical patients represent sexual things. For this purpose they took him to the

bedside of a female hysteric, whose attacks were an unmistakable imitation of the process of childbirth. But with a shake of his head he remarked: "Well, there's nothing sexual about childbirth." Quite right. Childbirth need not in every case be something improper.[4]

Freud's joke serves the purpose of allowing Freud to demonstrate the inherent absurdity of defining sexuality in accordance with the reproductive process and the equal absurdity in disregarding it altogether. Although sexuality is certainly concerned with the process of reproduction and its advocates—the genital organs—Freud is correct in pointing to the profound importance of the sexual perversions which, by definition, do not have reproduction as their goal. Freud ranges through the variety of perversions—homosexuality, cunnilingus, fellatio, anal intercourse, fetishism, necrophilia, exhibitionism, sadism, masochism, masturbation, voyeurism—in order to distinguish these acts from normal sexual intercourse: the insertion of the penis into the vagina in order to discharge the male semen into the woman's body.

Freud—who could hardly be described as a prude—held that all people are subject to committing perverse sexual acts, along with the so-called "normal" sexual practices. What is particularly striking is that there are people who have no desire—or ability—to engage in the normal, heterosexual act. More to the point, the connection between sexual perversions and psychopathology is more than a mere coincidence, since—according to Freud—sexuality and psychopathological symptoms are inherently entwined. Indeed, the intention, says Freud, behind all symptoms is the "satisfaction of a sexual desire." In other words, symptoms "are a substitute for satisfaction of this kind, which the patients are without in their lives."[5]

In order to grasp the subtle charm of this most profound assertion, we must understand how Freud stretched his definition of perversions so that human beings could be considered to be capable of becoming so "polymorphously" perverted. Thus,

The hysterical neurosis can produce its symptoms in any system of organs and so disturb any function. Analysis shows that in this way all the so-called perverse impulses which seek to replace the genital by some other organ manifest themselves: these organs are then behaving like substitutive genitals. The symptoms of hysteria have actually led us to the view that the bodily organs, besides the functional part they play, must be recognized as having a sexual (erotogenic) significance, and that the execution of the first of these tasks is disturbed if the second of them makes too many claims.[6]

Freud goes on to explain how sexuality thus pervades the various symptoms of psychoanalytic patients. In paranoids we find repression of homosexual desires; in obsessionals we find sadistic impulses and the repression of infantile acts of masturbation. Also, frustration of sexual satisfaction in general "brings out perverse inclinations in people who had not shown any previously."[7] Further, "Sucking at the mother's breast is the starting-point of the whole sexual life, the unmatched prototype of every later sexual satisfaction."[8] And so on.

Finally, Freud describes all sexual activity "as perverse if it has given up the aim of reproduction and pursues the attainment of pleasure as an aim independent of it."[9] Since children are incapable of sexual reproduction, the sexual life of all children "is bound to be of a perverse kind."[10]

Thus Freud neatly lays out his theory of sexuality in general and all-encompassing terms, defining as perverse any sexual activity whose goal is merely pleasure in itself and without the reproductive aim. According to this definition, the use of contraceptives between a couple otherwise engaged in a normal sexual act becomes perverse since the reproductive intent is explicitly avoided.

Ultimately, since the reproductive aim now is only marginal to the sexual activity, and because even the relation between one bodily organ and another can always be described as sexual, it is possible—indeed unavoidable—to ascribe sexual intentions to every human act, whether pathological or not.

While symptoms can indeed be interpreted by the analyst in terms of frustrated sexuality, the psychoanalyst, in conforming to these criteria, sometimes overlooks the more telling existential and interpersonal dynamics involved. He also overlooks the underlying structure of unconscious desire for recognition; a desire that is more pervasive than even erotic satisfaction.

In a study on sexuality, Merleau-Ponty describes the case of a young girl whose mother has explictly forbidden her to see her lover.[11] Subsequently the girl is unable to sleep, loses her appetite, her use of speech, and eventually succumbs to *anorexia nervosa*. Is was discovered that a similar loss of speech occurred earlier in her childhood following an earthquake and again after she experienced a severe fright.

A typical Freudian interpretation might refer to her oral phase of development, a time when events become arrested in the mouth. In the present moment, it is feasible that her body has become the stage of the sexual drama that has been arrested by her mother's intervention. Thus the girl's fear can be linked to her sexual desire which, due to the traumatic circumstances which frustate their fulfillment, compel her to associate (or confuse) her relation with her lover with an earlier time when events were captured by an oral orientation to the world. Following this line of thought, the psychoanalyst might then link her loss of appetite and failure of speech to an earlier terror (weaning or the earthquake possibly) which, by having become localized in her mouth, precludes its use in the present situation. The incredible power which the ruptured earth had over her life is now linked to the power her own mother has to rupture her world effectively (which includes her lost lover) or to frustrate her infantile desire. And so on.

But if we put aside for a moment the notions of the oral stage and polymorphous sexuality, we might discover that what is fixated in the girl's mouth is not merely her sexual existence but, more generally, those relations with others which have as their vehicle the spoken word. As Merleau-Ponty reminds us, if an emotion chooses to find its expression through a loss of speech, it is because, of all our bodily functions, speech is the one most intimately linked to communal existence. Thus a loss of speech stands for the refusal of coexistence, just as a fit of hysterics is a way of retreating from the situation: The girl breaks with relational life.

The girl, having lost her lover, her sleep, her hunger, her voice, more generally has broken with desire itself. Her inability to swallow food symbolizes her inability, literally, to swallow the prohibition which has been imposed on her. Since swallowing symbolizes for her the movement of existence which carries events and gives them significance, her love is caught in her throat. Her future is thus cut off, taking her back to her fear of the earthquake and her earlier response to the possibility of death, a stoppage of time, and a rupture between herself and the lost object of her desire.

This girl's hysterical response to her mother's prohibition is characterized by the function of an unrecognized desire, the purpose of which is to remove her from the scene she can no longer bear. This is a hopeful sign. The implied possibility of her refusal is that she may, once again, open herself to others by eventually overcoming her frustration.

Thus we can discover a sexual significance to a symptom embedded in a more general signficance in relation to past and future, self and others, desire and frustration, and the fundamental dimensions of our world. But the loss of one's voice is not simply a gesture, like that of a friend who, offended, refuses to talk to me. As Merleau-Ponty reminds us, losing one's voice is not just for the purpose of remaining silent because one can only do so if one was able to speak in the first place. The girl lost her voice in the same way that she lost her lover. Her object of desire has been forbidden to see her. The rejection which has been enforced by her mother has placed the girl in a new situation with definite bounds to her activities, just like the loss of an arm can remove from her grasp an object in the physical world. What has collapsed for this girl is not merely access to her lover, but her field of desire. The loss of her voice does not merely represent a refusal of speech or of life: It is a refusal of others and consequently a death of her desire.

This girl could not explain to us why she was unable to speak because she does not know why. Her object of desire has been lost, and with it any access which might give her a clue. Turning back on itself, her desire has effectively devoured itself and returned to that inaccessible region of consciousness which—due to the disappearance of its object— is virtually unconscious. This is why the psychotherapist does not succeed by trying to make the patient realize the origin of his illness. In any case, this coming to awareness, if we could provide it for him, would remain purely cognitive. Moreover, the patient would not accept the meaning of his disturbance without the personal relationship with the therapist, without the desire and recognition felt toward him, and without his desire to be recognized in his misery, and in his desire to be free to desire others in turn.[12]

The intensity of sexual pleasure would not be enough to explain the importance which it occupies in our lives unless it was seen as an opportunity, always available, for acquainting oneself with others. Thus, "sexuality conceals itself from itself beneath a mask of generality and continually escapes from the tension and drama which it sets up."[13] Desire permeates sexuality as sexuality permeates desire. At the heart of subjectivity resides a desire which is not merely bound to its own erotic pleasure but is bound to another who is encountered in his subjectivity and his desire also. Further, this desire may choose to use sexuality in order to reach this other, or alternately to abandon sexuality in order to achieve recognition by some other means. Indeed, sexual abstention is not synonymous with a fear of desire, since such circumstances are sometimes dictated by the conviction that to submit to sexual intercourse would foreclose the possibility of recognition as anything more than a sexual object. The young woman who struggles with the loss of her virtue is one example, the priest, or nun, another.

Thus, sexuality is a power which can make itself available for the purpose of experiencing an erotic situation by adapting sexual conduct to it. Our concern as practitioners is not merely limited to erotic behavior per se but rather to the course of a secret intentionality which follows the general structure of existence and yields to all of its movements. Sexual life is only one more form of desire, based on a certain attitude which endows experience with vitality and pleasure.

However, sexuality itself is not only biological but dialectical as well. The ultimate purpose of sexuality is to integrate one human being to another. Thus sexual life is not merely an effect of the genital organs, but "a general power which we enjoy, taking root in different settings and establishing itself through diverse experiences with other sexual creatures."[14] Insofar as a man has a sexual history which provides a key to his life, we discover his manner of being and his regard for others.[15] Freud insisted sexual repression was the cause of all neuroses. Yet these symptoms symbolize a whole attitude of being toward others, whether, for example, one of satisfaction or resentment.

Charlotte consulted me because she was desperately unhappy with her marriage, her husband, her life. She was frigid in her relation with her spouse who tended to blame her for the absence of a satisfying sexual relation. He insisted she "do something" about it and the result was her decison to undergo psychotherapy. That her heart was not in it was evident. Their sex had never been particularly passionate, but three years previously Charlotte ceased to give her body to her husband due to what she called a "loss of interest." She admitted that she had never in her life felt particularly aroused or truly satisfied sexually, and this was a source of profound insecurity.

She described a recurring sex fantasy. A stranger attacks her, attempts to rape her, and just at the final moment she suddenly turns round and takes over. It is revealing that her husband was never—nor could he be—an actor in this drama since, according to Charlotte, he was not a real man. Indeed, Charlotte insisted she wished—though she could not imagine—such a drama might occur in reality with her spouse, and that she would be capable of achieving orgasm instantly, thus depriving her husband of satisfaction, a truly sadistic fantasy. Indeed, there is always a touch of sadism in the frigid woman. Sadism is expressed against her desire and against a necessary accomplice to the subversion of her desire.

There is nowhere a more telling, blatant, and radical example of the sadistic impulse than in the work of the man who gave us its name: Sade. According to Serge Viderman

> Whereas his work is ostensibly a narcissistic exaltation of the uniqueness of the ego radically separated from its victim, it is obvious that his approach blinds him to the fact that the other is in reality the living focus of extremely highly charged emotional relations. His work celebrates, in its own way, the macabre sacraments of his love life, where one ends up by no longer being able to distinguish the executioner from the victim.[16]

The presence of sadism—however subtle it may be—always betrays a fundamental impotence: a failure of desire. As such, it is characterized by forms of behavior which have no specific end in themselves, but this is achieved by confusing the means for the end. The aim of sadism—the death of the object—has no other objective than to compel the other into submission and surrender. But it fails for the very reason that a dead object can no longer continue to submit. Ultimately, this is the failure of the sadistic impulse toward omnipotence because it leaves the perpetrator where he began: alone.

What is most remarkable about Charlotte is not her frigidity per se or a husband who is incapable of arousing her. Rather, it is the structure of her frigidity itself, a structure of vengeance and death. Her wish to avenge her empty existence cannot be construed as desire; what she demands is satisfaction, the same thing that a man who has lost his honor feels without. And yet Charlotte is already avenging herself by refusing to bed her partner. As she began to realize that her vengeance was complete, she left analysis satisfied that nothing or no one could touch her.

In the secret drama of sadistic revenge, Charlotte's sexuality is merely a means by which she refuses her husband her desire. Indeed, Charlotte never admitted that she did not *want* to be aroused. What she did want was to make the other suffer her suffering. The violence of her rape fantasy is enacted daily in her aggressive vindictiveness and in her refusal to recognize in her husband anything more than a reflection of her impotent ego. And by seeing in her husband a mere substitute for her emptiness, she effectively desexualizes their relation. And it is there that she finally achieved her power.

Charlotte is a prisoner of the satisfaction she elicits from her revenge. She substitutes her desire for a transitional satisfaction and forfeits the possibility of realizing her subjectivity as desire. She prefers the satisfaction of revenge to the possibility of a desire that can never completely belong to herself.

It would be misleading to infer that Charlotte has failed as a sexual creature. Indeed, her sexuality is a constant presence in its painfully obvious absence. It is a means through which she realizes her vengefulness by withholding her body's desire. Her satisfaction is triumphant in its desexed demands because her deadened desire is so deadly. Neither is Charlotte a victim of repressed sexuality because her sexuality is the only means of power that is left in her impregnable isolation. Her lust for revenge remains fulfilled only so long as she withholds the satisfaction of her body. If you were to ask her if she loves her husband, she would say yes, and she would fail to recognize the contradiction because she loves to deprive her husband of his pleasure just like she loves to deprive herself. For Charlotte love is a means of conquest rather than an act of surrender. It goes without saying that her views about love—like her views about sex—are extremely confused.

Charlotte's frigidity, the sadistic current which formalizes its underlying structure, and Freud's perversions all hold in common the project of transforming the subjectivity of the other into an object of resentful hatred. In fact, what binds the perversions together is not the absence of the procreative aim, but rather, the lack of a true subject of desire as an object of desire, a lack which is perpetuated through the objectification of the other by effacing a desire for their recognition. It is this—and only this—that constitutes a possible definition of what we take to be perverse in human relations. It is obvious that a perverse attitude can exist in any form of sexual activity—even in the act of procreation—if the other is conceived as merely a means to the achievement of a narcissistically satisfying experience. And we know only too well that masturbation can occur in many varied and assorted guises, including the most conventional (and respectable) modes of sexuality. It is equally obviously evident that fellatio, cunnilingus, homosexuality, and so on are not necessarily perverse if, for example, mutual recognition is coincident in the sexual act itself.

To be perverse is essentially to be either afraid or contemptuous of desire and anyone who is desirable, expressed by whatever means and subterfuge a "deadened" desire might take in a sexualized expression. This definition, of course, raises difficulties in the prevalence of pleasure which is achieved in the perverse act, an achievement that, according to Freud, is absent in the neurotic. There is the further difficulty in implying something obviously pathological in the perverse act, an implication which Freud was loathe to make, despite his and other analysts' reference to normal sexuality versus that which is perverse. While Freud refused to discuss the perverse act in terms other than those explicitly sexual (such as the moral, social, or characterological senses), we have seen how, in expanding the definition of what is to be regarded as sexual, virtually every human act can be included.

While adopting the sexual researches and descriptive categories of the perversions outlined by Krafft-Ebing and Havelock Ellis, Freud's singular originality lay in using his discussion of the perversions to challenge conventional ideas about sexuality itself. Freud's radical contribution lay in his hypothesis that young infants were sexualized and, what is more, that perversions themselves—which had always been regarded as "unnatural"—were conceived by Freud to be perfectly normal. According to Laplanche and Pontalis,

> The frequency of typically perverse types of behavior, and especially the persistence of perverse tendencies, whether these underpin neurotic symptoms or are integrated into the normal sexual act in the guise of "fore-pleasure," lead Freud to the idea that "the disposition to perversions is itself of no great rarity but must form a part of what passes as the normal constitution."[17]

Adult perversion is thus defined as merely a regression to infantile, pregenital fixations of the libido. This definition has never been satisfactory, though it is clearly an advance over previous definitions which defined perversions from moral or religious perspectives. For one thing, it is difficult to link all forms of homosexuality, extended foreplay, voyeurism, and sadism into precisely the same category, whether we conceive perversions to be normal or abnormal.

Furthermore, the notion that perversion is a reversion to a pregenital state is clearly refuted in the case of fetishism, incest, and forms of homosexuality. And lastly, while Freud goes to great pains to describe perversions as normal, he also speaks of normal sexuality when contrasting it with that of the perverse.[18] The margin is a rather thin one when oral sex, for example, can be classified either as normal or perverse, depending upon how long one decides to engage in foreplay.

If the concept of the perverse is to have any meaning at all, it must be contrasted to some other form of sexual practice that does not limit its distinction to the type of the sex act itself. There is a concept which is tenable, though it is necessary to step outside of the sexual act in order to formalize this distinction. What all perverse forms of sexuality hold in common is their singular denial of the other as a subject of desire. Instead, the other is perceived as merely an object of narcissistic pleasure. Virtually any sexual act can be construed as perverse in this respect, just as almost any sexual act can be free of perverse intent, save for two very obvious ones: sadism and necrophilia.

Viderman's study of Sade raises the suggestion that sadism, of all the perverse acts, is perhaps the one which is most prototypical. The sadist, who is essentially impotence in disguise, wants to dominate, to enslave the other, and does so only by turning the other into a thing. While pretending to dominate the other, the sadist in reality is totally *dependent* on him, in classic master-slave style. The reason for this is because the only power the sadist has is his threat to kill the love object; but if, in fact, he does so, he loses his love. According to Viderman, "Sadistic domination is a failure, which accounts for its desperate vehemence. The limits of violence are repeatedly reached and again and again pushed back, in a furious cycle refired by failure but in vain."[19]

The sadist's failure, however, is not what makes him perverse. Rather, it is his total disregard for the other save the other's ability to please him. It is this stance, which we can only regard as narcissistic, that fuels every perverse act. It is true that the pervert can indeed achieve pleasure where the neurotic cannot, but this does not make him any more superior or any less pathological than the neurotic. And it is at this juncture that the pleasure principle breaks down, as Freud came to realize in his revision which resulted in the death drive. Freud, as we know, was careful to draw clear distinctions between neuroses and the perversions. While he maintained that repression is absent in perversion, he did not fail to mention the other mechanisms so often found in them, such as disavowal and splitting, for example. These are mechanisms commonly found in psychosis.[20] Obviously, the pleasure of the sadist is not the same as the pleasure of the subject of desire. Concerning the former, we are witnessing the length to which narcissistic denial can go in affording itself the pathetically impotent pleasure at hand. It is a pleasure to be sure, but a pleasure devoid of desire, since its satisfaction is always complete in the deadened deadliness of its success.

If our thesis about the perversions is correct, the sadist is not the

prototypical pervert. The necrophiliac is. The point we are trying to
make is not the occasional cruelty that can be discovered in perversions,
but simply the absence of the other as anything other than an object—
in the purely objective sense—of satisfaction. What we are perceiving
here as objects of the pervert's desire are indeed things: the clothing of
the fetishist, the vanquished or conqueror of the sadist and masochist,
the dead body of the necrophiliac. All deny, nor do they require for
their pleasure, the desire of the other, but only the other's disposal,
willingness, availability, or, in the case of the voyeur, visual accessibility.
"Love" can indeed be spoken of during any discussion of the perversions because of the many elastic and ambiguous connotations that this
concept provides us. Perhaps it is valid to propose that the pervert
"possesses" his love object, while the subject of desire "dispossesses"
himself in favor of it.

Further, love, properly speaking, is not merely an infantile eroticism
which constantly insists on newer and newer proofs of attachment. It is
always a tender apprehension that takes the other person as he is and in
his subjectivity, without claims of possession or demands for submission. Since the infant's relation to others may be preestablished—as
Freud claimed—through those regions of the body which are least
capable of discrimination (the mouth and anus), there is no guarantee
that these primordial "means to an end" will cease to predominate in
the adult's relation to others. When the subject of desire becomes trapped in "the impasses of absolute immediacy, oscillating between an
inhuman demand, an absolute egotism, and a voracious devotion which
destroys the subject himself," it is hardly surprising that the sucks and
bites and defecation which originally accompanied the child's erotic
desires would once again take over and command the sexual conduct of
an adult estranged from his desire, and that he would no longer know
how to judge when to hold on or let go, or be capable of surrendering
his narcissistic needs for an apprehension of his desire for the other's
recognition.[21]

If we conceive the sexual history of the individual as the elaboration
of a general attitude to life, then psychological constituents will naturally enter into it because the genital life is geared to the whole life of
each person. Our question is not so much, as Freud proposed, over
whether or not human life does or does not rest on sexuality. Rather it is
one of determining what it is we understand by sexuality.

Thus sexuality is only one of the many currents of desire which is bound to be confused with existence unless it is particularized as a region of experience which is linked in turn to other avenues of knowledge through the body's apprehension of itself, the subject's desire for recognition, and the impasses of disarticulated experience.

CHAPTER EIGHT

THE LURES OF THE CURE AND THE DIALECTIC OF DESIRE IN LANGUAGE AND PSYCHOANALYSIS

If, as Heidegger suggested, to talk about language is even worse than to write about silence, then perhaps it is more forgivable to write about language than it is to speak about silence. Men have been talking to each other for a long time, yet most of what they say goes unnoticed. Why do we bother to speak at all, if not because we want to be heard? This question is ultimately one of understanding what in the world, and in ourselves, is the relationship between the word spoken and the word conveyed; in short, the relation between one human being and another.

What, then, is speech, properly speaking? This is a difficult question to answer. However, we know that without speech we could not see one another. When face to face with another person, the other is never really present to me. Even in the violence of an argument, it is not in his face with his grimace and pained expression that his existence reaches me. His voice, gestures, his eyes, are only impressions, while the man who conveys those effects lies elsewhere. His words reveal all that he has to show me about himself and his perception of himself and, of course, his perception about me. Whenever and wherever one man encounters another, he finds himself in language.

There are those who have reduced the act of speech to the mere utterance and communication of one's thoughts through the spoken word. They believe that speech is the manifestation of what lies hidden inside a person; that speech is a mere activity of a behavioral sort. They think that speech is the material of thought, a representation of reality or even ideal entities. This conception of language is at least as old as

Aristotle, who believed that words are the signs of the soul's experience. It is not for me to say that this view of language is wrong, or even misleading, but this conception does fall short of providing something of an understanding of the essence of language and, what's more, its relation to the essence of man himself.

In the modern era, phenomenology, psychoanalysis, and structuralism have provided something of a revolution in our understanding of language which, each in its own way, attempts to question traditional conceptions of speech and of the man who utters it. This understanding has a specific relevance to the psychoanalytic cure.

Merleau-Ponty, in his *Phenomenology of Perception*, characterizes two important concepts in the philosophy of language which preceded the current era of "linguistics."[1] According to the first, we witness the production of words aided by vocal organs arising from the brain and the nervous system. The production has been excited in the first place by external stimuli coordinated with mechanisms of association. According to this concept, speech is conceived as an activity, but man is thought to be essentially passive in that his speaking is determined by stimuli originating from outside himself. We have here an overtly causal explanation of speech that overcomes the speaker, as in the swoon of a lovesick damsel.

According to the second concept, we have an inner thought which is rooted not in the outside, but in itself. Language is conceived as a system of signs and symbols that communicate inner ideas to others, while the means of the speaker's communication fails to influence his style of thinking. Words are noted as the material experience of the speaker himself, but what is lacking is precisely to what these material signs refer, and with it the transcendental component to language.

Despite the apparent differences between these two conceptions of language, both conceive language predominantly as a mode of communication of thoughts which are already there: What is said exists prior to its expression. Thoughts—and meanings—exist either in the world or are constituted from within the mind. In either case, these primordial meanings are uttered after the fact by language. In both cases speech, a sensory-motor activity, neither contributes to nor constitutes meaning, but merely conveys it.

Nowhere in the hypothesis above do we discover in the use of language the means of revelation or disclosure. We find only transmission of the most primitive sort. Merleau-Ponty rightly criticizes these conceptions of language primarily because of the conception of man which they produce, an essentially positivistic conception which views words in much the same way as it does man, as a mere effect of causal determinants, originating from somewhere outside or inside, but, in either case, completely passive to the forces and laws of nature.

It is the view of man and of his use of language, described above, which dominated European psychiatry at the close of the nineteenth century when Freud was attempting to formulate his discovery of the talking cure. A close reading of Freud's early work reveals that his greatest insight was unquestionably that of the seemingly miraculous power of mere words to cure the most obstinate mental disorders. However, Freud's discovery of the potential curative power of language was couched largely in the Stoic theory of sign and signification which has persisted until the present century: the representational theory of language and perception.

According to the representational theory, words are viewed as pictures or signs of objects which we are assumed to know about from a source other than language itself. Words merely direct our attention from one object to the next. Language does not reveal as much as it designates things in the world we already know about. It was this theory of language that Freud wholeheartedly endorsed, convinced it could provide the foundation for his theory of the unconscious.

Scientifically trained, Freud wanted his insights into language to be scientifically respectable and believed that his theories were comparable to those of the natural sciences, as science was understood in the nineteenth century. But the dominant science at that time was physics. Thus, his linguistic structures were based on illustrations and analogies based on physics. As a consequence, Freud's most important work, *The Interpretation of Dreams,* yielded to conceptions of explanations wherein the language of energy dominates and obscures what Freud was in fact attempting to articulate: the meaning, or sense, of symptoms.

Freud's famous Signorelli parapraxis is a good example to demonstrate his conception of language and, in it, his explanation for memory loss and neurotic symptoms in terms of repressed contents and unconscious processes.[2]

In a conversation with a stranger, Freud failed to remember the name of a painter, Signorelli, and substituted instead the name of two other painters, Botticelli and Boltraffio, though he recognized them for the substitutes that they were. Thus he proceeded to apply his technique of associative investigation to attempt to recall the forgotton word from the substitutes which had come to mind. He surmised that the "Signor-" in Signorelli was related to "Herr" (which means the same thing) in Herzegovina, the province toward which he and the stranger were driving. Of primary significance, Freud later recalled that, "Light was only thrown on the forgetting of the name when I recalled the topic we had been discussing directly before, and it was revealed as a case in which *a topic that has just been raised is disturbed by a preceding topic.*"[3] The preceding topic concerned the customs of the Turks living in Herzegovina and the nearby province of Bosnia. Freud related to his companion that he had heard they were accustomed "to show great confidence in their doctor and great resignation to fate. If one has to inform them that nothing can be done for a sick person, their reply is: '*Herr* [sir], what is there to be said? If he could be saved, I know you would have saved him.'"[4] Thus Freud also surmised that the "Bo-" of Botticelli and Boltraffio derived from Bosnia.

Of further significance to the repressed artist's name and the Turkish provinces to which it refers was Freud's recollection that "Turks place a higher value on sexual enjoyment than on anything else, and in the event of sexual disorders they are plunged in a despair which contrasts strangely with their resignation towards the threat of death."[5] Freud explains that he finally realized that the reason he had forgotten (that is, repressed) the name of the artist in conversation with this stranger was because he did not want to allude to the topic of sexuality with a stranger. Further, the "-traffio" of Boltraffio's name was linked to the village of Trafio where Freud learned of the suicide of a patient of his, "over whom I had taken a great deal of trouble [and] had put an end to his life on account of an incurable sexual disorder."[6]

Thus, the forgotten word "Signorelli" was associated not only with the embarrassing topic (sex) but also was connected to the disturbing idea of death, a topic that Anthony Wilden, in a book on the work of Jacques Lacan, notes must have weighed heavily on Freud's mind since the Signorelli incident occurred at the time he has formulating his theory of the Oedipus complex.[7] The repressed topic of sex could then be expanded to include Freud's own desire for his mother as well as the desire for the death of his rivals—including his own death.

The incident served to demonstrate for Freud that, "Displacement is not left to arbitrary psychical choices but follows paths which can be predicted and which conforms to laws. In other words, I suspect that

the name or names which are substituted are connected in a discovera-
ble way with the missing name."[8]

Freud's intent in this example of the forgetting of words was to
establish a theory which would explain forgetting as a mental process—
repression—and to demonstrate unconscious mental processes generally. While much is said of the links and barriers to these links between
names of places and names of persons, couched in a representational
view of language, Freud was equally concerned with establishing the
unconscious intent behind forgetting and knowing in general. Thus,
psychoanalytic technique was envisioned by Freud as a process
whereby the patient, by saying anything that should come to his mind,
would eventually reveal through the associative meanings between one
word and the next the hidden meaning which had been repressed and
given rise to the symptom which had taken its place. This technique
then proves the, " . . . efficacy of psychoanalytic therapy, which aims at
correcting the repressions and displacements and which removes the
symptoms by reinstating the genuine psychical object."[9]

Numerous authors have had a turn at interpreting and improving on
Freud's account of the Signorelli story. As we shall see, it is possible to
reinterpret Freud's account of his talking cure by applying to it modern
conceptions of language which have only been made since Freud made
his. The linguistic theories of Ferdinand de Saussure, Roman Jakobson, Martin Heidegger, Maurice Merleau-Ponty, Paul Ricouer, Noam
Chomsky, and others have been applied to psychoanalysis and the social
sciences, such as anthropology, by a wide range of thinkers such as
Claude Lévi-Strauss, Victor Rosen, Marshall Edelson, Stanley Leavy,
Roy Schafer, Hans Loewald, and, of course, Jacques Lacan. This was
done in an effort to help us grasp an appreciation for the dramatic
powers that language and speech possess, a power most dramatically
revealed to us by Freud himself. Victor Rosen is a prime example of a
proponent of the ego-psychological theory toward language which assumes that interpretations are due to the rational (adult) part of the ego
vanquishing the irrational unconscious determinants of his neurotic
behavior. In a paper on the relation between language and unconscious
meaning Rosen examines the rudiments of language as originating in
presymbolic sounds.[10] He proposes that the early babbling of infants is
expressive of certain needs which are later transferred to ordinary language, thus conjecturing a link between primary process (infantile) and
secondary process (adult) meanings. The implication of this view is that

only childish (regressed) language is laden with ambiguity, while adult speaking is always rational, clear, and mature. Thus, analysis is a process whereby the patient's primitive presentations are transformed through interpretations into a more mature dialogue. Infantile babbling and gestures are associated with surrounding events and are related to specific objects in the infant's world.

Stanley Leavy was skeptical of Rosen's claim that nonpathological speech should be free of ambiguity:[11]

> A difficulty with Rosen's view is that it seems to grant too much maturity to language as symbolic process. It is all a bit *too* secondary, as though ordinary adult language were not laden with ambiguity all the time, recognized by analysts because of their attunement to redundances that more practically minded listeners prefer to ignore.[12]

Leavy is also somewhat critical of Rosen's appeal to reason which implies "that there is always an autonomous ego to which we need only speak reasonably for it to learn the error of the ways of the unconscious."[13] While Leavy detects a more positive side to Rosen's concern with language itself, suggesting an adherence to dialectics and the theories of Saussure, I view Rosen's approach to the linguistic element in psychoanalysis as essentially faithful to the pre-Saussurian view that language is a conveyor of meanings rather than their determinant. Rosen's prejudice toward rational and adult language is faithful to the ego-psychological perspective that sanity lies always outside the individual and that adaptation to the rational discourse of the analyst is representative of maturity and health. One merely has to get in touch with meanings of the analyst's discourse in order to grow up. This is the unfortunate line of thought proposed by Freud and promoted by most of his followers who view the unconscious, primary process as primitive, childlike, and so forth, so that rationality and health lie on the side of adapting oneself to a superior truth rather than by inhabiting one's own.

Picking up on the theme of ambiguity in language, Leavy refers to Marshall Edelson's application of the linguistic theory of Noam Chomsky to psychoanalysis. Leavy notes Edelson's comparison of the ambiguity in the dream to the ambiguity of sentences: "In the latter case, identical surface structures may reveal on syntactic analysis quite different deeper structures, and conversely it is possible for a single deep structure to be represented by different surface structures."[14]

Just as the manifest content of dreams may reveal disparate latent meanings, the manifest content of everyday speech also refers to disparate latent meanings. Indeed, it is precisely this conception of everyday discourse on which the entire psychoanalytic enterprise resides. In making interpretations, however, the analyst himself may be unaware of the origin of his own interpretations of the patient's discourse, confusing his latent understanding with that of the patient's. According to Edelson, "Much of the understanding the psychoanalyst attributes to empathy, intuition, or conscious or unconscious extralinguistic information actually derives from his own internalized linguistic (and semiological) competence of whose nature and existence he may be altogether unaware."[15]

Edelson examines the nature of language in more depth.[16] He raises the question: Is psychoanalysis a science of tropes? "No scientist, regardless of what discipline, needs to be convinced today of the importance of tropes. Metaphor, for example, is not only a figure or trope in rhetoric or poetics. Metaphor can be defined in the terminology of logic as an expression of identity or similarity in the form of relations among entities in different domains."[17] When metaphors are understood in the widest possible sense as a substitute for something seemingly unrelated to it, we have little difficulty in perceiving how the most seemingly innocent sentence ("I love you") can be a disguise for something quite different ("I hate you"). In professing love substituted for hate—a favorite theme of R. D. Laing's—its metaphorical equation may be perceived in terms of a reaction formation wherein the person unconsciously disguises from himself the absence of love in his life, or it may be viewed in terms of mystification, wherein the person in childhood equated the word *love* with the mental torture he received from his family. Thus symptoms are themselves metaphors, in that they disguise the desire whose place they have assumed.

Freud's genius was in recognizing the pervasiveness of disguised communication which exists in dreams, symptoms, and everyday speech. Edelson, following Chomsky, pays particular attention to the metaphorical structure of sentences in contrast, for example, to Freud's emphasis on individual words as we have witnessed in the Signorelli incident. Apparently influenced by Harold Bloom's insistence on the so-called "tropological" structure of language, Edelson recounts a conversation with him in which Bloom expressed skepticism that any linguistic expression was free of tropes or figures of speech. Edelson felt inclined to dissent from this view because it suggests that what we assume to be literal statements of fact are myths.

While Edelson suggests that his disagreement with Bloom is minor because he believes figurative forms of speech only make sense when contrasted with those which are literal, I would suggest that this disagreement is quite crucial to our conception of language, symptomatology, and the analytic cure, as we shall soon see in Lacan's adoption— and alteration—of Saussure's linguistic theory. This question hinges on whether there exists an external, literal reality to which speech is capable of referring, or if reality is in itself a personal construction of tropological equivalences with its own internal consistency or inconsistency. Edelson points out that in order, "to make the distinction between 'literal' and 'figurative' it is necessary to abstract from actual expressions that sense which they possess independent of any context."[18] In other words, we may contrast figurative or metaphorical speech from literal speech by situating the former in a context while the latter is able to stand on its own.

The disagreement between Edelson and Bloom takes us right back to traditional conceptions of language which suggest that signs refer to things rather than to what Saussure regards as concepts. In qualifying his adoption of the view that all language is rooted in contextual meanings, Edelson is suggesting that there are some real things to which words definitely refer, falling back in this instance on Rosen's claim that psychoanalysis should enable us to reclaim this lost, presumably universal, reality. Thus, Edelson is saying that both literal and figurative conceptions of language exist and influence the analytic enterprise. In pursuing his point, he goes on to emphasize that "a literal language is a regimented, formalized language. In such a language, one and only one object from a specified domain of unequivocally distinguishable objects is assigned to each name or definite description which denotes that object"[19] However, in his daily practice, the analyst is constantly confronted with ". . . the figurative, allusive language of the analysand. Certainly, when the analysand constructs a fantasy, a dream, or a neurotic symptom, names or descriptions are often used to refer or allude to other than what they customarily denote. . . . It is part of the competence of the psychoanalyst, which enables him to make clinical interpretations, that he understands the ways in which figurative language departs from literal language."[20]

In other words, according to Edelson, it is up to the analyst to

distinguish between fantasy and reality. In so doing, it is important that
the analyst himself remains faithful to a literal meaning of his conceptual framework while decoding the analysand's figurative utterances
into that framework: "The tension between the language of psychoanalysis as science and the language it studies is a tension between
literal language which as scientists is the language we try to use, and a
figurative language which belongs to the object world which we as
scientists try to describe."[21] In characterizing psychoanalysis as a
"science of illusion," Edelson suggests that "Freud's *The Interpretation
of Dreams* is an exemplification of a science of illusions."[22] Further, "to
have made the distinction between manifest dream-content and latent
dream-thoughts was to raise the question a science of illusions must
answer."[23]

However, Edelson cautions against accepting the notion that the analysand's illusion is true or false. Rather, he suggests that we consider to
what extent it is internally consistent or inconsistent in the overall context of the analysand's experience of his world, not of reality (such as,
literal meanings): "Psychoanalytic interpretation that is concerned with
a distorted illusion reconstructs what internal representation has been
dictated in an act or work; not truth or falsity, but fidelity, the direct-
ness or indirectness of a representation or a performance, are the alternatives to be examined."[24] Thus Edelson, in his roundabout way,
appears to have come full circle in assuming the very position for which
he criticized Harold Bloom. By invoking the notion of fidelity in the
analysand's discourse, Edelson is not concerned with the literal meanings to which the patients' illusions refer, but rather to the inner consistency of his (the patient's) own understanding of his reality. When
Bloom questions that words ever refer to literal (objective) fact, but
rather to a network of associative meanings which remain embedded in
the tropes and metaphors of the linguistic system we inhabit, he is
suggesting that words refer to other words, and to concepts which refer
to other concepts, and so on, but that literal expressions of reality are
nonexistent as such. Edelson himself makes it clear that he refuses to
believe in a clear-cut, objectifiably verifiable model of interpretive
meanings to which the analyst can refer to test the validity of his interpretations: "That there is no possibility for developing an automatic
procedure enabling the psychoanalyst, given a particular symbolic entity (e.g., the dream) to discover the right—or even a good—interpreta-

tion of it, I take for granted. An interpretation is always under-determined by the data."[25]

Thus, Edelson adopts the view that illusion is in itself based on metaphorical and metonymic associative meanings which have not diverted the analysand from a literal or concrete reality, but one rather ensnared in an internally coherent structure of meaning, which reveal an inherent contradiction in his discourse: "I am not what I am." Interpretations are intended to unravel this contradiction and free the patient to assume his own discourse. It is on this point that Leavy is critical of Rosen's adoption of the ego-psychological program of putting the patient in touch with reality, exemplified by the appeal to reason which the analyst attempts to indoctrinate his patient into: "It is not likely that alteration will come from our appeal to reason, but more likely that we can achieve our end by finding the right metaphor within the network of meanings in which he now stands."[26] It is this network of meanings to which Edelson refers in his adherence to the fidelity of the analysand's discourse.

Leavy, however, believes that Edelson's adoption of Chomskian linguistics is ultimately inadequate to the task of serving as a foundation for psychoanalysis, for the simple reason that psychoanalysis is not merely an analysis of sentence structures to determine their internal consistency. Rather, it is a dialectical relationship between the analysand's understanding of his words as well as of the analyst's. Seeking out the ambiguous elements of the other's discourse, embedded as it may be in metaphors, is not in itself enough, since the analyst is also punctuating, questioning, prying, and probing the patient's words from a position of his comprehension of psychical and linguistic structures. In other words, Chomsky's view of language fails to attend to the character of repression per se. That is, some remarks are perfectly capable of arousing the analyst's suspicions as to what the subject is saying. Leavy reminds us that if a patient were to say, "I certainly love my wife," "the Freudian contribution here is that words like 'certainly' arouse suspicion: Use of such a word *in such contexts* may mean what it says but also its opposite, or at least is likely to raise the question, 'Does he?'"[27]

While the context of the patient's discourse makes all the difference to the other meanings they may conceal, the analyst and his understanding is part of that context too. It is not a question of who is right or who is wrong, but what comes of the free play of all possible contextual variations of the words exchanged between them: "Like poetical creation, analytic method is an intensification, deepening, and sophistication of what we do in all dialogue. Linguistics in the larger sense is the basic science of psychoanalysis because it explores the processes by which the psychoanalytic exchange takes place."[28]

Nowhere has the significance of language been more forcefully applied to the nature of psychoanalysis than in the work of Jacques Lacan, who applied Saussurian linguistics to the analytic dialogue. The difficulty of Lacan's expression results in the kind of hostile reaction which Lacan himself would suggest parallels the nature of aggression in one's experience of frustrated satisfaction. Be that as it may, Lacan's treatment is all the more difficult because his application of Saussure differs markedly from Saussure's own conception and because Lacan generally fails to acknowledge his debt to Heidegger while posing a condemnation of phenomenological theories which approximate Lacan's own in ways he is loathe to admit. The battle cry of "structuralism versus phenomenology" tends to confuse rather than clarify the current debate in linguistic investigations of Freud's work.

It is due primarily to Saussure's vision of language as a system of signs that we owe the adaptation of linguistics to the social sciences more generally. Of course, Saussure was more interested in the laws of language, being careful to distinguish *la langue* from speech (*parole*). Phenomenologists, such as Merleau-Ponty, have tended to focus more concern on the speech act itself, and it is due to this diversion of interest that Lacan has attacked phenomenologists for not comprehending that the role of linguistic laws is critical to his own understanding of the Freudian unconscious. Perhaps the most important contribution of Saussure's thought lies in his situating within the linguistic sign two inseparable components. One, the acoustic sound, relates to a concept. This view differs rather radically from traditional conceptions which refer words to things. Thus, according to Saussure, the sound "tree" refers to a concept of tree and not to the thing we sensually experience as a tree.[29] This distinction is central to Lacan's linguistic theory and, indeed, to the science of linguistics itself.

Thus, the sound image, or word, is termed by Saussure as the "signifier" in speech, and the concept is the accompanying component of the sign, which is called the "signified." Further, the relationship between the two is entirely arbitrary. This is a crucial point, since the arbitrariness of the meaning of words is precisely what allows a word or

THE LURES OF THE CURE AND THE DIALECTIC OF DESIRE   *161*

concept to be freed of its definitive tie to things in reality, such as, the external, concrete, literal world. This shifting of emphasis from thing to concept (the signified) allows language a life of its own, rather than relegating it to serve as a mere indicator of that natural world which is regarded as preeminent over words in pre-Saussurian formulations.

Revolutionary as Saussure's conception of language was—it spawned the "structuralist" movement and influenced Merleau-Ponty's conception of language—Saussure believed the bond between signifier and signified to be unbreakable. As a result, the application of this theory emphasized language as a science of meanings, making the signified— the underlying concept to which all words refer—one's major point of interest. The problem with this conception, as Lacan saw, was that the word took precedence over the sentence and the context in which words were spoken.

Freud's analysis of words was to some extent remarkably similar to Saussure's. In some other ways it was more primitive. In other ways, Freud's analysis was more radical, since his conception of displacement and condensation could not be readily explained according to Saussure's model. To combat this error, Lacan altered Saussure's equation to the extent that he envisioned a signifier without a signified, words that are not readily related to underlying, or hidden, concepts but rather to other signifiers along what Lacan referred to as a signifying chain. Of course, Saussure was the first to recognize the associative link between one signifier and another and discovered two fundamental axes of language upon which these associations were enjoined: through combination and selection. But it was due largely to Roman Jakobson's development of Saussure's theory of language in the use of rhetoric and tropes, such as metaphors and metonymy, that Lacan was able to apply Saussure's theories to psychoanalysis.[30] Lacan's interest in linguistics became almost exclusively concerned with the relationships amongst signifiers, almost—but not entirely—unconcerned with the signified itself.

For one thing, by breaking the irrevocable bond between the signifier and the signified, Lacan was able to claim that what at first appeared to be signified turns out to be but one more signifier, which in turn is related to yet another, and then another, and so on. While Lacan goes into great detail in his investigation of these rhetorical structures of language, the revolutionary import of his own formulation is remarkably close to the Husserlian conception of knowledge in

general: that we must bracket the obvious or apparent meaning (signified) of a word (or experience) in order to examine its relation—via
Freudian free association, or Husserlian free variation—to the surrounding context in order to see where these words may lead. By sus-
pending ultimate reality we can follow the metaphoric and metonymic
train of associations to examine the effect of this combination of associations. Thus, in any discourse—such as the psychoanalytic—we may
engage in, there is always something missing: the signification to which
the present signifier refers. It is, according to Lacan, the combination
of these collective signifiers, most of which are hidden, which reveal the
signified.[31] Further, it is this collection and interaction of absent signifiers which accompany and are part of the discourse of the participants which Lacan designates the "Other." This is his conception of the
unconscious. It is this conception of the unconscious as a network of
signifying elements which relate to other signifiers which, in turn,
belong to a separate chain of signifying elements that allows Lacan to
define psychoanalysis as an enterprise which is less concerned with
restoring the hidden center of meaning of an original signified than
with reconstituting the structure of the subject's unconscious, e.g., the
structure of his desire.[32] Another way of putting Lacan's dictum, "the
unconscious is structured like a language," is that language is structured unconsciously. Lacan's pure subject of the unconscious, the subject of desire, is thus an effect of his absent discourse. It is the Other,
that is, the missing chain of unconscious signifiers, which occasion his
unarticulated or repressed desire.

Though torturous and enigmatic as his description of the unconscious may appear to be, Lacan is merely laying a foundation for a
purely linguistic formulation of what phenomenologists have been saying from the perspective of intentionality. Reality is not something we
can discover in any objective encounter; it must come from the articulation of our own construction of it. We shall now explore the implications of Lacan's use of tropes as formulated by Jakobsen and Saussure.

On closer examination, Lacan's alteration of Saussure is intended to
avoid the implication that any word denotes a meaning of its own, an
obvious discovery to anyone who seeks for definitions (signified) to
words (signifiers) in dictionaries, only to discover the use and reference
to other words, none of which ever arrive at any particular meaning
(signification) unless one is already working with a stock of fixed meanings with which to compare those presented. Saussure's system leads to

ambiguities for this very reason, since one is tempted to confuse a particular signified with its absent signification. Thus, the Saussurian signified can, for all practical purposes, be equated with a signifier after all. It is for this reason, according to Anthony Wilden, that Lacan chose to base his understanding of linguistics on a series of signifiers:

> He seems to have settled on signifier for a number of reasons: One, its clear implication that something is signifying something *for someone* (the intentionality of the discourse)—whether that something is an individual, a society, or language itself; two, its differentiation from "signal," too easily assimilated under the term "sign"; three, its implication that no direct or necessary relationship to a real object or to reality is involved.[33]

Jakobson's amplification of Saussure's two fundamental bases of language—selection and combination—was appealing to Lacan when he attempted to revise the primacy of signifiers in language. Of course, any study or appreciation of language and its intelligibility in psychoanalytic interpretation immediately implies a choice on the part of the analyst of one linguistic code over the other. If analytic interpretation is intended to explain to an analysand the meaning of his suffering, according to the analyst's "understanding" of mental illness, he is simply referring to a body of knowledge which he regards as more realistic than that of his patient. This is essentially a didactic approach to therapy. If, however, the analyst views his patient's words in much the same way he would a poet's, he is seeking the meaning of what the patient is saying about himself—rather than what the patient is failing to understand about health, or more realistic behavior. But having inserted himself into a metaphorical or tropological appreciation of language, there is no guarantee that he will resist the temptation to substitute the patient's meaning for his own. Metaphor can be used in many ways, such as, for example, disguised explanations. The importance in understanding Jakobson's or Saussure's contribution toward an appreciation of the richness and intricacies of language is not in order to apply a complicated linguistic technique to the practice of psychoanalysis, but rather in order to resist objectifying tendencies in ourselves which we might otherwise commit.

Saussure's inspiration lies in the insight that language can never really express some thing, but only relationships between words and our conceptions of them. From this perspective, we can see that words are being substituted for and combined with other words all the time, according to Saussure through combination and selection, such as, metonymy and metaphor. We structure our sentences according to a selection of words which, combined together, convey a collective meaning, while we also choose specific words which we feel are more appropriate or to the point, than others. The words of this sentence, for example, are stretched out in a linear fashion which suspends its full meaning to the end, when they collectively provide a meaning which transcends any one of them. However, I might be careful to select a particular word, such as *red* rather than *colorful* because I believe it to be more precise or revelatory to what I wish to convey. These two principles of combination and selection structure the language system from which we choose our utterances.

Jakobson discovered, for instance, that a study of aphasia utilizing this conception of language revealed the patient's speech to be deficient in either combination or selection. If we say that signifiers are related to each other either metaphorically or metonymically, we are merely attempting to show how words are always revealing something to which they refer but do not, as it were, describe. Metonyms, for example, allude to something that is missing, a part is often substituted for the whole as in the expression, "Would you like a drink?" The word drink refers to a drink "of something" which need not be added since the missing part is inferred. A metaphor, however, substitutes a word which ostensibly has no direct contiguous association, but may be more potent or dramatic. "The sky is electric tonight," for example, uses the metaphor electric to convey a meaning one would not ordinarily associate with sky, but adds a dimension of meaning which immediately conjures other signifying associations as well. In the expression, "He is the power behind the throne," we have the metaphorical use of power which, given the context, must be a substitute for authority or leader, while the word *throne* more immediately refers to something that is related to throne, such as the person who sits on a throne: the king or queen, for example.

This kind of linguistic analysis could become endlessly tedious except for the way Lacan suggested an equivalency between metaphor and Freud's reference to condensation in his study of dreams and between metonymy and Freud's concept of displacement. This is the kind of interpretive legitimacy which, up until now, one has had to do without, relying instead on fixed symbolic meanings for the dream content, such as a house is always a vagina, an elongated object is always a penis, and so on.

Thus dream elements can be seen to obey the laws of metaphoric and metonymic substitution which refer to other signifiers which these substitutions have disguised. What they ultimately refer to, of course, depends on the overall context of everything else the dreamer can think of to talk about. It is obvious that Jakobson's use of the signifying elements in language contained in metaphor and metonymy can vastly alter our understanding of the nature of discourse and any attempt to interpret its meaning.

Adding his own twist to Jakobson's fascinating argument, Lacan sees all symptoms—whether somaticized or psychical—as metaphors (since they replace one signifier for another) and the unconscious desire to which the patient's utterances refer as a metonymy. Thus, the tension between the present symptom and the missing desire can be articulated along signifying elements to which the laws of metaphor and metonymy constantly refer. Whether this formulation of Lacan's is essentially correct, it does suggest the enigmatic ways in which speech is used to both reveal and conceal the significations of the analysand's discourse.

To return to Freud, we may now begin to examine some of his utterances about the unconscious according to these linguistic revisions and the nature of desire itself. One of Freud's most startling insights into the link between language and subjectivity was derived from what has now become a popular reference point to the child's assumption of language: the famous "Fort!-Da!" game of Freud's gandson. There is perhaps no better example in Freud's work with which to examine the emergence of the child into a field of desire.

In the second chapter of *Beyond the Pleasure Principle,* Freud describes his observations of a seemingly strange habit of his grandson which occurred when his mother would go away.[34] This consisted in collecting small objects from his crib and throwing them somewhere in the room out of sight. While doing this the child would exclaim "o-o-o-o" (for the German "Fort") meaning "away." The child engaged in this activity with a great deal of joy and excitment.

The game became more intelligible when Freud observed the child playing with a wooden toy attached to a string. When he threw the toy over the crib so that it was out of sight, he said "o-o-o-o" once again, then he pulled on the string until the toy reappeared, greeting it with a joyful "da," meaning "here." Freud found the joy of the toy's disappearance quite mysterious, as it was this part of the "Fort-Da" game which was emphasized in the child's play. Further, Freud observed that the child never cried when his mother went away, expecting a one-and-a-half year old child to experience her disappearance with considerable distress. Finally, the meaning of the game became obvious. According to Freud,

> It was related to the child's great cultural achievement—the instinctual renunciation (that is, the renunciation of the instinctual satisfaction) which he had made in allowing his mother to go away without protesting. He compensated himself for this, as it were, by himself staging the disappearance and return of the objects within his reach.[35]

In Freud's eyes the child was in a position to accept the absence of his mother without distress because he did not experience her leaving passively, but rather gained "mastery" of the situation by assuming an active role vis-à-vis the game he himself controlled: "At the outset he was in a *passive* situation—he was overpowered by the experience; but, by repeating it, unpleasurable though it was, as a game, he took on an *active* part. These efforts might be put down to an instinct for mastery."[36] One detects in Freud's account of this discovery the brilliance of insight couched in so-called "physicalist" (instinctual) terms which is so typical in Freud's theoretical formulations. The full import of this discovery has been expanded upon by numerous authors, but the two most relevant for our present discussion are Winnicott and Lacan.

Freud's interpretation of the reel game inspired Winnicott's theory, called "transitional phenomena," which today represents probably his most brilliant contribution to psychoanalysis. Freud's interpretation of the child's "great cultural achievement" was taken up by Winnicott in reference to the importance of the child's ability to engage in such playful activity which serves to both symbolize the mother's disappearance as well as the child's tolerance of it. For Winnicott the child's assumption of play is a crucial step in acceptance of reality, i.e., the world outside the mother.[37] Disturbed children are unable to engage in such play and as a consequence fail to distinguish between "I" and "not-I." However, Winnicott's interpretation of the child's cultural achievement is couched in terms of the surrounding environmental milieu, which the child is able to enter only on condition of his experience of "good-enough" mothering. Not surprisingly, Lacan's understanding of this achievement is couched in entirely different terms, those which place the child in relation to absence, desire, and the assumption of language.

For Lacan, this cultural achievement is not merely a renunciation of instinctual satisfaction but the experience of the desire for the mother and the effort to cope with his frustration. In his essay, "The Function and Field of Speech and Language in Psychoanalysis," Lacan observes that Freud, in a flash of genius, revealed to us that the " . . . moment in which desire becomes human is also that in which the child is born into language."[38] The child's exclamation of "Fort!-Da!" expresses his experience of presence and absence, indeed, of presence through absence contained in that moment wherein he begins to make life *his own,* such as that moment in which "desire becomes human." In effect, the child begins to break his dyadic relation with his mother by inserting himself into a pluralized relationship with society in general, through his assumption of the most social of all institutions: language itself. In this, however, Lacan owes a tremendous debt to Claude Lévi-Strauss and his application of structural linguistics to anthropology, since it is Lévi-Strauss's conception of the unconscious which Lacan has formalized in his critique of Freud's.

According to Lévi-Strauss:

> The unconscious ceases to be the ultimate haven of individual peculiarities—the repository of a unique history which makes each of us an irreplaceable being. It is reducible to a function—the symbolic function, which no doubt is specifically human, and which is carried out according to the same laws among all men, and actually corresponds to the aggregate of these laws.[39]

For Lévi-Strauss, like Freud, it is crucial to distinguish between the preconscious and the unconscious, though his interpretation differs from that of Freud in that he eliminates from the unconscious any pretensions toward a seeming reservoir of instincts, impulses, emotions, and so on:

> The preconscious, as a reservoir of recollections and images amassed in the course of a lifetime, is merely an aspect of memory. The unconscious, on the other hand, is always empty—or, more accurately, it is as alien to mental images as is the stomach to the foods which pass through it. As an organ of a specific function, the unconscious merely imposes structural laws upon inarticulated elements which originate elsewhere—impulses, emotions, representations, and memories. We might say, therefore, that the preconscious is the individual lexicon where each of us accumulates a vocabulary of his personal history, but that this vocabulary becomes significant, for us and for others, only to the extent that the unconscious structures it according to its laws and thus transforms it into language.[40]

It is Lévi-Strauss's emphasis on the laws of language, which in turn structure the unconscious, which has profoundly influenced Lacan's revision of the unconscious as well as of the Oedipal drama, that moment in which the child assumes his role in society. Thus the father is much more than the third member of the Oedipal triad, he is also the symbolic representative of a larger social order into which the child, now equipped with speech, enters. This social order, according to Lévi-Strauss, is governed by relationships of human exchange (pacts, marriages, customs, etc.). The incest taboo, which is one of these pacts, of course dominates the Oedipal complex in the form of society's prohibition of the child's desire. More to the point, it is not desire that society prohibits but rather its satisfaction. Lacan gives great importance to the role of naming and that place from which names derive, since at birth our very identity is designated by and for someone else: the father. Lacan, following Lévi-Strauss, is merely saying that the law that establishes the pattern for customs and relationships is the same law which sets the pattern for human language. This, in turn, structures the laws of the unconscious. Thus, Lacan borrows a conceptual schema which he posits at the heart of language itself from phenomenology and structural anthropology to elaborate Saussurian linguistics. The subject is not so much structured by real events or external reality as much as it is by society's comprehension of the events which we experience.

Lacan views the subject as subordinated to the laws of language, which allows him to defer the distinction generally made between interpersonal and intrapersonal relations by situating the second within the first through the chains of signifiers which link them. Thus, the fundamental drive of the human subject is not the libido in the Freudian sense but rather desire for the other's recognition as conceived by Hegel. This distinction is important, for if desire is to be conceived in terms of the subject's relationships to language and the social dimension, then the subject's attitude toward and comprehension of others is central to our understanding of desire.

Contrary to Freud, Lacan (relying on Hegel) conceives of desire not so much in terms of a satisfaction of instinctual urges as in those of the uncertainity of not knowing who we are in relation to our conception of ourselves and the *other's* conception of who they perceive us to be. If we were to adopt the biological view, our experience of doubt would appear to be impossible. After all, Darwinism rests on the notion that differences do indeed exist between one individual and the next. Yet, this principle appears to fail us in the field of the social sciences. Francois Roustange raises the question: "Why must we register an uneasiness, the torment of having to distinguish ourselves from the rest of our kind or, contrariwise, our incoercible need to melt into the mass?"[41] Indeed, the differences we are required to maintain in relation to others is something we typically dread. As we have seen, according to Hegel, man is specifically human due to the uncertainty of his self-definition. His relationships with others are plagued by the incessant ambivalence between attempting to posit himself as something for the other, and his attempts at escaping this very positing in the eyes of the others in the form of self-objectification. According to Kojève's interpretation of Hegel—an interpretation that markedly influenced Lacan's reading—man is self-consciousness. He desires to be recognized by others as something other than a thing. This recognition is not marked by an act of knowing but rather in an act of desire. We will examine the implication of this conception of desire later, but suffice it to say for the moment that the question of subjectivity is at the center of the structuralist conception of language. Just as things in the world must be mediated to us in a form of knowing, which is essentially linguistic, our conceptions of ourselves and others must equally be mediated in and through the linguistic expression of our subjectivity. We shall now return to Freud and his theory of parapraxes in light of Heidegger's conception of language.

As we have seen, Freud believed that slips of the tongue and other parapraxes (as well as dreams and symptoms) contain a hidden motivation. The application of free association in psychoanalysis should enable the analysand to trace his way back to an assumption—or knowledge—of this motivation. Freud was concerned with an origin, or cause (Freud uses these two concepts interchangeably), of the underlying impulses, such as unconscious impulses, which gave rise to the parapraxes in the first place.[42] Thus, the notion of a hidden truth which psychoanalysis allows us to reveal reigns supreme in Freud's conception of the analytic cure. According to Heidegger, too, the notion of a hidden truth bears equal weight in the plight of man's feelings of uneasiness over his existence, but, whereas Freud was concerned with repression in the unconscious regions of the mind, Heidegger studied the undisclosed truth which is hidden in language itself. As we shall see,

Heidegger's conception of language has had considerable influence on Lacan's reading of Freud, as well it should, since there is much to be gained by applying Heidegger's theories to the Freudian notion of the unconscious.

Like Aristotle, Heidegger viewed the function of discourse as that of letting something be "seen." In keeping with his lifelong interest in the phenomenological conception of language, Heidegger believed the connection between perception, language, and thought to be inextricably entwined. While the earlier portion of his career was devoted to studies pertaining to the nature of Being and thought, his researchers after 1950 were predominantly concerned with language, particularly with what he referred to as the relation between saying and showing. In his essay, "The Way to Language," Heidegger says that, *"The essential being of language is Saying as Showing.* Its showing character is not based on signs of any kind; rather all signs arise from a showing within whose realm and for whose purposes they can be signs."[43] Heidegger's main thesis in this essay, as in virtually everything he wrote on the nature of language, concerned the notion that to encounter language is not merely to master a habit or tool for communication, nor is it, strictly speaking, an effort to expand intellectual or cognitive abilities. Rather, it is concerned with what he calls undergoing experience with language: "When we talk of 'undergoing' an experience, we mean specifically that the experience is not of our own making; to undergo here means that we endure it, suffer it, receive it as it strikes us and submit to it. It is this something itself that comes about, comes to pass, happens."[44] The reference to experience was a theme that always occupied Heidegger's interest (earlier in his career he wrote a book on Hegel's conception of experience).

Even in Heidegger's conception of understanding, elaborated in his earlier work, *Being and Time,* he believed that it was necessary for the subject to participate in that which he wants to understand. The theme of submitting oneself to something, whether to language or to experience, is also a favorite of Heidegger. For example, we must *accept passively* that which we *want* to experience.[45] It is this theme of "submission to experience" which led to the more famous "Heideggerianisms" picked up by popular existentialism in the form of: Man is not born, but thrown into the world.

So what did Heidegger mean when he talked of an experience with language? He explained that to undergo an experience is to allow it to overwhelm and transform us by experiencing it. Thus, if we speak of receiving an interpretation, he means that we submit ourselves to it, experience it and undergo it. If so, that interpretation should strike us, move us. Then, perhaps, we will understand something differently than we did before. Of course, for Heidegger to understand something means to be transformed by it. There is no such thing as purely cognitive understanding. If we were to say that we understood something but that it did not make any difference, that it did not change anything, Heidegger would simply say that we did not hear it, even if we thought we did. Seen in this vein, accumulating information or know-how about language is not nearly the same as undergoing an experience with it; having someone explain to us what it is we are failing to understand about ourselves is not the same as seeing it for ourselves. So what does this mean in the case of parapraxes, when we forget a familiar name? According to Freud, we should try free association in order to allow the word or its associations to come to mind. In Heidegger's terms we simply submit to language by playing with language in order to allow the forgotten word to come into play so that we might expereience (remember) it. In our everyday use of language this does not ordinarily occur. J. M. Heaton compares the Freudian and Heideggerian conceptions of language to throw light on their respective views on the nature of parapraxes and to demonstrate how Freud's concept of free association is indeed quite similar to Heidegger's theory of language itself.

According to Heaton,

> When we use language to describe, order, calculate, express our feelings and all other everyday use we put it to, we are not submitting to language itself but are using it to deal with each other and things in the world. In these cases language itself has, so to speak, got to hold itself back in order that we may use it. But when we submit to an experience with language, langugage bares itself to us and so we may glimpse its essence.[46]

In other words, Heidegger's admonition of allowing ourselves the opportunity to undergo an experience with language is extraordinarily similar to what Freud characterizes in psychoanalysis as free association: "Thus we let language speak instead of using it to speak with and this experience may transform us and give us insight as shown by Freud in innumerable examples in *The Psychopathology of Everyday Life*."[47]

We can now begin to see the similarity between Lacan's view of the unconscious being "structured like a language" and Heidegger's notion that language is that dimension of our experience which reveals to us that which we have forgotten (repressed). Indeed, Heidegger's studies into the nature of language, from *Being and Time* to his most advanced formulations, emphasize the ways in which language both reveals and conceals that which is closest to us: ourselves. When Heidegger says that saying is showing, however, he is not referring to showing and seeing as a mere perceptual apprehension but as an experience with language itself. For Heidegger, to experience language and to see what it reveals are inseparable. In drawing our attention to this dimension of Heidegger's usage, Heaton explores this revelatory aspect of language:

> To speak to someone means to say something, show something to him and to entrust one another mutually to what is shown. In saying, everything present or absent announces, grants or refuses itself, shows itself or withdraws. In speaking which is saying, we listen to the language we speak and this listening is not a listening while but "before" we speak—we then speak thoughtfully. Speech which is not listened to says nothing and is thoughtless. So in speaking which is showing the speaker is present in his speaking with those to whom he speaks—he stands behind what he says, as we say colloquially.[48]

Freud required the suspension of our everyday casualness to the power that language contains from his analysands. He persuaded, cajoled, and reminded people again and again to listen to language when they had committed parapraxes. In order that they could carry out free association, it was crucial that they cease—if only for 50 minutes—going about their usual business in order to hear what language had to say and to see what it might show them. His interpretations were not intended to explain what they themselves could not see, but rather to show them the way to language itself, so they might see it for themselves. If there were indeed some thing to which their words referred, then bringing their attention to it would surely be enough in itself. What Freud wanted to show them was that the word itself would reveal to them the nature of the subject who spoke it.

If the termination of analysis involves the patient's discovery that only he possesses his own truth, it is because he is the truth he possesses, and this truth is the language he himself utters.

> The ordinary spoken discourse exchanged by two subjects has as its ideal norm what Chomsky calls "immediately comprehensible utterance" or "well-formed sentence." This norm implies that the speaking subject over-

sees the meaning of his utterance and understands it at the very moment
he profers it. Husserl turns this hypothetical norm into the model of the
subject's relation to discourse, arguing that speech is nothing more than
the act of making available to others a meaning that is already constituted
in the self, silently and without any necessary recourse to language.[49]

The passage by John Brinkman quoted above describes the problem
language poses as perceived by structuralists in their attack upon phenomenologists—led by Husserl—who, the structuralists claim, fail to
appreciate the autonomy of language as a system over and above the
autonomy of the human who merely utters his words. Structuralists
make a heavy attack against phenomenology—which is ultimately a
phenomenology of perception—for positing at the center of its program an investigation of experience, or man's immediate presence to
himself as well as to that which is other than himself. Structuralists
deny any such notion as presence because presence itself must be mediated through language via a network of signifiers which exist prior to
speaking and perceiving and, indeed, determine one's experience and
one's utterances. While phenomenology posits the primacy of consciousness (*cogito*), structuralism posits the primacy of the unconscious
(or its referent language). In turn, phenomenologists have generally
condemned structuralism for its thesis that man's subjectivity lies outside a specifically human dimension, but in a nebulous, abstract structure without a center.

As a result, phenomenological investigations of language have tended
to focus on the act of speech as uttered by man rather than on the
linguistic laws in which the speech act is embedded.[50] The question of
subjectivity and of the unconscious lies at the heart of this controversy.
Lacan, who was originally influenced by phenomenologists such as
Sartre, Heidegger, and Merleau-Ponty, later swore allegiance to the
structural linguistics of Saussure and Lévi-Strauss, claiming ascendency over the many phenomenologically oriented psychiatrists (Henry
Ey, Daniel Lagache, A. Hesnard, to name a few) of his day.

At first glance, the battle lines seem clearly drawn and the possibility
of reconciliation impossible. The structuralists perceive that the unconscious actually exists, not as an instinctual drive but rather in the
structures of society and language. It is not a question of a divided
subjectivity as envisioned by Freud between conscious and unconscious, ego and id, but of the illusion of a conscious subject subsumed
under the real subject—a decentered subject—located in language,

which in turn is conceived as a structure, for example, a subject without a center, without a heart. For their part, the phenomenologists conceive of the unconscious as a metaphor, a figure of speech, a confused term designating at least two entirely different concepts. First, the unconscious is used as a subject which is not to be mistaken for an ego or self but as a consciousness-of. This subject is not to be confused with the reflective act per se—the act which reveals the ego in its stead—but rather in the prereflective act which is conceived prior to self-revelation. This is indeed a hidden subject which lies at the heart of intentionality itself.

While the above formulation is not contained in Husserl's notion of a transcendental ego of the type that Brinkman referred to earlier, it has been posited by Sartre and Merleau-Ponty as the foundation for the phenomenological conception of the *cogito:* a consciousness without an ego. According to Ricouer, even Husserl ". . . recognized this negative side of the signifying relation; he called it 'suspension,' 'placing in brackets,' 'placing out of bounds,' and he applied it directly to the natural attitude in order to cause the *phenomenological* attitude to spring from it through differences. If he called the being (i.e., subject), born of this difference, *consciousness,* this difference was . . . required by the sign as such. But this consciousness offers no egological character; it is only a 'field,' the field of *cogitations.* Absolutely speaking, a *consciousness without an ego* is perfectly conceivable, and Sartre's well-known essay *The Transcendence of the Ego* has demonstrated this perfectly."[51] In other words, contrary to Lacan's attacks against phenomenology, the phenomenological concept of consciousness does not imply a philosophy centered in a personal ego, but rather in a prereflective consciousness of the world.

Second, the unconscious refers not to consciousness itself but rather to the world of objects which includes potential objects of consciousness (Freud's preconscious) as well as to those which are inaccessible to consciousness (the Freudian as well as the Lévi-Straussian unconscious—as well as others). The notion of a decentered subjectivity which resides on the periphery of the prereflective cogito is considered absurd by Merleau-Ponty.[52]

Lacan's position in this controversy is both confusing and somewhat evasive in that he is neither a structuralist in the sense of Lévi-Strauss nor a phenomenologist in the sense of Husserl. To say that language is a system of signs which is autonomous of the human *cogito* as in the

Saussurian scheme raises difficulties which Lacan himself recognized and attempted to correct. Wilden has pointed out that Saussure, who refused to posit a definitive reality to which signs refer, while at the same time erasing a human subject who bears the meaning of his discourse, ended up with a circular argument ultimately contained within itself, providing no way to establish a relation with either reality or a human subject. Saussure's structural theory, ". . . implies a circularity of meaning, a system of signification arbitrarily related to 'reality' and in fact only related to itself. It is this implied circularity and autonomy of language that leads Lacan into postulating a sort of fault in the system, a hole, a fundamental lack into which, one might say, meaning is *poured*."[53]

As we have seen, Lévi-Strauss's application of Saussurian linguistics to anthropology posits a decentered subject whose heart is in fact located in the laws and customs of social institutions. His unconscious is not a subject who desires so much as a subject who is an effect of the social and linguistic forces which surround him. According to Wilden,

> For Lévi-Strauss a structure is totally autonomous, a system of interchangeability permitted by a sort of internal free-play, but lacking the "center" or fixed point (the transcendental referent) implied in all the traditional notions of structure. . . . It is a sort of Newtonian universe without any God to wind it up, or better, a whole system of utterances without a speaking subject. This is precisely the same sort of paradox for which Saussure has been reproached by linguists: a system without a center is unthinkable, and the diacritical system of meaning has no center.[54]

Lacan obviously realized the problem Wilden refers to and the implication it must inevitably give rise to. The implication would be a social theory which ultimately sees man as a helpless, passive victim of social forces, powerless to change his situation without first altering the social forces themselves. This theory would dismiss out of hand the psychoanalytic concept of radical subjectivity which views man's malaise in the very belief that he mistakenly sees himself as a victim of external forces. In order to correct this possible death blow to the psychoanalytic enterprise, Lacan posits a center without a center inspired by Hegel's concept of a subject who is a no-thing, a subject who is constituted by his desire to be something, a desire which can never be satisfied.

Lacan's notion of a primordial "lack" is precisely the "lack of a fixed point" (the impossibility for desire to recover the lost object) toward which desire and consequently the metonymic movement of discourse is aimed. It is a lack providing for the absent center (the object) and is thus simply a reversal of the fixed point. Lacan's view does not seem to dispense with the transcendental referent presupposed in psychoanalysis: for him this referent is the lost object at the origins. *Presence becomes absence.*[55]

It is in this sense that Lacan posits a de-centered subject rather than in the Saussurian and Lévi-Straussian sense, since, for Lacan, the Hegelian dialectic of a consciousness (subject) who is ruled by his desire to become an object of consciousness for the other, but not enslaved by the other, and who in turn occupies an objectified position in respect to the desiring other, situates the human subject in a place that is neither an egotistical substance nor a mere effect of social forces.

Lacan's attack on phenomenology defines the latter as a humanism which posits a substantial subject who is potentially independent of what the other perceives him to be: "The Freudian discovery is that of a de-centering"; and, "The true center of the human being is no longer where a whole humanistic tradition has put it"; or, "Man is essentially an ex-centric being." But why does Lacan find it necessary to posit his incorporation of Saussurian linguistics into a Hegelian theory of desire in the name of an attack against the supposed humanism of phenomenology?

It is precisely to the humanism of phenomenology that Lacan turns to transcend Saussure's circularity, in order to "ground" his conception of subjectivity as profoundly human, though the definition of this humanism can more accurately be described as a theory of interhuman or cohuman subjectivity. It is this concept of subjectivity which Heidegger, Sartre, and Merleau-Ponty, each influenced by Hegel's dialectic of desire, attempt to delineate when they speak of a pre-reflective consciousness which is neither inner nor outer, but both. Lacan, who can hardly be regarded as a structuralist in the proper sense of the word, has proferred a conception of subjectivity and language which is a sort of synthesis of the phenomenology of Hegel, Heidegger, Merleau-Ponty, and the linguistics of Saussure and Jakobson, which in turn is integrated into Freudian psychoanalysis. An exemplary achievement, but one wonders why Lacan, who easily alienated himself from the international psychoanalytical community, chose to separate himself from a philosophical tradition that bore him the very concepts he needed to overcome the circularity of structuralism. It is true that phenomenologists have generally failed thus far to integrate the more useful discoveries of Saussure into the psychoanalytic enterprise.[56] (Ricouer described the problem in great detail.) But Lacan's indebtedness to phenomenology is so vast that one must conclude he divorced himself from it for political reasons. Enough said. It is time for us to move onto the place of desire and the meaning of the cure in psychoanalysis.

According to Heidegger, man is less a rational animal than a speaking animal. Thus, the Word occupies a central place in his philosophy. He defines Logos (commonly interpreted as "word" or "thought") as discourse, which means, "to make manifest what one is talking about *in* one's discourse."[57] What does the word Logos say to us? According to Heaton, "It has come to mean reason, thought, logic, saying, a discussion, an oracle or maxim, a fable, a story, calculation. Logos is connected with the word '*legein*.' This came to mean talk, say or tell, but more originally, nearer to Heraclitus' time, it meant to lay down, to lay in order, to arrange, to gather oneself, to lay asleep (one gathers oneself to fall asleep)."[58]

How did the notion of "to lay" come to mean saying, talking, and discourse? To lay is a gathering, as in gathering oneself to make a speech or to take a plunge: "But gathering is not a mere amassing, it is not jumbling a whole lot of things together higgledy piggledy. Gathering involves a selection, a sorting of that which has to be gathered. So laying and telling became associated in '*legein*' because the appropriate word lets things fall into place."[59]

Thus the process of selection and sorting can be likened to the metonymic and metaphoric structuring of language which allows proper words to emerge. But to what avail? Heidegger was struck by a saying of Heraclitus which he believed threw light on this question: "When you have listened, not to me but to the Law (Logos) it is wise to agree that all things are one."[60] Heaton takes this to mean that when you have truly listened, you will be in agreement and feel yourself to be at one with the situation. But Heraclitus emphasizes that it is the Logos to which one must listen and not the voice of the speaker himself. Thus being at one does not imply a strictly interpersonal nor an egocentric experience. But to what, then, does it refer? Heidegger stresses man's essential relationship to Being through the Word which discloses the

Truth. Our concern, however, is with the words which disclose the truth about ourselves. It is in turning to Hegel's dialectic of desire that we will find the answer.

Unlike Freud, who viewed desire as essentially sexual and biological, Hegel saw desire as essentially intersubjective. But the subject of desire is not an ego but rather a void at the heart of being. Since man is a conscious as well as a talking animal, it is not enough that we simply exist but that we discover who or what it is that we exist as. If we look for this answer within ourselves, all we see is a descriptive characterization of ourselves which we have appropriated from others: an ego or self-identity. What we seek from others is couched in ambivalence, since we want to make ourselves into something while at the same time we wish to escape the gaze of objectification which results when we are seen as someone or something. What I am beneath this objectification is a questioning, what Hegel—as explicated by Kojève—calls the desire for recognition. But it is a desire for recognition as what?

To the extent that others fashion me in the image of their demands and expectations, I establish an identity which I can accept or refuse, but I am not free to remain indifferent. It makes no difference whether the thing, or ego, that I am made into is attractive or repugnant, whether I promote it or resist it, the result is still the same in that my ego becomes a reference point from which I offer myself to others and to which the others are inclined when they address me. And how is it that this ego is formed? Through the words that are passed between us. This ego fixes me in a deterministic way which results in my assumption of two possible alternatives in response to my self-identity: I can either conform to its form, or I can rebel against it. There is no other option.

There is a problem, for even if I like my self and others like it too, Hegel believes that I still remain alienated from my fundamental desire, which is a desire to be recognized (not objectified) as someone other than myself. This cannot occur if the other, in seeing me, only concerns himself with surface appearances, initial impressions, his own preconceptions, and so on. He must look beyond his initial impressions in order to recognize me as my desire to be recognized by him. He can only do this through a questioning of who I am in reference to what I am not. What constitutes me as a subject of desire is *my* question. If I am only concerned with answers, then I will never recognize his desire because my answer will have fixed him in place, frozen in time; it will momentarily relieve me of my frustration at not knowing. However, my answer will be a lie, an illusion, and one which is bound to catch up with me as a consequence of my own misconceptions.

Thus Hegel conceives language to have but one purpose: to ask each other who we are; the function of language is to evoke and provoke, not to inform or conform. The words passed between us do not refer to who it is I really am but rather to what we make of each other. We have the choice of objectifying each other or exploring what we might reveal beneath what we conceal. Who I am beneath the appearances is necessarily ambiguous; to resist objectification we must allow for uncertainty and relativity in determining who we are in what we are not. Since I am not a thing to be identified, it is only in the context of my interaction with others that I will discover my desire to be recognized in my specifically human reality. But in order to discover the nature of my desire it is necessary that the other recognize it. Hegel believed that the anxiety of doubt behind this question is so great that men are willing to kill in order to resolve it.

In the master-slave dialectic Hegel presumed that the only way to resolve man's desire for recognition was for one person to submit to the other in order to escape death. Thus, on a purely interpersonal level, he could not conceive of a mutually beneficial resolution. Since I want the other to desire me and not merely enslave himself to me, even the victor turns out to be the loser. In the end no one wins. In Kojève's reading of Hegel, the master fell sway to a so-called "existential impasse." What he wanted was the recognition of an autonomous free agent who would recognize his desire as human, but what he ended up with was merely a servile, pathetic recognition of the slave.[61]

Psychoanalysis does not recognize this impasse as absolute or inevitable but rather as the impasse of neurotic man, an impasse which can be eliminated by the subject's surrender not of his desire but of his egoic fixations which are rooted in defense mechanisms. But to this we will turn later.

Though we might fail to do so explicitly, the words that pass between us imply names, not in a formal sense but in the implication that we know who it is we are addressing. We reveal what we think of one another in the way we address each other, by what we say and what we omit to say. I transform the other person each time I address him in that he becomes what I conceive him to be. It is in this sense that one may read Hegel's notion of the servitude to which each of us must submit in the simplest, seemingly innocent exchange with others. I cannot make the other recognize my desire nor can I stop him from objectifying me. Our words invest in the other a new reality, such as, "You are my salvation," or "You are a despicable creature." With every exchange the other becomes located within the calculus of my possible experience. Even if he ignores me, he can do so only in reference to my address; he still assumes a posture vis-à-vis me. In any case, his reality is transformed, whether insignificantly or dramatically, by the way I experience him for myself.

Thus, I am not what I think I am nor who others think I am. If I choose one or the other, I fall prey to a dualism which is neurosis, per se. Nor am I a combination of the two. This would lead to psychosis. I am neither one or the other, but rather the release from having to be one or the other that makes me specifically human and which evokes my unconscious desire to be liberated from this primal ambivalence. The symbolic function of language always makes me something other than what I appear to be, from a place other than where I seem to originate, along the "signifying chain" of my desire. Insofar as my discourse is the medium of desire, its realization must occur in a place excentric to my egoic identifications, which have no other purpose than to fix me in a false situation. If discourse can decentralize my ego from its place of privilege in my life, it can do so only by deepening my awareness of its place and of its function: in self-objectification.

What, then, is the subject if not an ego or a self? The subject is a subject of desire, not because the subject is located in the laws and customs of society, or in a language which is extrinsic to itself, but because the subject can never know itself, nor can it assume consciousness of itself for the reason that the subject is always a wanting which is directed toward anything but itself. When the subject does attempt to posit itself, it merely creates an illusion in the form of a lie which it calls itself. The subject is the "I" who speaks, but it can sometimes tell a lie when it posits itself, not as itself, but as an ego which takes its place. The "I" can never gain consciousness of itself but only of its desire to be other than itself.

But due to the paramount importance of discourse in the life of the subject and of the dialectical structure of desire, subjectivity is always an intersubjectivity. The other is not only the medium of my desire. The other *is* my desire. If I hide from my desire for the other's recognition, I can do so only by putting forward another *in my place,* an ego which the other is then bound to objectify because I have already objectified myself. This is why Lacan refers to the ego as originating from the realm of the imaginary, because we each enter into an imaginary discourse which serves no other purpose than to uphold an illusory conception of what it is we are doing with each other: the dichotomy between full (symbolic) and empty (imaginary) discourse. When my discourse is symbolic of my desire, I am at one with the Logos; but when my discourse is entrapped in the defiles of my ego, I am merely talking to myself or, to put it differently, from my self.

Heidegger says that when we speak in such a way that ignores the Logos, we merely talk about things but fail to talk *to* the things themselves. He refers to this way of talking as "gossip, passing the word along," idle talk. We become authorities about things we know nothing about in order to avoid true understanding: "That something has been said groundlessly amounts to perverting the act of disclosing (e.g., revelation) into an act of closing off (e.g., concealment). This closing-off is aggravated by the fact that an understanding of what is talked about is supposedly reached in idle talk. Because of this, idle talk discouraged any new inquiry and any disputation, and in a peculiar way suppresses them and holds them back."[62]

This statement by Heidegger is reminiscent of something Nietzsche once said, that "It is not doubt, but certainty, that leads to madness." In other words, Heidegger conceives of idle talk as a form of fixing our attention to things which deter us from the task at hand, to live the truth we discover about ourselves. There is certainly an element of idle speech when we speak to or from our egos, when we conceal our desires beneath a mask of generality and mystification. In avoiding the ambiguous nature of who we are, we cling to identifications instead, what Lacan calls the "imaginary," and for Neitzsche is certainty. This kind of self-certainty is nowhere more tellingly exemplified than in the paranoiac: the only one who knows for certain what is happening.

Yet, empty speech, as characterized by Heidegger, was intended to describe the common man. It was not intended to be disparaging in the sense of willfully engaging in lies or story telling: We do so automatically, unknowingly, unconsciously. But that does not make it any less effective. What does this say about psychopathology?

We know that language can both reveal and conceal. When we suspend our certitudes about ourselves and each other, we open a questioning of what we mean to one another. When we use language in this way, we engage in full speech. But when we use language to obstruct the emergence of full speech, by utilizing our egoic fixations and certitudes about who we and others are supposed to be, we conceal our desire from ourselves and from each other, so our speech is emptied. It does not say anything. The variations of empty speech characterize the variations of psychopathology.

In all forms of psychopathology, the subject undertakes to construct for himself a false self, an imaginary ego. Thus, everything he says is designed to evoke from others affirmation of his self. But given its illusory nature, the subject is rooted in anxiety for fear he will be discovered—not by another, but by himself. Now the subject who is not so enslaved in conformity to his ego is not any more certain of himself than, let us say, the neurotic is. But the difference between them is that the neurotic craves this certitude, to conform to the formations of his ego, to the achievement of himself as something substantial, secure, permanent. The uncertainty of life frightens him. He does not know himself but believes he must, or he does not know himself and cannot bear it, or he thinks he knows himself and is fooling himself. It is not a question of raising himself from unconsciousness to a consciousness of self, since the subject is unconsciousness itself: a primal lack. Nor is it a question of replacing a false self with a true self—but rather with overcoming the domination of his self (e.g., defenses, identifications, superego, etc.). Thus, he no longer *needs* to be something. Even if the subject were successful—as are many neurotic people—in putting his false self forward and having it recognized, he would become all the more alienated for having done so, as his malaise would be all the less obvious. It is not the lack of a true self, or a good self, or a strong ego which characterizes the various forms of psychopathology, but rather the state of alienation that ensues when we imagine ourselves to be selves at all.

The foundation for all forms of psychopathology, whether neurotic, psychotic, narcissistic, perverse, or otherwise, is essentially paranoiac. (I am something that I am not and am tormented, in its projected form, by it.) Or, it is narcissistic (I am captivated by and alienated within this persona I need to maintain). This conception of the ego, or self, was not developed by Lacan; it was proposed originally by Sartre.

It is worth noting that this theory was first put forward in 1936, during the heyday of Husserlian phenomenology, and that it was repeated and expanded in 1946, 1949, and 1951, during the heyday of Sartrian existentialism. One recalls the importance of the *regard de l'autre* in the early Sartre . . . Lacan's view of the *moi* as an alienated self makes an interesting commentary on the early Sartre's conception of the ego as transcendent and not interior to consciousness, that is, as something we are conscious *of*. Lacan's *moi* corresponds to the internalization of the other through identification; we are conscious of this self, but unconscious of its origins. Lacan shows the dual relationship between *moi* and other as a dual relationship of objectification (and inevitably, of aggressivity) along the lines of Sartre's analysis of our sadomasochistic relationship to the other who is an object for us, or for whom we make ourselves an object. The *moi* is thus another, an *alter* ego.[63]

When Lacan says that, "The subject begins analysis by talking of himself without talking to you or by talking to you without talking of himself," and that, "when he will be able to talk to you of himself, the analysis will be terminated," he is merely alluding, in his peculiarly elusive way, to the fact that the neurotic is always talking about himself (his ego) *as though* it were himself (his desire), but to no one in particular because his aim is to persuade the analyst (projected father, mother, or even himself) that he really is this alienated self that, of course, he is not. When he has finally discovered that there is an otherness within which is the figment of imagination par excellence, and is able to reveal to the analyst (as analyst and not as maternal benefactor) the vastness and wonder of his discovery, he will be cured of his captivation. But what does this captivation entail in terms of neurotic and psychotic structures?

The neurotic is essentially frustrated in a repressed desire for recognition which has become transformed into a need, or a demand, to be what he is not. He is unable to accept that he is what he is not: a lack at the heart of being. He wants to be recognized, but, because he wants his desire to be fulfilled, he tries to enslave the other to become his slave, or he gives up and becomes a slave to himself. In the view of Fredric Jameson in his *The Prison-House of Language,* "Neurosis becomes a movement of repression which fails to recognize itself, and which attempts to stem the flight from one signifier to another by fixating on a single one, by choosing for itself in one form or another a transcendental signifier, or a God."[64] This tendency of the neurotic to gain control by trying to become the omnipotent master by virtue of his inability to surrender himself to the signifiers of his uncontrollable desire is most clearly exemplified in the obsessional, though the same dilemma is more frantically expressed in the hysterical attempt to turn over control to another, who, in turn, must be resisted, and eventually discredited, in order to free himself of the other's control.

The neurotic's relationship to the other is a reminiscence of the original master-slave battle for recognition with his mother, which he lost, in the Oedipal conflict. These wounds, and the scars which cover them over, emerge later in the form of neurotic symptoms. As before, such symptoms are signifiers for the wounds which occasioned his desire for recognition, and which become signified in his loss. The neurotic is always inhibited in his desire for recognition because the other (in the form of his mother) must first approve of the form his desire is to take before it can be lived. He is essentially a conformist. In giving himself over to his imaginary ego (which is the slave to the mother's mastering of his desire) his symbolic relation to others can express only and whatever that which will maintain his subjectivity in the form of the original dialectic, which was lost. The fact that the neurotic subject is striving to maintain such a master-slave relation with others is necessarily not among the things he is free to express, since to admit consciously that he is working to keep up this kind of (imaginary) relationship would require him to accept that he is not the self he wishes to project. This projection, in all its three forms of the project of his labor, the image of himself he wishes to project, the images of his mother which he unconsciously projects onto others, conceals from him the truth that he is not the self he strives to project, which would set him free. It is this truth which is signified in relation to the patient's symptoms as signifiers. In other words, it is the results of the original master-slave struggle with his mother which is projected onto his material reality, barring the symbolic emergence of his desire—not to dominate—but to desire for the sake of desiring itself.

Hegel viewed the compulsion to dominate or submit as a disease, and it is the chronic ambivalence between the two poles which characterizes neurosis, per se. The cure consists neither in learning how to dominate nor in accepting one's servitude—the pole between satisfying one's desire, on the one hand (in effect, "killing" it), or denying one's desire, on the other. Rather, it involves accepting the reality of one's desire: an unquenchable regard for an elusive recognition, the very emergence of which is its own reward. The Oedipal knot is resolved when the subject stops trying to please the mother who dominated his desire and stops trying to become the father whom he believes to be the master of desire, but instead arrives at the truth that no one owns or controls his desire—not even himself—that, in fact, his desire is to be discovered in the logic of its movements, in the dialectical search for its realization.

Psychosis is another matter, since the psychotic is not embroiled in the frustrated emergence of his desire. He has given up altogether the desire to be recognized and has completely surrendered himself to the imaginery ego which has mastered his desire. Indeed, one can speak of a sort of merger between the psychotic as subject and as ego. He wants to be the slave who lost the master-slave dialectic and maintains in his style and his vocation the fate he has accepted; the helpless nonagent in society. Having failed to maintain his destiny as his mother's child, he has, in effect, become society's child, in all of the infinite forms and variations. But the psychotic is also a contradiction, since the child he needs to maintain in himself is often a rebellious child, an angry child, in the words of Scheler, a resentful child, who has had to pass through the most incredible forms of rationalization and mutilation in order to ordain himself in his crippling position. His words are, ". . . simply a waiting out of all possible variations of a given paradigm."[65] It is a conglomeration of every possible explanation he has heard, hated, accepted, rebelled against, parodied, and appropriated in the name of his utterly defeated—and defeating—position. He makes the perpetrators of his condition pay for their crime by holding up his mutilated form for everyone to see. In his infinite servitude, he is anything but a conformist. Having nothing left to lose, he removes himself from the social order and refuses society its demand to remedy their discomfort in the face of his spectacle. By sacrificing his desire, he makes them pay with their failure to bring him into being.

The neurotic and psychotic share one thing in common: their failure as a result of adhering to the normative alternative of conformity fashioned by the blind delusion which denies the very condition they lose themselves in. The alienation of the normal man takes flight not in a past which has captivated his desire, nor in a future salvation that will never come into being, but in the everyday milieu of contemporary discourse which serves to mirror what he himself has become. In the glory of his own alienation, he denys that there is anything the matter. What is most insidious about this person is that he often poses as normal. Indeed, this is what he is because he is the norm of the empty aspiration so commonly conveyed in the media, magazines, television, and every conceivable form of regressive and vicarious experience. He has so perfectly conformed to the image of what everyone commonly adores and admires that he shines in the glow of his superficial success, the banality of being well thought of, in a word, popular. Having enslaved himself to the admiration of all those fools who do not know any better—and who would not dare tell him if they did—he is free to gossip and belittle everyone outside of his immediate self-interest; and the more anonymous they are, the better! This is the sort of man who cries out at or is outraged by the latest news report of the latest atrocity to mankind, but who cannot recognize the atrocities which are occurring beneath his very nose—often at his own hand. His words, as Heidegger says, are merely passed along, but they say nothing. He merely repeats what he has heard but never thinks a thought of his own. This normal man is in a hopeless state, since, as far as we know, there is no cure for normality.

So what of the cure in psychoanalysis? As we have seen, the neurotic remains captivated by the Oedipal experience, in the words of Jameson: "The experience of the mother as one of an initial plenitude from which the infant is brusquely severed. Thus the separation from the mother results in a kind of primal lack, a gaping, and it is this traumatic experience which is customarily felt (by both boys and girls) as a castration."[66] Learning to use language itself represents an opening into a desire for the absent other, precisely the opposite of a plenitude, an incompleteness which is never filled but rather experienced and in turn submitted to in order to discover one's desire elsewhere, in its most humbling—and humble—configuration. Thus, neurosis, ". . . is essentially a failure to accept castration, a failure to accept the primal lack which is at the center of life itself: a vain and impossible nostalgia for that first essential plenitude."[67] In other words, neurosis is a perpetual demand that this plenitude can indeed be reestablished. Genuine desire is an acceptance of incompleteness, whereas neurosis is a vain attempt to keep the delusion of ultimate satisfaction alive, an attempt to achieve ultimate certainty. The neurotic remains enslaved to the signified of his satisfaction, while denying the signifiers of his desire. It is to this absent signified that the neurotic addresses his discourse in the many forms of his egoically driven fixations. When he addresses the psychoanalyst, he appears to be talking about someone (his ego) who, even if he were to become it, could never become one with his desire. It is his vain attempt to persuade the analyst to authenticate this alienated self that constitutes the lure of his hoped-for cure.

The analysis of the neurotic consists in the telling of his history: his misfortunes, failed aspirations, traumas both remembered and repressed, explanations, rationalizations, and disappointments, none of which convey a history necessarily experienced so much as one noted, remembered, and understood according to a particular logic which is his and his alone. Through words, analysis links the neurotic's discourse, rooted in a logic of this history (real or imagined), to his present predicament—his castration. Based on this logic, we will see where it is intended to take him. Once the internal consistency of this logic is revealed, the patient must accept it or give it up. This is why psychoanalysis is not concerned with what really happened in reality but rather with the specific ordering of reality which the neurotic has himself assumed. The cure lies not in overcoming the traumas of his past, but in recognizing the contradictions and inconsistencies within this particular logic, his logic, which, once unveiled, he must see as his own. Thus, the cure lies in revealing the significations that have rendered him impotent to his desire, which will be conveyed in the metaphors and metonymies which order the reality he experiences. What is at stake is his being made aware that this logic has created the egoic identifications which perpetuated his castrated position. The distinction between the true subject of desire—the "I"—and the ego—that which conceals the "I"—is crucial to the psychoanalytic enterprise. The object, then, of psychoanalysis is the recognition by the analysand of himself as a true subjectivity who, in effect, orders his own experience of reality and no longer as a victim of objectifications which, as we have seen, is the personification of his own ego. The ultimate termination of the analysis is made when the patient discovers that only he himself—and not his ego—possesses his own truth. Since psychoanalysis rests on recognizing the imaginary character of the ego in order to free the subject toward his desire, it is crucial that the analyst himself be capable of performing this distinction instead of collaborating with the patient's misapprehension.

The neurotic is consumed with fantasies and memories which keep his servitude alive. Until they are put into words, so that their logical structure can be unveiled, they command his current attitudes and behavior. By bringing these relationships into the flesh of speech, they are revealed for what they are, and the source of these commands, prohibitions, rationalizations, and misunderstandings are seen to be none other than that internal dialogue which has perpetuated them, in the form of his egoic aspirations (for omnipotent satisfaction) and superegoic prohibitions ("Be what we tell you to be.") in the dead voice of his parents, which turn out to be none other than himself.

In order to be rescued from his hopeless situation, the patient strives to have his expectations substantiated by the analyst to rationalize his helplessness to do anything about it. Having lost the master-slave conflict with his mother, he now repeats this conflict—and its outcome—after the mother is no longer there, projecting her position onto the analyst who now becomes the authority who can release the patient from servitude by satisfying his omnipotent demands. His egoic identifications are structured in precisely that fashion which compels him to maintain the helpless position he experiences himself to be in. By the analyst's refusal to acknowledge this image the patient has of himself, he must eventually abandon this position and rediscover his desire that had been surrendered at the Oedipal crisis.

But how does the analyst avoid repeating the same objectifying relationship that the patient experienced with his mother? He can do so, in part, because he is himself liberated while the mother was not. The mother needed her child to remain under her domination, and succeeded by suggesting she could satisfy his (or her) desire. Herself bereft of recognition, she projected her own neurotic aspirations onto her child, thus prohibiting the child's emergence into the laws and the dialectic of desire. It is not the father, per se, that the child turns to in order to resolve his Oedipal dilemma, but to the social ordering of unsatisfiable desire which the father represents. The father is merely symbolic of the world the child turns to once the way to satisfaction is barred. This is why the analyst cannot—and must not attempt to—satisfy the analysand's desire where others have failed (such as in "friendly" or sexual caresses). He must merely serve to introduce the analysand to the nature of desire itself in all its ambiguity. While the mother had needs of her own in attempting to prohibit the child's emancipation, the analyst has no such need. So long as this principle is assumed, and maintained, throughout the analytic experience, what is actually said is of no crucial importance.

Of course, if the analyst believes he has recourse to a reality which his charge is lacking, his interpretations will allude to the expediency of adapting to something he himself is lacking. The scandal of Kleinian and other interpretive paradigms which couch their interpretive structures in inviolable signifieds—breasts and penises or whatever—is that they serve to inhibit the analysand's assumption of the logic of his own reality; a reality which, in its primordial presence, silently orchestrates the laws of his mental behavior. It is the emergence of his truth—not that of society—that will guide his eventual emancipation.

Returning to Heidegger, the analyst has the privilege of remaining silent most of the time because he assumes that symbolic position which disillusions the patient of his neurotic fantasies, and by disappointing him in his expectations of achieving such things as fulfillment and self-satisfaction, by disengaging him of his demands that someone else relieve him of his chronic experience of helplessness and futility, in a word, of his experience of alienation. Further, in his reticence to talk, the analyst avoids the kind of idle chatter that serves to obstruct the emergence of the patient's own understanding of his truth. This truth is unconscious not because it is a thing to be made conscious, or a signified that defies signification, but because this truth is an unformulated way of knowing which is already in place and operating according to the dialectic of his desire between a subject who defies objectification and an ego which serves to protect him from this very fate—and whose achievement is at the heart of his folly.

Similarly, words serve the cure in psychoanalysis, but not because they are chained to a signified which defies comprehension. We neither master the word, which is the neurotic's demand, nor do we enslave ourselves to it, which is implied in the structuralist argument. Rather, words can lead to a cure because it is in the listening to words that we discover this unformulated way of knowing which is ourselves. It is in this sense that we might say the subject has a history which indicates a destiny whose path can never be made fully conscious (in the sense of direct apprehension), but can only be witnessed in the effects of its insistent creations, in the form of dreams, slips, errors, feelings, in short, in the formations of existence itself. It is in his tending to the utterances of this discourse that the analyst discovers the only tool he has, which is why it is necessary that he be capable of hearing it, in order that his patient hear it also. In his respectful silence toward the other's speech, the analyst assumes the position of interlocutor who merely punctuates the voice of the Logos in the signifier of the other's desire.

As a consequence, what the analyst does say assumes tremendous importance, increasing the attentiveness of the analysand toward the words of the Other and, in turn, to the words he himself utters. As the analysand engages in this activity—the result of which can be anything but what he might expect—he will encounter frustration at the hands of his recognition that his ego, which he had previously assumed to lie at the foundation of his subjectivity, is in fact an other within himself, another he talks to and maintains, that he keeps alive at the expense of his own death, in short, an imaginary construct. The effect is both dazzling and scary. He becomes disoriented and unsure of himself. He reacts in two ways. First, he becomes upset, perhaps petulant and angry, or cynical and obstinate, he feels his life is a waste and that nothing or no one can save him, or that the analyst merely refuses to save him. This is the heart of the negative transference where the analysand will attempt every ploy in his power to seduce or blackmail the analyst into doing something—anything—to help him. Second, as his ego slowly disintegrates and his defenses become all the more ineffectual, he becomes increasingly dependent and more awkward in his day-to-day affairs. This decomposition of the ego has been traditionally described as regression, and sometimes it alarms those analysts who conceive the cure in terms of ego strength and facility. This transitional phase must be allowed to find its own resolution if the analysand is ever to give up the remnants of his demand for some intervention by the good Doctor.

It is at this point that the analyst, above all, must avoid any temptation at seduction. This is not easy and the risks are tremendous if he is at all unsure of his task. It is at this point, perhaps more than any other, that the analysand is likely to attempt an amorous seduction or, alternately, threaten suicide or premature termination. If the analyst leaps to the rescue, all is lost. He may have saved his analysand from even an imaginary leap into the void, but his emergence into desire will most likely have been forfeited forever.

This tact will, perhaps, appear a bit strange—even brutal—to those analysts couched in ego psychology, or who adhere to the medical tradition of having as its project the saving of lives. This bias has no province in the psychoanalysis and liberation of desire. First of all, the aim of analysis is not to save lives. This is, perhaps, the province of the priesthood or the surgeon, or the Good Samaritan, but this purpose has little, if any, relevance to the production and elimination of neurotic, or even psychotic, phenomena. Second, the aim of analysis is not to relieve suffering, but rather the relief of alienation and its crippling consequence: impotence and castration, male or female. If our goal were to relieve pain or suffering, we would be more effective in doing so by prescribing pills which the physician is only too ready to provide. The goal of analysis is rather to bear the pain and suffering which naturally occasions the assumption of knowledge that our lives are ours to live in the dialectic of our aspirations and limitations. This is not a simple matter to resolve. Indeed, it defies resolution since there is one form of suffering in psychopathology, and another in life itself. We can only say that the kind of suffering that is the consequence of desiring is far preferable to that which occasions the death of desire itself.

Further, any attempt to strengthen the ego, or self, of the analysand, which is so popular in current ideology, is doomed to perpetuate the analysand in the endless alienation of his desire. An inevitable consequence of this view is the so-called "analysis of resistances" so common in current practice which, at best, is a waste of time and, at worst, encourages the analysand to reform his ego into something that is presumably modeled on the aspirations of the analyst himself. And to whom does the analyst address himself in such interpretations other than that self who craves such guidance? If the analyst directs his analysand at all, it is surely in the assumption of his own truth rather than the reality of another.

In the end, the analysand will never be able to put his desire into words but will only come to its realization through words. That is to say he will be freed of his self-absorption when he recognizes that it is the desire of the other which holds the key to the emergence of his own desire. While he previously believed that his salvation lay in becoming someone who would be more acceptable to others, he comes to realize that it is his interest—and questioning—of others which reveals to him the assumption, and recognition, of his desire as a subject who is not to be localized in this signified or that, but rather in the context between one subjectivity and another which, together, undertake to resist the lures of objectification. His desire is not contained in satisfying himself or filling himself up but rather in assuming his role in the social dimension, a dimension which is already there, and yet a dimension which is, in the form of tropes, his own construction. The history to which the analysand is constantly referred is not so much a history objectifiably experienced, as much as a history lived according to the solutions which previously occasioned the implications he himself derived from it. That is, it is a future which is a barrier to his desire. Analysis is a collaboration between analysand and analyst wherein this history is told, interpreted, and revised according to a possible future which the analysand himself is prepared to undertake. His future is thus a future he either chooses, takes up, and *assumes* as emancipatory in the face of life's ambiguous possibilities. Or, it is a future in which he is resigned to his fate: the seal of his servitude to a history which remains the closure of his desire which is death itself.

Finally, the goal of psychoanalysis is not to facilitate getting along with others—the nightmare of a narcissistic conformity which perpetuates the prophecy of life's endless disappointments. Rather, it involves bringing about the discovery in others of their questioning what he himself is comprised of. This is not to say that the privilege of the analyst lies in changing the course of a destiny which for the patient has yet to be determined, but rather in preparing the patient for a destiny which is there for him to assume. To the extent that he is successful in erasing the captivation of his egoic personality which, after all, is his own creation, he will no longer remain obsessed with fulfilling desires as in realizing them, since the point of life is not to fill things up, but rather to make it more real. Having abandoned all claims to omnipotence and the suspicions to which it gives rise, he will have become a far less frightened person while, paradoxically, open to ever greater dangers.

Notes

[Note: All references to Freud refer to *The Standard Edition of the Complete Psychological Works of Sigmund Freud* (J. Strachey, ed. and trans.). 24 volumes. London: Hogarth Press, 1953–73. Hereafter referred to as "Standard Edition".]

CHAPTER 1: THE IDOLATRY OF THE EGO

1. Turkle, S. (1978). *Psychoanalytic politics: Freud's French revolution*. New York: Basic Books, p. 7.
2. Ibid., p. 29.
3. Ibid., pp. 30–31.
4. Freud, S. *Project for a scientific psychology. Standard Edition,* Vol. 1.
5. Freud, S. *Standard Edition,* Vol. 20., p. 196.
6. Freud, S. *The question of lay analysis, Standard Edition,* Vol. 20.
7. Freud, S. *The ego and the id, Standard Edition,* Vol. 19, p. 26.
8. Ibid., p. 26.
9. Loewald, H. (1980). *Papers on psychoanalysis*. New Haven: Yale University Press, p. 6.
10. Mannoni, O. (1971). *Freud*. New York: Pantheon, p. 184.
11. Hartmann, H. (1964). *Ego psychology and the problem of adaptation*. New York: International Universities Press, p. 28.
12. Ibid., p. 23.
13. Ibid., p. 23.
14. Ibid., p. 27.
15. Ibid.
16. Ibid., p. 6.
17. Rapaport, D. (1958). A historical survey of psychoanalytic ego psychology. *Collected papers.* p. 749.
18. Ibid., p. 749.
19. Ibid., p. 749.
20. Hartmann, H. (1950). Comments on the psychoanalytic theory of the ego. *Psychoanalytic Study of the Child, 10,* pp. 9–29.
21. J. Laplanche and J.-B. Pontalis, (1973). *The language of psychoanalysis.* New York: Norton, pp. 131–132.

22. Lacan, J. (1977). The mirror stage as formative of the I as revealed in psychoanalytic experience. *Ecrits—A selection*. New York: Norton, pp. 1–7.

23. Frings, M. (1978). Husserl and Scheler: Two views on intersubjectivity. *Journal of the British Society for Phenomenology, 9*(3), pp. 143–149.

24. Ibid., pp. 143–149.

25. Scheler, M. (1923). *The nature of sympathy.* London: Routledge & Kegan Paul.

26. Lacan, J. The mirror stage as formative of the "I" as revealed in psychoanalytic experience. *Ecrits—A selection*. Op. cit., pp. 1–7.

27. Winnicott, D. W. (1971). *Playing and reality.* London: Tavistock, pp. 111–118.

28. Muller, J., and Richardson, W. (1982). *Lacan and language—A reader's guide to* Ecrits. New York: International Universities Press, p. 30.

29. Ibid., pp. 31–32.

30. Lacan, J. The mirror stage. . . . Op. cit., p. 2.

31. Melanie Klein also suggests that the suckling infant experences his mother's breast to be a part of himself.

32. Lacan, J. Aggressivity in psychoanalysis. *Ecrits—A selection*. Op. cit., pp. 8–29.

33. Ibid., p. 24.

34. Ibid., p. 22.

35. Ibid., p. 23.

36. Ibid., p. 23.

37. Sartre, J.-P. (1957). *The transcendence of the ego.* New York: Noonday Press, p. 31.

38. Kojève, A. (1969). *Introduction to the reading of Hegel.* New York: Basic Books.

CHAPTER 2: THE PRIMORDIAL SUBJECT OF UNCONSCIOUS DESIRE:
A RECONNAISSANCE OF THE UNCONSCIOUS

1. Ricouer, P. (1970). *Freud and philosophy.* New Haven: Yale University Press.

2. Freud, S. (1915d). *Repression, Standard Edition,* Vol. 14, p. 147.

3. Sartre, J.-P. (1956). *Being and nothingness.* New York: Philosophical Library, pp. 47–54.

4. Sartre, J.-P. (1957). *The transcendence of the ego.* New York: Noonday Press, pp. 48–49.

5. Ibid., pp. 48–49.

6. Ibid., p. 59.

7. Kojève, A. (1969). *Introduction to the reading of Hegel.* New York: Basic Books, pp. 3–30.

8. Sartre, J.-P. *The transcendence of the ego.* Op. cit., pp. 93–94.

9. Jameson, F. (1972). *The prison-house of language.* Princeton: Princeton University Press, pp. 137–138.

10. Merleau-Ponty, M. (1962). *Phenomenology of perception.* London: Routledge & Kegan Paul, pp. 380–381.

CHAPTER 3: THE LOST OBJECT OF DESIRE

1. Lacan, J. (1977). The function and field of speech and language in psycho-analysis. *Ecrits—A selection.* New York: Norton, pp. 30–113.

2. Klein, M., and Riviere, J. (1964). *Love, hate and reparation.* New York: Norton, pp. 58–62.

3. Ibid., pp. 58–62.

4. Lacan, J. The mirror stage as formative of the function of the "I" as revealed in psychoanalytic experience. *Ecrits—A selection.* Op. cit. pp. 1–7.

5. Merleau-Ponty, M. (1964). The child's relations with others. *The primacy of perception.* Evanston, Ill.: Northwestern University Press, pp. 127–129.

6. S. Schneiderman (ed.) (1980). *Returning to Freud.* New Haven: Yale University Press, pp. 1–8.

7. Leclaire, S. (1959). Philo, or the obsessional and his desire, in S. Schneiderman (ed.), *Returning to Freud.* Op. cit., p. 117.

8. As reported to Leclaire by a patient. Ibid., p. 123.

9. Ibid., p. 124.

10. Kernberg, O. (1975). *Borderline conditions and pathological narcissism.* New York: Aronson, p. 232.

11. Sullivan, H. S. (1973). *Clinical studies in psychiatry.* New York: Norton, pp. 363–364.

12. Hegel, G. (1967). *The phenomenology of the mind.* New York: Harper & Row, pp. 217–227; Hyppolite, J. (1974). *Genesis and structure of Hegel's phenomenology of spirit.* Evanston, Ill.: Northwestern University Press, pp. 156–171.

13. Ibid., Hegel, pp. 217–227; Hyppolite, pp. 156–171.

14. Lacan, J. (1977). The function and field of speech and language in psychoanalysis. *Ecrits—A selection.* Op. cit., pp. 30–113.

CHAPTER 4: THE SUBVERSION OF DESIRE IN THE
APPREHENSION OF THE OTHER

1. Sartre, J.-P. (1962). *Sketch for a theory of the emotions.* London: Methuen, p. 63.

2. Ibid., p. 65.

3. Ibid., pp. 65–66.

4. Scheler prefers the French term *ressentiment,* borrowed and considerably expanded from Nietzsche's concept of the term. *Ressentiment* refers to the heart of the resentful tendency in psychopathological behavior and is used in contrast to everyday usage of the term which conveys no particular pathological tendency.

5. Scheler, M. (1972). *Ressentiment.* New York: Schocken Books.

6. Ibid., p. 47.

7. Riviere, J. (1964). Hate, greed and aggression, in M. Klein and J. Riviere, *Love, hate and reparation.* New York: Norton, p. 21.

8. Scheler, M. Op. cit., p. 52.

9. Klein, M., and Riviere, J. Op. cit., pp. 26–27.

10. Due, no doubt, to the Kleinian preoccupation with so-called "innately determined dynamics" of the child's relations with others (other part objects rather than with other subjects).

11. Klein, M., and Riviere, J. Op. cit., pp. 27–28.

12. Scheler, M. Op. cit., p. 47.

13. Ibid., pp. 48–49.

14. In this regard, the term "self-esteem" would refer to that situation we might characterize as the "loss of the other."

15. Ego psychologists include Anna Freud and Heinz Hartmann, and, many in the American school of ego psychology.

16. Scheler, M. Op. cit., p. 58.

17. "The ressentiment experience is always characterized by this 'transparent' presence of the true objective values behind the illusory ones—by that obscure awareness that one lives in a *sham world* which one is unable to penetrate." Scheler, M. Op. cit., p. 60.

18. Ibid., p. 74.

19. Sartre, J.-P. Op. cit., p. 71.

20. Ibid., p. 72.

21. Ibid., p. 73.

22. Klein, M. (1981). *Love, guilt and reparation and other works*. London: Hogarth, pp. 306–343.

23. In other words, the patient expects the therapist to bolster his ego, to confirm that he is all right as he is. That is to say, the therapist is to collude with him in his own avoidance of his Truth.

24. Lacan, J. (1977). Aggressivity in psychoanalysis. *Ecrits—A selection*. New York: Norton, pp. 8–25.

25. Ibid., p. 13.

26. "For in this labor which he undertakes to reconstruct *for another,* he rediscovers the fundamental alienation that made him reconstruct it *like another,* and which has always destined it to be taken from him *by another.*" Lacan, J. The function and field of speech and language in psychoanalysis. *Ecrits—A selection*. Op. cit., p. 42.

27. Lacan, J. Aggressivity in psychoanalysis. *Ecrits—A selection*. Op. cit., p. 23.

28. Evans, M. (1953). Introduction to Lacan's "The Neurotic's Individual Myth." *The Psychoanalytic Quarterly,* vol. 4 1979. p. 399.

CHAPTER 5: ONCE REMOVED TO THE SECOND POWER: PSYCHOSIS

1. Apologists such as Britain's Harry Guntrip and Charles Rycroft go to great lengths to suggest that virtually every original idea that has occurred in this century is implied in Freud's work. That one can read Freud as a humanist or mechanist, phenomenologist or positivist all at the same time is an issue of debate within psychoanalytic circles. Rycroft, C. (1966). *Psychoanalysis observed.* London: Constable;Guntrip, H. (1971). *Psychoanalytic theory, therapy and the self.* New York: Basic Books.

2. French intellectuals generally, whether of a structuralist, phenomenological or Marxist persuasion, have tended to regard Freud's ego as a foil to consciousness, rather than the reverse.

3. Heaton, J. M. (1979). Theory in psychotherapy, in N. Bolton (ed.), *Philosophical problems in psychology*. London: Methuen.

4. Laing, R. D. (1965). Mystification, confusion, and conflict in I. Boszormenyi-Nagy and J. Framo (eds.), *Intensive family therapy*, New York: Harper & Row.

5. Ibid., p. 344.

6. Ibid., pp. 344–345.

7. Ibid., pp. 347–349.

8. Freud, S. (1924). *Neurosis and psychosis, Standard Edition*, Vol. 19, p. 149.

9. Macalpine, I., and Hunter, R. A. Trans. (1955). *Memoirs of my nervous illness*, by D. P. Schreber. London: Dawson and Sons.

10. Freud, S. Psychoanalytic notes on an autobiographical account of a case of paranoia (Dementia Paranoides), *Standard Edition*, Vol. 12, pp. 62–63.

11. Schatzman, M. (1973). *Soul murder, persecution in the family*. London: Avon.

12. Macalpine, I., and Hunter, R. A. Op. cit., pp. 145–146.

13. Schreber, D. G. M. (1852). *Die Eigentumlichkeiten des Kindlichen Organismus (The characteristics of the child's organism)*. Leipzig: Fleischer, p. 40.

14. Macalpine, I., and Hunter, R. A. Op. cit., p. 139.

15. Schreber, D. G. M. (1858). Kallipädie oder Erziehung zur Schonheit durch Naturgetreue und Gleichmassige Förderung Normaler Körperbiklung (*Education towards beauty by natural and balanced furtherance of normal body growth*) as reported by Schatzman, M. (1971, June). Paranoia or persecution: The case of Schreber. *Family Process, 10*(2), p. 182.

16. Ibid., p. 184.

17. Ibid., p. 184.

18. Ibid., p. 188.

19. Schreber, D. G. M. Die Eigentumlichkeiten . . . Op. cit., p. 60.

20. Schreber, D. G. M. *Education towards beauty*. . . . Op. cit., p. 192.

21. Ibid., p. 192.

22. Ibid., p. 192.

23. Ibid., p. 197.

24. Schatzmann, M. Paranoia or persecution: The case of Schreber. Op. cit., p. 188.

25. Will, O. A., Jr. (1971, June). Commentary on Schatzmann's article in *Family Process, 10*(2), p. 209.

26. Waelhens, A., de (1978). *Schizophrenia*. Pittsburgh: Duquesne University Press.

27. Ibid., p. 137.

28. Ibid., p. 137.

29. Ibid., pp. 19–20.

30. Ibid., p. 138.

31. Ibid., p. 138.

32. Ibid., p. 22.
33. Ibid., p. 22.
34. Ibid., pp. 132–133.
35. Mannoni, M. (1970). *The child, his "illness," and the others.* New York: Random House, pp. 3–4.
36. Laing, R. D. (1969). *Self and others* (2nd ed.). New York: Pantheon Books, pp. 72–78.
37. Ibid., p. 77.
38. Mannoni, M. Op. cit., p. 13.
39. Ibid., p. 13.
40. Ibid., pp. 27–30.
41. Freud, S. *Analysis of a phobia in a five year-old boy, Standard Edition,* Vol. 10.
42. Mannoni, M. Op. cit., p. 28.
43. Ibid., p. 16.

CHAPTER 6: THE TEMPORALITY OF THE SUBJECT

1. Heidegger, M. (1952). *Being and time.* London: Basil Blackwell.
2. Sartre, J.-P. (1956). *Being and nothingness.* New York: Philosophical Library, pp. 107–129.
3. Hamilton, W. (ed.). (1940). *Works of Thomas Reid.* London: Routledge & Kegan Paul. Vol. 1., p. 348.
4. Ibid., p. 348.
5. Ibid., p. 348.
6. Husserl, Heidegger, Sartre, Merleau-Ponty have made such studies, to name only a few.
7. Merleau-Ponty, M. (1962). *Phenomenology of perception.* London: Routledge & Kegan Paul, pp. 410–443.
8. Ibid., p. 411.
9. Ibid., pp. 411–414.
10. Ibid., p. 412.
11. Ibid., p. 413.
12. Bergson, H. (1910). *Time and free will.* New York: Humanities Press, pp. 117–139.
13. Merleau-Ponty, M. Op. cit., p. 413.
14. Ibid., p. 415.
15. See Sartre's discussion of Proust in *Being and nothingness,* recounted by Merleau-Ponty, M. Op. cit., p. 425.
16. Freud, S. (1912). "The dynamics of transference." *Standard Edition,* Vol. 12. pp. 99–108.
17. Freud, S. (1914). "Remembering, repeating and working through," *Standard Edition,* Vol. 12. p. 147.
18. Ibid., pp. 147–148.
19. Kirsner, D. (1983). Freud's concept of transference and linguistics. *Australian Journal of Psychotherapy,* vol. 2.

20. Ibid., pp. 2–3.

21. Heaton, J. M. (1979). Theory in psychotherapy, in N. Bolton (ed.), *Philosophical problems in psychology*. London: Methuen.

22. Freud, S. (1917). *Introductory Lectures on Psychoanalysis, Standard Edition*, Vol. 16. p. 444.

23. Kirsner, D. Op. cit., p. 8.

24. Ibid., p. 10.

25. Lacan, J. (1977). *Ecrits—A selection*. London: Tavistock; (1977). *The four fundamental concepts of psychoanalysis*. London: Hogarth Press.

26. Culler, J. (1976). *Saussure*. London: Fontana.

27. Freud, S. (1915). *Observations on transference love, Standard Edition*, Vol. 12, p. 168.

28. Laplanche, J., and Pontalis, J.-B. (1973). *The language of psychoanalysis*. London: Hogarth Press, p. 78.

29. Ibid., p. 78.

30. Ibid., p. 78.

31. Freud, S. (1909). *Analysis of a phobia in a five-year-old boy, Standard Edition*, Vol. 10, p. 122.

32. Merleau-Ponty, M. Op. cit., p. 410.

CHAPTER 7: UNMASKING DESIRE OF ITS SEXED EXPRESSION: PERVERSION

1. Freud, S. (1921). *Group psychology and the analysis of the ego, Standard Edition*, Vol. 18, p. 90.

2. Hegel, G. (1967). *The phenomenology of mind*. New York: Harper & Row, pp. 218–227; Hyppolite, J. (1974). *Genesis and structure of Hegel's phenomenology of spirit*. Evanston, Ill.: Northwestern University Press, pp. 159–168.

3. Freud, S. (1917). *Introductory lectures on psychoanalysis, Standard Edition*, Vol. 16.

4. Ibid., p. 303.

5. Ibid., p. 299.

6. Ibid., p. 308.

7. Ibid., p. 310.

8. Ibid., p. 314.

9. Ibid., p. 316.

10. Ibid., p. 316.

11. Merleau-Ponty, M. (1962). *Phenomenology of perception*. London: Routledge & Kegan Paul, pp. 154–173.

12. Ibid., pp. 160–162.

13. Ibid., p. 168.

14. Ibid., p. 167.

15. Ibid., pp. 169–171.

16. Viderman, S. (1980). The subject-object relation and the problem of desire, in S. Levovici, and D. Widlocher (eds.), *Psychoanalysis in France*. New York: International Universities Press, p. 189.

17. Laplanche, J., and Pontalis, J.-B. (1973). *The language of psychoanalysis*. London: Hogarth Press, p. 307.

18. Ibid., p. 308.

19. Viderman, S. Op. cit., p. 191.

20. Freud, S. (1940). *An outline of psychoanalysis, Standard Edition*, Vol. 23, pp. 202–204.

21. Merleau-Ponty, M. (1964). *Signs*. Evanston, Ill.: Northwestern University Press, p. 228.

CHAPTER 8: THE LURES OF THE CURE AND THE DIALECTIC OF DESIRE IN LANGUAGE AND PSYCHOANALYSIS

1. Merleau-Ponty, M. (1962). *Phenomenology of perception*. London: Routledge & Kegan Paul, pp. 175–181.

2. Freud, S. (1901). *The psychopathology of everyday life, Standard Edition*, Vol. 6, p. 2.

3. Ibid., pp. 2–3.

4. Ibid., p. 3.

5. Ibid., p. 3.

6. Ibid., p. 3.

7. Wilden, A. (1968). *The language of the self*. Baltimore: Johns Hopkins University Press, p. 247.

8. Freud, S., op. cit.

9. Freud, S. (1898). *The psychical mechanism of forgetfulness, Standard Edition*, Vol. 3, p. 295.

10. Rosen, V. (1969). Sign phenomena and their relationship to unconscious meaning, *International Journal of Psychoanalysis, 50*, pp. 197–207.

11. Leavy, S. A. (1983). Some linguistic approaches to psychoanalysis. *Psychoanalytic Quarterly, 3*, pp. 34–55.

12. Ibid., p. 39.

13. Ibid., p. 40.

14. Ibid., p. 43.

15. Ibid., p. 43.

16. Edelson, M. (1978). What is the psychoanalyst talking about? in J. Smith (ed.), *Psychoanalysis and language*, New Haven: Yale University Press, pp. 99–120.

17. Ibid., p. 103.

18. Ibid., p. 107.

19. Ibid., p. 108.

20. Ibid., p. 108.

21. Ibid., pp. 108–109.

22. Ibid., p. 113.

23. Ibid., p. 114.

24. Ibid., p. 129.

25. Ibid., p. 134.

26. Leavy, S. A. Op. cit., p. 40.

27. Ibid., p. 44.

28. Ibid., pp. 45–46.

29. Saussure, F. de. (1966). *Course in general linguistics.* New York: McGraw-Hill.

30. Jakobsen, R. (1974). *Main trends in the science of language.* New York: Harper & Row.

31. Lacan, J. (1977). The agency of the letter in the unconscious or Reason since Freud. *Ecrits—A selection.* New York: Norton, pp. 146–178.

32. Brinkman, J. (1977). The Other and the One: Psychoanalysis, reading, *The Symposium. Yale Freud Studies,* Vol. 55/56, pp. 431–443.

33. Wilden, A. Op. cit., p. 235.

34. Freud, S. (1920). *Beyond the pleasure principle, Standard Edition,* Vol. 18, pp. 14–15.

35. Ibid., p. 15.

36. Ibid., p. 16.

37. Winnicott, D. W. (1971). *Playing and reality.* London: Tavistock, pp. 1–25.

38. Lacan, J. (1977). The function and field of speech and language in psychoanalysis. *Ecrits—A selection.* New York: Norton, p. 103.

39. Funt, D. (1973). The question of the Subject: Lacan and psychoanalysis. *The Psychoanalytic Review, 60*(3), p. 400.

40. Ibid., p. 400.

41. Roustang, F. (1984, Spring). Uncertainty. *October,* p. 91.

42. Freud, S. (1901). *The psychopathology of everyday life, Standard Edition,* Vol. 6, pp. 239–279.

43. Heidegger, M. (1971). *On the way to language.* New York: Harper & Row, p. 123.

44. Ibid., p. 57.

45. Heidegger, M. (1962). *Being and time.* London: Basil Blackwell, pp. 172–174.

46. Heaton, J. M. (1982, May). Freud and Heidegger on the interpretation of slips of the tongue. *Journal of the British Society for Phenomenology, 13*(2), p. 130.

47. Ibid., p. 130.

48. Ibid., p. 131.

49. Brinkman, J. Op. cit., p. 437.

50. Ricouer, P. (1974). *The conflict of interpretations.* Evanston, Ill.: Northwestern University Press, pp. 236–268.

51. Ibid., p. 260.

52. Merleau-Ponty, M. (1962). *Phenomenology of perception.* London: Routledge & Kegan Paul, pp. 369–409.

53. Wilden, A. Op. cit., p. 217.

54. Ibid., pp. 217–218.

55. Ibid., p. 218.

56. Heidegger appears simply to have ignored it while Merleau-Ponty, who was clearly influenced by Saussure, virtually distorted it to suit his own ends. See James Edie in Merleau-Ponty, M. (1973). *Consciousness and the acquisition of language.* Evanston, Ill.: Northwestern University Press, pp. xxx–xxxi.

57. Heidegger, M. *Being and time.* Op. cit., p. 56.

58. Heaton, J. M. Op. cit., p. 138.

59. Ibid., p. 138.

60. Heidegger, M. (1975). Logos (Heraclitus), Fragment 050J. *Early Greek thinking.* New York: Harper & Row.

61. Kojève, A. (1969). *Introduction to a reading of Hegel.* New York: Basic Books, p. 19

62. Heidegger, M. *Being and time.* Op. cit., p. 213.

63. Wilden, A. Op. cit., pp. 160–161.

64. Jameson, F. (1972). *The prison-house of language.* Princeton: Princeton University Press, pp. 138–139.

65. Jameson, F. Op. cit., p. 139.

66. Ibid., p. 172.

67. Ibid., p. 172.

Bibliography

Auglaugnier, P. (1964). Remarques sur la structure psychotique. *La Psychanalyse, 8*.

Bergson, H. (1971). *Time and free will*. New York: Humanities Press.

Boszormenyi-Nagy, I. and Framo, J. (eds.) (1965). *Intensive family therapy*. New York: Harper & Row.

Brinkman, J. (1977). The other and the one: Psychoanalysis, reading, The Symposium. *Yale French Studies,* Vol. 55/56.

Culler, J. (1976). *Saussure*. London: Fontana.

De Waelhens, A. (1978). *Schizophrenia*. Pittsburgh: Duquesne University Press.

Evans, M. (Fall, 1979). Introduction to Jacques Lacan's lecture: "The Neurotic's Individual Myth." *The Psychoanalytic Quarterly.* Vol. 4.

Freud, S. *The standard edition of the complete psychological works* (24 vols.). (J. Strachey, ed. and trans.). London: Hogarth. 1966–1974. (Hereafter: "*SE.*")

Freud, S. (1950a). Project for a scientific psychology. *SE*, 1.

Freud, S. (1898b). *The psychical mechanism of forgetfulness. SE*, 3.

Freud, S. (1900a). *The interpretation of dreams, SE*, 4 and 5.

Freud, S. (1901b). *The psychopathology of everyday life. SE*, 6.

Freud, S. (1909b). *Analysis of a phobia in a five-year-old boy. SE*, 10.

Freud, S. (1911c). *Psychoanalytic notes on an autobiographical account of a case of paranoia* (Dementia Paranoides). *SE*, 12.

Freud, S. (1912b). *The dynamics of transference. SE*, 12.

Freud, S. (1914g). *Remembering, repeating and working through. SE*, 12.

Freud, S. (1915a). *Observations on transference-love. SE*, 12.

Freud, S. (1915d). *Repression. SE*, 14.

Freud, S. (1916–1917). *Introductory lectures on psychoanalysis. SE*, 15 and 16.

Freud, S. (1920g). *Beyond the pleasure principle. SE,* 18.

Freud, S. (1921c). *Group psychology and the analysis of the ego. SE,* 18.

Freud, S. (1923b). *The ego and the id. SE,* 19.

Freud, S. (1924b). *Neurosis and psychosis. SE,* 19.

Freud, S. (1925d). *An autobiographical study. SE,* 20.

Freud, S. (1926e). *The question of lay analysis. SE,* 20.

Freud, S. (1940a). *An outline of psychoanalysis. SE,* 23.

Frings, M. (1978). Husserl and Scheler: Two views on intersubjectivity. *Journal of the British Society for Phenomenology. 9*(3).

Funt, D. (1973). The question of the subject: Lacan and psychoanalysis. *The Psychoanalytic Review, 60*(3).

Hamilton, W. (ed.) (1940). *Works of Thomas Reid.* London: Routledge & Kegan Paul. (Vol. 1).

Hartmann, H. (1950). Comments on the psychoanalytic theory of the ego. *Psychoanalytic Study of the Child, 10.*

Hartmann, H. (1958). *Ego psychology and the problem of adaptation.* New York: International Universities Press.

Hartmann, H. (1964). *Essays in ego psychology.* New York: International Universities Press.

Heaton, J.M. (January, 1972). Symposium on saying and showing in Heidegger and Wittgenstein. *Journal of the British Society for Phenomenology, 3*(1).

Heaton, J.M. (1972, May). Insight in phenomenology and psychoanalysis. *Journal of the British Society for Phenomenology, 3*(2).

Heaton, J.M. (1979). Theory in psychotherapy. Bolton, N. (ed.), *Philosophical problems in psychology.* London: Methuen.

Heaton, J.M. (May, 1982). Freud and Heidegger on the interpretation of slips of the tongue. *Journal of the British Society for Phenomenology, 13*(2).

Hegel, G.W.F. (1949). *The phenomenology of mind.* New York: Macmillan.

Heidegger, M. (1962). *Being and time.* London: Basil Blackwell.

Heidegger, M. (1971). *On the way to language.* New York: Harper & Row.

Heidegger, M. (1975). *Early Greek thinking.* New York: Harper & Row.

Husserl, E. (1958). *Ideas—general introduction to pure phenomenology.* New York: Macmillan.

Hyppolite, J. (1974). *Genesis and structure of Hegel's* Phenomenology of Spirit. Evanston, Ill.: Northwestern University Press.

Jakobson, R. (1974). *Main trends in the science of language.* New York: Harper & Row.

Jameson, F. (1972). *The prison-house of language.* Princeton: Princeton University Press.

Kernberg, O. (1975). *Borderline conditions and pathological narcissism.* New York: Aronson.

Klein, M. (1981). *Love, guilt and reparation and other works.* London: Hogarth.

Klein, M. and Riviere, J. (1964). *Love, hate and reparation.* New York: Norton.

Kojève, A. (1969). *Introduction to the reading of Hegel.* New York: Basic Books.

Lacan, J. (1977). *Ecrits—A selection.* New York: Norton.

Lacan, J. (1977). *The four fundamental concepts of psychoanalysis.* New York: Norton.

Laing, R.D. (1960). *The divided self.* London: Tavistock.

Laing, R.D. (1961). *Self and others.* London: Tavistock.

Laing, R.D. (1965). Theory and practice: The present situation. *Psychotherapy Psychosomatic Medicine, 13.*

Laing, R.D. (1967). *The politics of experience.* New York: Pantheon.

Laplanche, J. and Pontalis, J.-B. (1973). *The language of psychoanalysis.* New York: Norton.

Leavy, S.A. (1983). Some linguistic approaches to psychoanalysis. *Psychoanalytic Quarterly, 3.*

Leowald, H. (1980). *Papers on psychoanalysis.* New Haven: Yale University Press.

Lebovici, S. and Widlocher, D. (eds.). *Psychoanalysis in France.* New York: International Universities Press.

Macalpine, I. and Hunter, R.A. Trans. (1955). *Memoirs of my nervous illness* by D. P. Schreber. London: Dawson and Sons.

Mannoni, M. (1964). *The child, his "illness," and the others.* New York: Pantheon.

Mannoni, O. (1971). *Freud.* New York: Pantheon.

Merleau-Ponty, M. (1962). *Phenomenology of perception.* London: Routledge & Kegan Paul.

Merleau-Ponty, M. (1964). *The primacy of perception.* Evanston, Ill.: Northwestern University Press.

Merleau-Ponty, M. (1964). *Signs.* Evanston, Ill.: Northwestern University Press.

Merleau-Ponty, M. (1973). *Consciousness and the acquisition of language.* Evanston, Ill.: Northwestern University Press.

Muller, J. and Richardson, W. (1982). *Lacan and language—a reader's guide to* Ecrits. New York: International Universities Press.

Pontalis, J.-B. (1981). *Frontiers in psychoanalysis.* New York: International Universities Press.

Rapaport, D. (1958). A historical survey of psychoanalytic ego psychology. *Collected Papers.* New York: International Universities Press.

Ricouer, P. (1970). *Freud and philosophy.* New Haven: Yale University Press.

Ricouer, P. (1974). *The conflict of interpretations.* Evanston, Ill.: Northwestern University Press.

Rosen, V. (1969). Sign phenomena and their relationship to unconscious meaning. *International Journal of Psychoanalysis, 50.*

Roustang, F. (Spring, 1984). Uncertainty. *October.*

Rycroft, C. (ed.) (1966). *Psychoanalysis observed.* London: Constable Press.

Sartre, J.-P. (1956). *Being and nothingness.* New York: Philosophical Library.

Sartre, J.-P. (1957). *The transcendence of the ego.* New York: Noonday Press.

Sartre, J.-P. (1962). *Sketch for a theory of the emotions.* London: Methuen.

Saussure, F. de (1966). *Course in general linguistics.* New York: McGraw-Hill.

Schatzman, M. (June, 1971). Paranoia or persecution: The case of Schreber. *Family Process, 10*(2).

Schatzman, M. (1973). *Soul murder—persecution in the family.* London: Allen Lane.

Scheler, M. (1972). *Ressentiment.* New York: Schocken Books.

Scheler, M. (1979). *The nature of sympathy.* London: Routledge & Kegan Paul.

Schneiderman, S. (ed.) (1980). *Returning to Freud—Clinical psychoanalysis in the school of Lacan.* New Haven: Yale University Press.

Schreber, D.G.M. (1852). *Die Eigentumlichkeiten des Kindlichen Organismus (The characteristics of the child's organism).* Leipzig: Fleischer.

Smith, J. (ed.) (1978). *Psychoanalysis and language.* New Haven: Yale University Press.

Sullivan, H.S. (1973). *Clinical studies in psychiatry.* New York: Norton.

Turkle, S. (1978). *Psychoanalytic politics: Freud's French revolution.* New York: Basic Books.
Wilden, A. (1968). *The language of the self.* Baltimore: Johns Hopkins University Press.
Winnicott, D.W. (1971). *Playing and reality.* London: Tavistock.
Winnicott, D.W. (1976). *The maturational processes and the facilitating environment.* London: Hogarth.

Index